Thera

WITH INSIGHTS AND STRATEGIES FOR
ANYONE LIVING OR WORKING

With

Troubled Kids

C. S. Belle ~ LMHC

BRIGHTON PUBLISHING LLC
435 N. HARRIS DRIVE
MESA, AZ 85203

Therapy in Action

With Insights and Strategies for Anyone
Living or Working

With

Troubled Kids

C. S. Belle ~ LMHC

Brighton Publishing LLC
435 N. Harris Drive
Mesa, AZ 85203
www.BrightonPublishing.com

ISBN13: 978-1-62183-328-4

ISBN 10: 1-62183-328-3

Printed in the United States of America

First Edition

Cover Design: Tom Rodriguez

Table of Contents

Disclaimer

Names and identifying details have been changed to protect the privacy of individuals. Any resemblance to actual persons, living or dead, or actual events is purely coincidental. I have tried to recreate events and conversations from my memories of them. In order to maintain their anonymity I have changed the names of individuals and places. I have changed some identifying characteristics and details such as physical properties, occupations, places of residence, and assigned the substance of conversations to different speakers. This book is not intended as a substitute for the advice of physicians, psychiatrists, educators, or mental health professionals. The reader should regularly consult a physician, psychiatrist, or mental health professional in matters relating to his/her mental health and particularly with respect to any symptoms that may require a medical or mental health diagnosis or medical attention. The information in this book is meant to supplement, not replace, proper training in mental health counseling, parenting, and classroom management. The author and publisher advise readers to take full responsibility for their actions and interactions and know their limits. Before practicing the skills described in this book, be sure that you are well informed, and do not take on tasks or individuals beyond your level of experience, aptitude, training, and comfort level.

Reviews

C. S. Belle's "Therapy in Action" is a work well suited to the task of introducing new graduate students to the mental health counseling profession.

I found her case studies format a very effective way to engage the reader and convey the information, her questioning of the use of medication and certain practices an accurate reflection of a serious problem within our field, and the interventions she illustrated in the text were practical, creative and on point.

Speaking as a clinical supervisor in a mental health counseling program, I encourage my colleagues to add "Therapy in Action" to your required reading list.

Stephen A. Giunta, Ph.D., LMHC, NCC, CCMHC

Immediate Past President, American Mental Health Counselors Association.

~ Belle addresses racism, prejudices, stereotypes, and many other serious issues plaguing our country and our world. ~

"This is not like other books of its kind because there are no other books of its kind. The author writes in a captivating way, pulling me in and wrenching my heart but, somehow, leaves me feeling more knowledgable and more capable on the other side. It's an easy read, I couldn't put it down."

Amazon Review

~ Excellent read explaining several different situations and how to treat... ~

"Excellent read explaining several different situations and how to treat not just the children but the whole family. A useful educational tool for both experienced and new clinicians alike."

Amazon Review

~ Profoundly Touching... ~

"This book is a profoundly touching account of how our children and their families are often misunderstood, over-medicated or mis-medicated, and the systemic societal issues that cause our "troubled" children and their families to often end up without the attention and help they need. We have to realize that, when we turn our backs and close our eyes to the darkness in their [troubled kids'] lives, we also shut ourselves off and apart from their light. We lose what they have to give.

We need to protect and embrace the troubled ones with all of our might and wisdom."

Amazon Review

~AN EXTRAORDINARY ACHIEVEMENT~

"In an intimate glimpse of case studies "C. S. Belle creates an extraordinary achievement that is passionate, profound, and deeply moving."

Publisher

Dedication

I dedicate this book, to Alicia, Kelsea, Jennifer, and Steve.

Acknowledgements

Therapy In Action is the product of more than three decades of encounters with troubled children and the many adults in their lives. Without their trust, this book would not have been possible.

Don McGuire, my acquisitions editor, and my publisher Kathie McGuire, have been wonderfully supportive in helping me to make my book suitable for publication. I have enjoyed a close professional relationship with them that was both inspirational and educational. I could not be more pleased with the graphic designer's interpretation of what my book is about as it was illustrated on the cover. I have also been immeasurably impressed with the collaborative effort of their entire publishing team, including the production staff, literary editors and marketing staff.

I will forever be grateful to my daughters, Kelsea and Alicia, still at home, during the years that I wrote the book, for their infinite patience with me, their intuitive and compassionate regard for the children and families I served, and for providing such inspiration and delight to my life and my work. My heartfelt gratitude also goes out to my first born daughter Jennifer, for her candor and grace, as she forged the path for her younger siblings. I can never thank them enough for their love, many years of sacrifice, encouragement and support. I am very proud of all three of them.

I will always be grateful to Steve Ellman, my dear lifelong mentor and friend, who has always been a stalwart source of vision, strength, love, and kindness.

I also want to thank my dear friends Sam and Carol for their encouragement and support as I worked my way through the entire editing process.

Michael K., Edward W. and Carl Z, Gary L., Michael C. and Russell L., "*May The Force Be With You.*" forever and ever!

I am deeply indebted to the supervisors and colleagues I have encountered, in the course of my profession, who share my regard for the people we serve.

Introduction

A troubled child is like a single pebble that sends ripples across a still lake, disturbing all that lies within its spheres. There is no escape. Whether your eyes are closed or your body is numb, the ripples will move you all the same. They come in the form of unwanted influences on you and your own children, in your child's school and in your community. They come in the form of crime, untreated mental illness, substance abuse, and in immoral and unethical practices imposed on children by caregivers and professionals assigned to their care. They come in an ever-increasing population of professionals and caregivers who cannot identify their own shortcomings and who lack the skills to effectively manage troubled kids.

This book is a window through which you will be able to see the psychodynamics and environmental factors that contribute to that ripple effect. You will also discover within yourself all that it takes to make a difference in the lives of those with whom you interact, on both a personal and professional level, every day.

I have worked with acting-out children for over thirty years in family homes, on school grounds, in classrooms, in the screening area of crisis stabilization units, or wherever my sessions took me. These are the settings where I have learned the enabling and destructive dynamics of relationships that trouble troubled kids. I teach and demonstrate, by example, how to empower troubled kids and the adults in their lives, to heal, learn, and grow.

I challenge those who deal with troubled kids to look beyond the obvious and to refrain from snap judgments. I check reactive interventions and ineffective traditional decrees and practices. I expose and redirect reactive responses that erupt from unexamined biases and personal prejudices. I encourage a team approach that embraces and engages rather than condemns and alienates troubled kids and their caregivers. I describe and then work to create an environment inside the home and classroom that opens its arms to troubled kids who have learned to feel alienated or to feel that they have nowhere safe to turn for understanding and refuge.

I challenge the misuse of specific medications and behavior management techniques. I question the practices of sentencing troubled kids to indefinite terms in special education classes. I also challenge the use of corporal punishment and the shame and blame tactics often used to modify the acting-out behaviors of troubled kids.

In the chapters that follow, I have presented families of varying economic advantage. My experience has taught me that the most damaging type of poverty is to be found, not in the economic aspect of the home, but in the felt impoverishment of spiritual awareness in some of the most religious homes, and in the absence of expressed genuine regard and affection in some of the most affluent homes.

I invite the reader to follow me into the classrooms, homes, and other arenas where my observations, assessments, interventions, and didactic discussions have taken place. I invite you to challenge yourself to keep an open mind and to consider a new approach to interpreting the nature of, and then intervening in the outcome of, the challenges troubled kids face.

I hope to awaken those who employ ineffective practices to a new way of looking at troubled kids and a new and more effective way to address their needs. I demonstrate how to root out the information needed to prevent mislabeling. I challenge trends that lead to misdiagnoses and ineffective treatments of troubled kids. I advise guardians and professionals to team up with the psychiatrist, psychologist, or therapist in their own community, as well as with the clients and the adults in the lives of troubled children, and to keep an open, inquiring mind. In order to learn the best approaches we must know the questions that need to be answered.

Parents have come to me whose child has been on medication for five to eight years for ADHD, with multiple referrals at school, placement in special education, increased oppositional defiance, and decreased governability at home. In many cases excessive punishments and consequences have been enforced and privileges taken away, one by one, until there are no privileges left to remove. And yet, the child's behavior has escalated further until the whole family is out of control.

Perhaps the proper diagnosis isn't ADHD. Perhaps the symptoms only mirror ADHD and are masking a more accurate diagnosis. I ask questions in a way that leads to a disclosure of historical and current traumatic events or levels of stress that the child or adult has suffered or is suffering that have never before been disclosed.

I have had similar experiences in the schools. I have to say to the teachers, "If the behavior management techniques aren't working, perhaps we aren't identifying the actual problem. Perhaps we are identifying the symptoms and trying to get rid of them without identifying and getting rid of the underlying cause."

In our efforts to be original with our behavioral and cognitive treatment approaches, we minimize the affective impact of historical life experiences. We fail to recognize the affective roots of a child's current mental and emotional state and how those are reflected in their behavior.

We have grown calloused in our response to the way children feel; yet we demand that they behave. We are masking the problem by treating the symptoms that way.

Some professionals and guardians inadvertently escalate troubled children in their efforts to de-escalate them. The focus needs to then shift from the child to the adults in the child's life. We need to educate them on how to implement the self-control and environmental controls that will help to de-escalate the troubled child.

I developed an instrument I call the Telling Wheel (described in Chapter Two). It is used for identifying the people who influence the lives of troubled children. I discovered that many adults in the life of a troubled child lacked the knowledge they needed to improve their lives and the lives of the child in their care. I did not step back from that lack of knowledge with an arrogant air; instead, I embraced it. We have to give adults and children more credit for being able to learn.

I discovered that many of the people influencing troubled children suffered from depression or substance dependence—or a combination of the two. Those and other mental and personality disorders can severely compromise their ability to maintain a healthy environment for the development of the children in their care. I speak to this as well and demonstrate ways to empower that population to seek and benefit from counseling services in their local community.

When confronted with children, adolescents, and adults who demonstrate that they have little hope for a healthy and productive life, I have to ask, "What phases of their development are they stuck in, and why?" Are they presenting the emotional age of a three- to five-year-old? If so, perhaps something happened at that stage that harnessed them to that level of emotional development. It could be something as wonderful as the birth of a sibling or something as shattering as the death of a parent or a divorce. There could have been an isolated incident of abuse or a sequence of abusive incidents in that child's past.

Freud taught that the affect that occurred at the time of a deeply disturbing or traumatic event is sustained in the personality and consciousness of the person for as long as the memory of the event is repressed. Once the content of that event or events is recalled and exposed, we can identify how much of the affect that we see now is carried over from the response to that historical event. We can then validate it. What I mean by that is that we can stop minimizing the affect of the person. We can stop condemning or diminishing the person for being outraged, mortified, or in excruciating pain, and instead reach out and comfort the person right at the source of that pain. Not only is the comforting long overdue, but it is the hook that engages the whole person in the process of treatment.

Once we have hooked the person, we can begin to demonstrate and teach that such a degree of despair or fear is no longer warranted by current or present circumstances. Until that happens, a minor inconvenience can be seen as a catastrophe. A minor itch or irritation can be felt as a lightning bolt. A look of preoccupation can be seen as loathing or indifference. A scolding or even the facial expressions of disapproval can be felt as a death threat.

When I explain to guardians and teachers how repressed phenomena are reflected in current behavior, the response is one of reflection and then, shock. I see that shift in their eyes. What follows is an uninvited self-awareness and deep remorse for the way they had responded up to that moment. I also see a deep sense of relief in response to the realization that they are not the sole cause of how the child is behaving. I use that instance of vulnerability to say, "When I see that a patient or his caregiver is demonstrating such a degree of despair, pain, or fear, I stop, step back, sit down, and contemplate an individualized course of action. The action I choose will focus on healing how the person feels, and then on the behaviors that need to change."

The cliché that people don't change baffles me. When you help a person change the way he or she feels, they want to behave better. We are mistaken to think that they enjoy negative consequences. We make another mistake: expecting them to change their behavior automatically. They can't because certain behaviors that were felt at one time to be essential to their existence have become as involuntary as breathing.

Children want to please and, for the life of them, cannot explain why or how they could do the thing again that they had resolved to never do. When they say they are sorry, they really mean it. This is a truth troubled children have proven to me time and again. Once released from the affect of trauma, the troubled child then has to identify and deliberately break the patterns or habits of behavior that they acquired during the traumatic period. Such behaviors were at one time felt to be necessary for their mental, emotional, or physical survival. When we attempt to change or charge them to change those protective behaviors without removing the affect that brought them about, we are perceived by the child to be threatening his or her very survival. No wonder we have such a battle on our hands. Behavior management and cognitive therapies alone do not work for them. Even the medications they're on will either have no effect or worsen the situation.

I have introduced the reasoning behind my interventions through discussions that empower rather than enable or condemn that population. I presume on the receptivity and intelligence of my readers now, just as I presumed on the intelligence of my patients and clients over the years. I am using the word intelligence to describe not just the wealth of knowledge they possess but also their capacity to learn. The receptivity of my patients and clients was there for the most part, owing to the fact that their way was not working. They were asking for help.

It is true that not everyone demonstrates a capacity to learn. No amount of education will make its way through deaf ears. No stone will absorb nurturing. There are vast populations of us who are deaf to the best counsel. There are also those of us who are too numb, too guilt ridden, or too hurt or angry to feel another's pain or rage. While it may be that they could, one day, benefit from an intervention, they won't benefit from it now, no matter what you do. But there is a way to approach that inspires them to seek help, sooner or later. They may not seek the help from you, but down the road all you have said and done will begin to ring true in real-life situations. They often come up with ideas as if they were their own—ideas you imparted days, months, even years ago. Positive interventions, whether immediately successful or not, are never wasted on the suffering.

My intent is to reach out to more families and professionals through this book. I have been very successful in awakening individuals to new and more effective responses to troubled kids in my face-to-face contacts. I hope to achieve the same result, here and now, with my readers.

Chapter One

Billy, Amy Lynn, and Kevin

I've often wondered, *Whatever happened to Billy, Amy Lynn, and Kevin?* Billy and Amy Lynn's cases were presented on the last day before I resigned from my position at a community-based mental health agency. Kevin's second visit to that same agency had been on my last day there as well. Did they receive the care and counseling services they needed? Or, like so many other little ones, did they slip through the cracks of our child protective system for too long?

If they didn't get the help they needed, in time, then it is likely that, by the time any intervention was offered, they wouldn't be spared a lifetime of reactive thought and behavior patterns that compromised their ability to learn, to function in any meaningful way, to secure gainful employment, or to have even a smidgeon of a notion of what a healthy, loving, and satisfying relationship might be like for them.

So many children coming from similar circumstances slip through our fingers or hide behind their fears so well that we don't discover them until they are grown and struggling out in the world on their own. Many more come within our spheres but trigger such defensive reactions in us that we miss the opportunity to hear the secrets they hold. By missing those opportunities, one by one, we inadvertently place so many bricks in the wall between us and them that we—guardians, teachers, and other professionals—can't even begin to see, hear, or understand what is troubling them.

I begin with snapshots of the three of them because they represent countless children suffering similar circumstances for no good reason. They live just beyond our reach and scope of vision, right now, somewhere, not too far from where we live. Their stories, as they were told that day, inspired me to write this book. They aroused in me a deep sense of responsibility to expose the injustices they and so many others endure.

Little Billy is five years old. His father is an alcoholic and his mother is on crack. His sister walks the avenue to pay for Daddy's beer. She pays for Mommy's drugs, too, and the shirt on Billy's back.

Billy got in trouble for fighting in school today, after another little boy tried to grab a French fry from his lunch tray. His teacher didn't know that lunch was the first and only meal Billy would receive that day. All she knew was what she saw, and what she saw was Billy pushing the other little boy so hard that he almost fell backwards off the bench. It took her less than a minute to pull him out of the lunch room and down to the principal's office, where he was ordered to sit on his hands and to be still, while she called his father to come pick him up.

Even more unfortunate for Billy was that his father had been drinking all night and was passed out when the call came in from the school. His teacher had to call three times before he answered the phone. When he did, he wasn't happy to hear that, because of Billy's behavior, he was going to have to get up, get dressed, and drive all the way to Billy's school while hung over. Daddy was so angry by the time they got home that he picked Billy up and threw him against the wall. Billy lost consciousness and had to be rushed to the hospital. Now his father is in jail and his mother says, "It's Billy's fault!"

Amy Lynn is thirteen years old. Her parents are the owners of a very successful business. She lives with her family in a seemingly secure and extremely affluent neighborhood where everyone enjoys the luxuries of an exceptionally high-end lifestyle. And yet, despite all the material comforts of her home, she is miserable. She was suspended from school for being belligerent and defiant with her teacher after getting caught sleeping in class. Having been warned several times that day to sit up straight and pay attention, she lashed out with a stream of defensive speech because her teacher had scolded her in front of everyone.

In response to Amy Lynn's defensive speech and inappropriate word choices, her teacher proclaimed that Amy Lynn had been warned enough. As her teacher left the room to call Amy Lynn's mother, she called back over her shoulder, "Today is the last straw!"

To Amy Lynn's mother the teacher said, "If she keeps refusing to pay attention, she shouldn't be here at all."

How was her teacher to know that Amy Lynn slept in class because her father kept her up at night? Her teacher couldn't possibly know because Daddy tells her, over and over again, that if she tells anyone about what he's doing, Mommy will make him punish her for lying. He scared her into silence and secrecy, saying, "Who would they believe, anyway—the successful businessman, or some silly girl who obviously couldn't care less about getting an education?"

No, there was no way for Amy Lynn's teacher to know. Night after night, Amy Lynn cried after her father left her room. She did care about getting an education. She wanted the other kids to stop laughing at her. She ached to have friends. She wanted to be able to giggle, chat, and carry on as if she too hadn't a care in the world, like all the other girls. These thoughts ran through her mind every night as she lay in bed, sobbing on her pillow.

When Amy Lynn was suspended from school, her mother told her father to take a belt to her. He told Amy Lynn he was sorry he had to do this, but she didn't believe him. She made up her mind she wouldn't cry this time, so when he ordered her to go to his room and to lie across his bed, she obeyed, determined not to so much as wince. Instead, she clutched the blanket and held her breath while he belted her again and again.

In response to her deliberate silence, he hollered, "You're enjoying this!" She still wouldn't respond, so he whispered, "If you don't cry, your mother will get suspicious. Please don't make me do this."

She dug her nails even deeper into the bed and remained silent. He got so exasperated that he threw his belt down on the floor and told her to get out of there. She got up and slowly left the room, hoping that by the time her three days of suspension were up, no one would see the welts.

As she walked to the stairs that led up to her room, which was at the end of what now seemed a very long hall, she saw her mother standing at the top of the stairs. She was peering down, as if she were listening, waiting, and searching Amy Lynn's face for tears. Not wanting to give her mother the satisfaction of seeing her cry, Amy Lynn deliberately fixed her eyes on her bedroom door at the end of the hall. As she passed her mother, she half expected her to lash out with a slap to her face or a tug on her hair. Instead, her mother screamed at her.

"You can just stay in there and serve out your three days of suspension! You'll never amount to anything—girls like you are a dime a dozen!"

Kevin, aged nine, was taken to the Intake Department of the Crises Stabilization Unit (CSU) in the middle of the night, by a Child Protective Services (CPS) investigator. I was working there part-time as an evaluation for admission screener.

After reporting that Kevin's father had tried to strangle him, the investigator said he wanted me to admit Kevin into the CSU so that he wouldn't have to disturb a foster home at that late hour. It was immediately clear, however, that Kevin didn't want to be there. From the minute he was brought in, he threw a terrible temper tantrum. He kicked the door, threw himself on the floor, and kicked and knocked over two of the chairs. He cried, screamed, and pleaded with everyone in the room to please take him back home "right now!"

To protect him from hurting himself or anyone else, the staff technicians threatened to put him in seclusion in four-point restraints. They told Kevin they could restrain him using cuffs on his arms and legs that are fastened to straps on the bed. One of the technicians said he wouldn't be able to move and asked how he would like that.

I objected and suggested to Kevin that he slip into my office, instead, where he could tell me why he needed to go home. The idea calmed him down. In my office I asked him to tell me what had happened to him.

He told me his mother and father had gotten into a fight. When he tried to break them up, his father grabbed him by the throat, slammed him up against the wall, and said he'd kill him if he didn't get the hell out of there. Kevin said he ran to his grandpa's home, two blocks down the road, and called 911. It was 3:00 a.m., but he hadn't stopped to think how dark and scary it was out there.

The father had left the home by the time the police arrived. They called CPS despite his mother's denial that the fight had involved any of her children after a report was made about what Kevin had alleged the father did to him. He was then taken from the home until they could complete the investigation.

I let Kevin know how sorry I felt for what he had gone through. I reached my hand out and gently felt the area where I could see the finger burns around his neck. He must have been scared for his life when he ran out of the house in the middle of the night. I wanted him to know that he was safe now with us. But no matter what I said, he wouldn't be consoled. He kept repeating that he had to go home. He begged and pleaded for me to tell them to take him home.

I gave him some paper and a box of crayons and told him I would go out and see what I could do about the situation. I tried to make him feel better by giving him at least a ray of hope that I would do something, if I could. I was puzzled, though. Why did he want to go back there when his father had nearly strangled him and threatened to kill him? Why wasn't he relieved now that he was safe?

As soon as I returned to my office, I got my answer as he explained the figures in his drawing. His mother was drawn bent over on the floor. His baby sister was upside down on the couch. His sister, aged seven, was drawn hiding under a bed. I understood in that instant why he was being so willful and defiant. He wasn't thinking of himself at all—he was afraid for them. He truly believed that his father could kill the whole family if he got angry enough. He was scared for his sisters. He had to get back there so he could protect and watch out for them.

I flashed back to the reaction of the staff and thought to myself, *And for this he could have been put in seclusion and four-point restraints.*

"You don't understand!" he stammered, insisting that his sisters needed him. "Nobody understands!" And then he began to cry enormous sobs. He kept repeating, "No one will be there to take care of them. If they cry he'll hurt them. They don't cry when their brother is there." He pounded his nine-year-old chest with his thumb and cried, "I'm the only one that can keep them quiet."

I told him I would ask the investigator again if he would go back to take his sisters out of the home.

When I got back to the waiting room, I approached the investigator, showed him the drawing, and asked that he go back and check on Kevin's sisters. He said, "No." He then qualified his stance, saying, "The report said nothing about the girls."

"Well, he is saying something now," I argued. "He's afraid for them. That is what all the commotion was about. He's scared their father will hurt them. That is why he feels he needs to get back there, right now."

"I can only go by what is in the report, ma'am."

"But Kevin thinks his father will be back, and when he does return, there's a good chance the fight will start up again. Why don't you go in and talk to him?"

Seeing he was unmoved, I continued, "He'll tell you enough to warrant going back to get the rest of them. There are finger burns on his neck that are more prominent now than when he first came in."

The investigator shrugged, rolled his eyes, and then said, "I'll take a look at the marks and put it in my report, but as far as it goes for the rest of them, I can't go by what he thinks is going to happen." He shrugged and rolled his eyes again, holding both of his hands out, palms up, as if to say there was nothing he could do about it. But then he said, "Look, we have twenty-four hours to file a report on cases like this. I'll go by there in the morning after I take care of him."

I was able to tell Kevin that the investigator would go back and check on his siblings for him. I thanked Kevin for trying to protect his sisters and told him they were lucky to have him for a brother. I then began the paperwork I needed to complete in order to admit him on the unit for the night. He did seem to meet the criteria for an involuntary admission when he first arrived. We weren't a quick stop for children en route to foster homes. But Kevin had been through so much that night. I wanted to keep him for observation even though he had settled down.

The investigator picked him up later that morning, and Kevin was placed in a local foster home so he wouldn't have to change schools.

A couple of weeks later, two law enforcement officers returned him to us in handcuffs. Kevin had threatened to kill himself during an altercation with his teacher, and he had acted out until she finally threatened to have him evaluated for special education. She told him his mother should ask his doctor for Ritalin or something to calm him down. He had been unmanageable in the foster placement, too, because of the way he felt about being separated from his mother and siblings when he was taken out of the home. He felt punished by our efforts to protect him.

I was relieved to learn later that Kevin was referred to our home-and school-based intervention program, once he was deemed stable enough to be released from the Crisis Stabilization Unit.

Troubled children such as Billy, Amy Lynn, and Kevin haven't made the news. They aren't lost causes yet. They haven't murdered anyone or sold their parent's furniture for drugs. They haven't vandalized the schools or robbed anyone on the bus. They haven't stolen anybody's car for a joy ride around the block.

Children who have committed such offenses are regarded as trouble with a capital "T" and often end up in Juvenile Justice Intervention programs. But children such as Billy, Amy Lynn, and Kevin are living among us, suffering within our reach, in our schools and neighborhoods. If they are lucky enough, they are referred into family home intervention programs.

I used to have both types on my caseload. I used to say, "The delinquent kids are the kids we missed in our home intervention program."

Troubled children live in high-risk environments where they are subjected to verbal, emotional, and physical violence. They experience turmoil, neglect, and chaos, almost daily.

Some people regard the kids that are trouble and the troubled ones all the same. They think the kids targeted for home intervention belong in the delinquent category, "because that is where they are obviously headed anyway." But while they don't belong with delinquents, they don't fit in with the more fortunate or normal kids either. They are different and require more thought in our approach to governing and educating them. They are not trouble—they are the troubled ones.

Troubled children such as Billy, Amy Lynn, and Kevin have learned to expect to be hurt. They've learned to expect to be told to shut up, to be made to feel small and worthless, to be embarrassed, ashamed, rejected, dejected, abandoned, scared to death, and alienated from their peers. They have learned to look right through you and not hear a word you say. They know that, if they did hear you, what you say would hurt them deeply. They have learned that, if they look you in the eye, you will be looking back at them with a disgusted, mean, or vacant expression.

Many of them are severely neglected and denied their basic needs; others are verbally bashed or physically beaten every day. They learn to turn their ears off and their eyes away from the people they are supposed to trust for sustenance and security. In time, they turn their backs on anyone in authority—or they counterattack in passive and aggressive ways.

Some of the troubled ones are taught to believe that God won't love them unless they try to understand and forgive the adults who cause their pain. They have been taught to forgive and not to complain. They aren't allowed to speak of the trouble they are having at home. But while some troubled children are often afraid to express their thoughts and feelings to anyone, others can't help but express their pain, no matter how good they are trying to be. Others refuse to speak on their own behalf, fearing that they'll put their siblings at risk of losing the parent who commits the acts of violence against them.

In many of the homes I serviced, family members rarely spoke to each other. They yelled at each other instead, even when they were having an ordinary conversation. Often the TV and stereos were on, dogs were barking in the yard or right underfoot, babies were crying, and cars and sirens could be heard in the background—all at the same time.

Troubled children can still hear the noise of a fight that occurred at home, days, even years, after it happened. For them, trying to pay attention in school is the same as trying to listen to someone talk while the radio is blasting. Someone needs to show them how to turn that "radio" down. Someone needs to go into their homes and turn the volume down on all the yelling that is going on.

I have been in the homes and schools of troubled children in rural, urban, and suburban communities as a home- and school-based counselor and as a professional therapist for over thirty years. I have worked as an evaluation screener as well, diagnosing and admitting patients into Crisis Stabilization Units. I've been an eye and ear witness to what these children are going through.

The circumstances of troubled kids are different from those of the other kids, and they see themselves as being different from the other kids. They are different! They hurt more—and they have more secrets.

I have seen the challenges they present, too. Teachers have the hardest time of all. They are faced with the daily burden of identifying, understanding, and managing the behaviors of those who act out like Billy and Kevin, and of those who suffer in silence like Amy Lynn.

Some troubled children do act out in ways that are a danger to themselves and others. Some are so disruptive that the others in the class can't hear the teacher give the lesson. The disruptive ones interrupt them time and again. My own children complain that the teachers are so busy managing behaviors that they have little time left over in the hour for covering the lessons. Most of the lesson is copied and given as homework. The students who succeed are often the self-motivated and self-taught.

For a person who wants to be a successful teacher, this prospect is mortifying. The most conscientious of the teachers are too often the first to fall prey to frustration and disillusionment about their professional choice.

In good faith, teachers make referrals and employ the intervention tools available to them. They access school- and home-based counseling services for the troubled children and their families through their community mental health centers. They enlist the help of campus-based behavior management specialists and implement the behavior management plans and techniques those specialists provide for them. They even refer troubled children to their primary care physician or psychiatrist for medication when inappropriate behaviors continue to manifest, despite other interventions.

When all of these efforts are spent to no avail, teachers lose faith in reaching out for help. They find that despite the employment of counseling, behavior management, and medication—independently or combined—there is little to no change in the disposition and behavior of the troubled children in their classes. Parents point their fingers at the teachers. In turn, teachers point their fingers at the parents. To avoid argument and unpleasantness that might embarrass the guardians or the school administration, they then point their fingers at the child.

Teachers have all but slammed the door in my face when I've appeared to discuss a child who's been assigned to me. After some foot shuffling and a plea to "give me a chance," I am given the explanation: Counselors have come and gone and done nothing about the problem; teachers say these counselors showed up once or twice but never really stayed long enough to discuss the situation, and the teachers never got their names. Guardians had the same complaints. Counselors either hung out at the schools during recess time or sat themselves down in the living rooms of troubled kids for an hour of Tiddlywinks or Candy Land. Issues weren't addressed. Behaviors weren't identified or even monitored for change.

I've found it's a good icebreaker to sit down with a family and play a game, but it isn't something I did every time I went into the home. I did make it an objective on my treatment plan that the family would play a game every Wednesday after dinner, or every Sunday afternoon. But I didn't waste the time that I had to effect a change in the family atmosphere of a troubled child's home, playing Tiddlywinks and Candy Land.

I discussed this with some of my associates from time to time and cringed when they defended that approach. I could do nothing but sympathize with the teachers' and guardians' reaction to me when I came in behind them.

Some counselors appeared to be assigned only to take down names and lodge complaints with the Department of Children and Families. They criticized the guardians, teachers, and children, shaking their heads—conveying that the whole situation was hopeless. They served out their two- to four-month interventions only to accomplish nothing time and again.

It most certainly must be said that most counselors work diligently and are extremely dedicated and effective. Nevertheless, the number of ineffective therapists is great. We can't afford to waste our taxes on them, and teachers don't have time to put up with them—there is just too much at stake.

The security of the programs, as well as that of the troubled children, is at stake. Counselors fresh out of school are the most likely to be hired for programs servicing the underprivileged, as they have low expectations for compensation. I understand that, and they have to earn their wings somehow, but they need case-specific training and supervision.

A courtesy customer satisfaction checklist could be attached to the progress note of every social worker and therapist who services families and schools. The program coordinators and supervisors would then have the information they need to improve the integrity of services provided and ensure the highest possible quality of care.

Behavior management is another area that needs to be discussed. It can be an extremely effective tool when used properly in the classroom and at home. The idea is to provide and follow through with negative consequences for inappropriate behavior and positive reinforcement for appropriate behavior. It sounds simple enough. What can go wrong? Why isn't it working with troubled kids?

In order to ensure successful outcomes using behavior management plans, it is important to make the distinction between kids that are trouble and those who are troubled. I submit there are kids that present as being more trouble than they are troubled. They are so self-destructive or dangerous that it's necessary to access services through the Department of Juvenile Justice. Negative consequences might be the only way to get their attention long enough to effect a change and keep them and their communities' safe at the same time.

In contrast, when negative consequences are applied in the management of troubled kids, they rarely bring about the expected behavioral change. At best, they simply force a change of venue for where the acting-out behavior will occur.

I have heard people say troubled children need more authority and discipline. The word discipline was thought of as another word for punishment instead of its true meaning, which is to improve and educate. The lack of "discipline" was thought to be a primary consequence of the increase in single parent homes where the father was absent, because historically the father has been viewed as the disciplinarian. Without a father present in the home, it seemed reasonable to conclude that children weren't being disciplined enough. What I learned is that, in most cases, the opposite is true.

The truth is this: a consequence of the collapse of the institution of marriage and the nuclear family is that many children have been subjected to the discipline of multiple strangers. It's not that they are lacking any punitive form of discipline; rather, most troubled children have had too much. Children of single mothers have been subjected to the punitive practices of not one but multiple father figures. When there wasn't a father figure, older siblings and extended family members were given full reign to "discipline" them. I've known troubled toddlers to have as many as nine different adults living in and near the home correcting and disciplining the little ones with corporal punishment.

Discipline doesn't always come in the form of whippings and spankings. Parents are admonished for beating or spanking their children without being taught healthier and more effective alternatives. The result is that children often aren't disciplined until the parent is at their wits end, and then the child is hit with a fist or any object close at hand. In some homes and schools where troubled kids are found, the use of corporal punishment is avoided, but verbal beatings, emotional withdrawal, and distancing are used instead.

These tactics don't work with troubled children. Those who are acting out or withdrawing as a result of being hurt will respond better to positive reinforcement. We simply cannot extinguish behaviors that are a result of their hurt, by hurting them more.

Children such as Billy, Amy Lynn, and Kevin need guardians and teachers who know how to reach out and pull them in to where they can feel safe. They need to feel that they belong. There has to be a place they can go, where they can feel safe and know they won't be hurt. Any attempt to raise and educate troubled children without these essential ingredients would be the same as making a cake without sugar or butter. You'll be able to say you made the cake, but who will want some?

Their behavior is a cry for help. To put it more precisely, it is a cry for love and everything we have from within ourselves to give. It is not the first sign of evil to be exorcised, contrary to what one teacher had the nerve to say to my face. They aren't possessed by the devil. The last thing they need is punishment. Punitive consequences are the least effective response for these kids, whether it comes in the form of a public reprimand, a loss of a possession or privilege, a dismissal, or a verbal or physical slap. These remedies only compound the emotional problems troubled children already have.

Without the essential ingredients—feeling safe, sound, and that they do indeed belong—the inappropriate behaviors often escalate. When they do, the frequency and intensity of the reprimands increase at school as well as at home.

Behavior management can either emphasize negative consequences for inappropriate behavior or positive reinforcement for the desired behaviors. When the emphasis is placed on using behavior management techniques to punish a troubled child in the name of discipline, it is about as effective as it would be to use the handle end of a hammer to remove a nail. You could pound the nail until it comes out, through the other side of the board. It would work eventually, but not without a lot of wear and tear on you and some considerable damage to the board.

Everyone wants a quick fix, but there is no magic wand. There is no remedy that will instantly remove the challenges troubled children suffer and present. And yet, that seems to be the expectation when children are referred to doctors or psychiatrists for medication. It isn't uncommon, either, for a child to have been medicated by his primary care physician prior to any other intervention taking place. Countless children are treated with Ritalin and other medications because they exhibited behaviors that matched the lists circulated by school-based therapists and social workers, for the purpose of identifying Attention Deficit Disorder (ADD) and Attention Deficit Hyperactivity Disorder (ADHD).

Many of the families on my case load learned that if criteria for either of those diagnoses could be established, the child would qualify for SSI for the rest of his life. That check came in handy when it came time to pay the rent. At least something good came out of it. The unfortunate thing about it was that many of the children were mislabeled and misdiagnosed. These children remained untreated for the emotional disorders and environmental factors that contributed to their suffering and acting-out behaviors. The result was that the behaviors stayed the same or got a lot worse.

Counselors circulated lists to teachers and guardians, indicating the behavior clusters that would fit the criteria for the diagnoses without any mention of how to identify or manage the powerlessness, helplessness, despair, and pain that often cause the troubled kids to behave in the same way as the ADHD kids behave. When teachers were able to observe and document that a child was off task and appeared to be distracted by external stimuli, they had no idea that it was internal stimuli that actually was disturbing him.

Children who suffer from ADD or ADHD are easily distracted by external stimuli. This is not true for most troubled kids. They are distracted, yes, but more often it is by internal stimuli, such as the noise of a fight or a succession of fights that occur in their homes at night. Any external distraction for them is more the result of hypervigilance than it is from hyperactivity. They have felt so unsafe in their homes that they are constantly on alert for what might be coming up behind them.

Ritalin and other medications designed to reduce a child's distractibility from external stimuli don't quiet the domestic noise reverberating inside the heads of troubled kids. Medications make them drowsy and slow them down physically, yes. But medications don't have the effect of making them feel or act better as they do for the ADD and ADHD kids. Instead, medications often make them even more defenseless against the noise imprinted in their heads.

It's easy to dismiss these facts and simply insist that these kids learn how they are supposed to behave. We can switch their medications and then switch them again; we can tell them over and over to "pay attention!" We can ask rhetorically, "Are you listening to me?" We can continue to complain, "He just won't listen!" We can insist that the child knows how to behave but just doesn't want to.

But what happens when we react in these ways? Greater consequences and restrictions are enforced. The teacher scolds and reminds until she is hoarse. Guardians scream and stomp around the house. Everyone else in the family home wants to bail out. Foster parents isolate and admonish until they are ready to pass them on to someone else's home. It isn't uncommon for foster children to have been placed in ten to fifteen homes in the first year or two of foster care.

It also isn't uncommon for children to be placed in special education classes because of their reactive behaviors, without any understanding that they might be reacting to the unidentified and untreated emotional or mental disorders of their caregivers. No matter how many programs the child participates in, and no matter how many different medications have been tried on him, if the illness lies with the guardian, then, it is the guardian who should receive the medication and counseling intervention. That has proven to be true for many of the troubled children on my case-loads.

The most effective approach to the treatment of troubled kids is to form a team that includes the child, guardians, counselors, physicians, psychiatrists, and teachers who see them every day. We can't assign the problem to the parents or to the teachers alone. There has to be a team approach.

It's just as important for us to recognize when everything we have in place—such as counseling, behavior management, and medication—is having an adverse effect or no effect at all. Guardians have told me that their child has been treated for ADHD for years and that none of the medications worked

We can't blame the physicians when they only see the child for a short visit, and then base their diagnosis, on the information provided them by the guardians, teachers, counselors, and the troubled child. If the guardian fails to disclose that the child has been a witness to episodes of violence, how is the physician to suspect anything but that the child is acting out from a chemical imbalance?

When a team has been formed, there is a better rapport between everyone concerned. Children tend not to be on the wrong medications for long. Everyone is on the same page when it comes to implementing the tools of positive reinforcement, as well as monitoring and measuring the outcome.

The home- and school-based therapists are the bridges between each of the various adults involved in the lives of troubled children. Once that bridge and that level of communication are established, things can begin to change for the better for the child. That is the level of support needed for guardians, teachers, and troubled kids. Then, once those teams are formed, there needs to be an overseer to ensure the quality of care. There is no room for thieves to bond with thieves here, and yet, I have seen this happen. Everyone is on the same team but moving in the wrong direction.

There are professionals and guardians who have a lot of resistance to changing their approach to troubled children. I don't want to leave the reader with the impression that this group defines the majority. I have been inspired by how dedicated guardians and professionals are in their pursuit of solutions to the problems these children endure and present. Children, natural parents and other guardians, teachers, counselors, social workers, judges, law enforcement officers, psychiatrists, psychologists, and primary care physicians have all taught me what works with these kids. I am passing on to the reader what I have learned from them.

But also, in the next chapter and throughout the rest of the book, I expose the postures, prejudices, and practices I have witnessed that threaten the healthy development, education, and treatment of troubled kids.

Chapter Two

Little Demons?

Most guardians and professionals involved with troubled kids have a vision of creating a healthy environment for them to heal, learn, and grow. But I have encountered too many who are thinking and operating in ways that are contrary to that end, even in my own profession.

One example: I overheard a counselor complaining to her supervisor about a mother named Julie who had missed her on-site appointment with our psychiatrist. The counselor said she couldn't call and leave a message because Julie didn't have a phone, so she drove to her apartment to put a note on Julie's door to remind her of the appointment. The note had included a warning that if she didn't show up for the appointment, she wouldn't be eligible for home-based counseling services. The Department of Children and Families had clearly stipulated that the mother would lose her children if she didn't participate in counseling.

In the most condescending tone the counselor could muster, she yelled, "How could any mother be so lame and stupid as to not at least call to cancel or reschedule the appointment?" She then went on to say, "Obviously, that woman doesn't want the help or care if she loses her kids or not."

I held out my hand to calm her and then attempted to give her a different perspective. "If the mother had the wherewithal to make, confirm, and keep appointments, she wouldn't need our help in the first place. Perhaps that could be one of her treatment goals." I then encouraged the counselor to consider how hard it must be to live without a phone or car and no way to get anywhere. After all, her transportation problem was one of the qualifying factors for our services.

The Counselor shrugged off my arguments and accused me of being one of those dreaded bleeding hearts. Ignoring her slight, I offered to go to the apartment with her that afternoon, to see if we could set another appointment for when one of us could provide the transportation. She reluctantly agreed to that.

When we got to Julie's apartment, we found her sister, Heather, was there, collecting Julie's belongings. We learned that, on the night before her appointment, Julie had been a victim of domestic violence. Heather then explained that Julie had found refuge in a woman's shelter.

In response to the counselor's posturing about the missed appointment, Heather turned to her and said defensively, "Julie is confused as to what day it is and where she'll go from there. The children are crying to go home and demanding to see their father, but he's the one who beat her and he isn't to know where they are."

I nodded and, in the most empathetic tone I could use, expressed our apologies while nudging my associate toward the door. When we got back to our car, my associate appeared dumbfounded, tsk-tsked, and then, under her breath, declared, "They all deserve each other!"

There are professionals and guardians among us who expect appropriate behavior from adults and children, no matter what their conditions are at home. They wall themselves off from the real world in which troubled children and their guardians live, and they aren't the least bit receptive to learning about what the children and their families are going through. They don't want to know about their living conditions. They feel it isn't their problem or that it's none of their business.

Such professionals and guardians butt their own heads against those self-sustained walls until they can't see straight. In doing so, they cause themselves tremendous headaches. They then blame the troubled children and their families for the fact that their heads hurt. They subsequently become frustrated because they can't achieve the success they expected to achieve or that is expected of them. Too often, they then unwittingly take that frustration out on the troubled children.

Such professionals and guardians tend to stereotype that population and regard them within the narrow parameters of their own prejudices and biases.

In one school where I tried to bring this travesty to light, I was asked to resign. They told me I was obviously not one of them, and they didn't need or want my kind at their school. The school was in a community that was particularly affluent. It isn't surprising to me that many of our hate crimes and a high rate of suicides come from children who have been raised in similar environments.

The postures and attitudes of the teachers and administration of that school defied affirmation and desegregation laws. To be one of them, you had to share in their biases, of which they weren't ashamed. Their hatred and anger was evident in everything they said and did in response to the troubled kids. They argued against taking a more progressive approach to managing the children. They weren't afraid to express their disapproval to my face.

I kept a journal of comments made to me during my brief employment at their school. I have included some of them below:

> "We do not want to hear them cry. We have work to do!" one teacher barked, in defense of my concern for a withdrawn child. She continued to argue, "When troubled children withdraw inside their shells, we appreciate them for not acting out. When the children do act out, we'll admonish them and group them off, so that they are not a disturbance to the rest of us."
>
> Another teacher was angry about having sent a child to the school psychologist for an evaluation, only to find out the psychologist didn't agree with her impression that the child had ADHD. She argued vehemently and tangentially against his opinion:
>
> "We feel we have done all we can to make sure the difficult kids get an education and a fresh start in life. We refer them to the school psychologist and counseling programs. We demand that the parents get their doctors to give them Ritalin or some other form of medication to calm them down. We hope these efforts will make it easier for us to manage them. But, if those children continue to not fit in or to not get an education, then, that is their problem. To hell with them! Sooner or later, they will join their kind in unemployment lines, in homeless shelters on welfare and social security supplements, or better yet in prison, where most of them belong."
>
> I heard another teacher say, "Their parents send them to church and give them all kinds of religion. Then they go home again where they learn to live in sin."

> Another teacher once told me, "They are little demons and of the devil's clan." She said it wasn't her job to get the devil out of them. She continued to defend her position, saying, "We don't have to feel sorry for them just because they don't have angel wings. We just have to make sure that our own little angels don't turn out to be like them."

The sentiments expressed above contribute to the weight, breadth, and depth of the problems we are facing in our schools, family systems, and communities. We all need to increase our knowledge base, sensitivity, and insight into the nature of what we are up against, when addressing the needs of troubled children.

We need to be more conscientious and informed when providing care and guidance to troubled children. We need to stop and think when we hear such sentiments expressed. Will we go along with that way of thinking, or will we be able to step back and form our own more educated opinions? Will we be as frustrated, hateful, and angry? Will we react to them in negative ways, too? Or will our response to them be to take a more compassionate and creative action?

For guardians, teachers, and counselors who live or work with troubled kids, that is our challenge in a nutshell. We need to observe, question, and examine ourselves and then deliberately put our conditioned responses and emotional reactions in check. Once we have identified them through our own self-observation, self-awareness, and scrutiny, we need to set a more enlightened and creative example for others to follow. We won't progress until we have tackled our own biases and debasing attitudes.

To do this, we need to look at the world through the eyes of troubled kids. We need to seek, visualize, and understand what is troubling them. As we begin to recognize and allow ourselves to feel their pain, our own tears will fall as we come closer to unveiling their innocence.

We need to look for the truth of what they must endure and then take a solution-based approach that actually improves their circumstances and furthers them. We can't afford to ignore what is going on behind closed doors at home or at school. The predominant force behind the behavior of troubled kids is often what goes on when no one else is looking. We need to take a look behind those doors if we are going to make a difference.

We need to evolve as individuals first and to question our own attitudes as well as those of our mentors. We need to clear our own minds and hearts in order to open ourselves to a more progressive and compassionate perspective and response. We need to challenge ourselves to ask more questions for every answer we think we have. Once we've developed less judgmental and more inquiring minds, we need to choose and follow good and creative examples. We need to stop being so sure we've tried everything and that our way is the only way.

Above all, we need to stop trying to make troubled children conform to what we have created. We need to create something that actually conforms to their needs instead, when our way hasn't been working for these kids.

My hope is that the cases presented in this book will motivate the reader to explore and implement positive and effective responses to troubled kids and their families. I do offer and demonstrate alternatives that I have implemented with remarkable success. There are options and we do have choices. We don't need to return to what we have already learned doesn't work. We need to protect troubled children from excessive disciplinary measures. We need to learn and practice alternatives to the excessive use of corporal punishment. We need to open our mind's door to a greater understanding of what kinds of questions to ask when forming our expectations of these kids.

I am not suggesting that we do away with behavior management tools and techniques. Rather, we need to have a greater awareness of the life situations of troubled kids when implementing them. We need to provide a support system for troubled children, and then, we need to be an integral part of that system.

When we begin to see them as troubled rather than as trouble, our approach will bring about an entirely different result. We need to question each other and ourselves. We need to seek clarity and direction rather than to judge, sort, and build fences. We need to want to heal these children from the inside out, and then we need to ask, "How can we heal them?"

As guardians, teachers, counselors, and other professionals alike, we need an opportunity to learn how to identify and manage troubled kids, but it's not just with ourselves and the children that we must be concerned. We can't reach the children without connecting with all the people who are influencing them.

When assigned a child, I would put myself in the shoes of that troubled child and then imagine myself looking up and around at all the adults influencing him. I wanted to explore what he might think and feel about them. Only then did I begin to understand how those thoughts and feelings could affect the way he behaved and who he might one day become.

I discovered that with all the comings and goings of the adults in their lives, it wasn't unusual for children to feel quite abandoned and alone. Often the interaction, hustle and bustle, and comings and goings of the adults made them feel as if they were invisible. It was equally common for the child in such circumstances to tune out, ignore, and remain seemingly unaffected by every one of them. In homes where five to fifteen adults wandered in and out, a child might report that he lived there alone with his mother and that she was never there.

By getting inside the child and looking around and up at all of the adults in his life, it was easy to see how he might feel as if he didn't count very much.

I wanted to know who played what role in the family home. Not only did I want to know what the child thought of each adult in his life, but also, what he believed each one of them thought of him. So I devised a tool called the Telling Wheel, which I found to be remarkably useful with even the youngest children.

On my fist visit with a child, I would pull out a few colored pencils and a piece of paper. I drew a heart in the middle of the paper and put the child's name in the center of the heart. I always asked the child to pick the colors for his and others' names. I found I could infer a lot, not only from the colors the child picked, but also from the order in which the child named significant people in his life. Sometimes "mother" wasn't named at all. Why?

The children often seemed to be as amazed as I was to see how many people were actually involved in their lives. As they named a person, I'd draw a line from the heart to the one-o-clock position and go all the way to twelve in the same manner. If more people were named, I'd draw a second but longer line at one-o-clock and begin to go around the wheel again. Those who came to the child's mind first were often the closest to the child and therefore appeared closest to the child's name.

Children were extremely receptive to this "game." Even those who were withdrawn or reserved responded with enthusiasm. Every child who made such a wheel with me wanted to keep a copy. So, once I had the names in place, I would make a copy of the wheel. I would then ask whatever questions came to mind.

On my copy, I would write the answers verbatim, under the name of each child or adult reported to me as being either a resident or guest of the home. For example, I would ask, "Of all these people, who makes you laugh the most?" "Do any of these people ever tickle you?" "Who?" "Tell me which ones." The children almost always smiled or giggled when I asked that question.

Already, by incorporating the Telling Wheel into the initial phase of treatment, I had begun to build a rapport that would serve to help me design a treatment plan.

Once I had earned the child's trust and built his or her confidence, I would ask more poignant questions, such as, "Who in your wheel makes you mad?" "What does this one or that one do when they are mad or sad?"

One of the more difficult questions to ask was, "Who spanks you?" The answer to that one often revealed that several people were allowed to discipline a child, ranging in age from twelve to seventy-five years old or more.

I could ask, "Who is home when you get home from school?" "Who is there when you go to bed at night?" "Who is there when you wake up in the morning?" "Who was there when you woke up this morning?" "Who made your dinner last night?" (Many times, the answer to that last question was that they hadn't had dinner.) The parameters of this particular tool are infinite and limited only by the imagination of the one who uses it.

The Telling Wheel can be a dangerous tool. If the child's confidence was recklessly breached, the child could be at risk for repercussions at home. I would offer to hold the copy with the information on it for them, and I would promise to keep it safe. I would place it in a folder marked with the child's name, and then I would write "Private" on the cover, right there in front of the child. If the child wasn't able to read, I would ask her to pick a color. I would tell her what I was writing and let her watch me write the word PRIVATE in big, bold letters. I would often hear a great sigh of relief as I got to the last letter.

I used my wheel as a map that gave me the direction I needed to connect with the people who were influencing the child. It wasn't designed to judge the adults in their lives, or to be used as a weapon against them. I was careful in approaching the adults. At times they were defensive and resistant to treatment. This was true in homes where the adults were abusing illicit substances. It was also true in homes where the very idea of therapy was unheard of and beneath them. And it was true in all the cases in between, where the parent was too full of self-importance to accept counseling, or too distressed or too dysfunctional to believe anything or anyone could begin to fix the problem.

Their level of resistance often faded in the light of my acceptance and understanding of them. I approached them with the idea that they were doing the best they could with what they knew at the time. And I had to approach them with the idea that we were all on the same team. I wouldn't allow triangulation, one-upmanship, or "I win, you lose" games that are so often played out in dysfunctional family systems.

By the time a therapist is assigned, as I said before, most everyone is at their wits' end. They feel helpless and powerless and see no end in sight to the difficulties that have come to light. The invasion of professionals from the outside often confirms their sense of powerlessness and helplessness. It tells them they have failed and that the therapist has been assigned to come in and fix everything they've been unable to fix themselves.

I didn't see that as my role as a therapist. I understood that I was to teach them to identify and draw from their own strengths and resources. I taught them how to identify, acknowledge, and use their own strengths and resources to reduce the level of stress and difficulties in their situations. In helping them to identify and acknowledge their strengths, I was able to teach them something that could be generalized to situations that arose in the future. I was not there to subordinate the authority of the guardians; I was there to serve the children and their families.

This aspect of a professional's role is often the hardest for some to swallow. After all, the professional is the one with the power to find that the environment is unfit. They have the power to recommend that the children be removed from the home. They are the ones with the education and gainful employment, so they obviously have their lives "together" and are therefore superior and an authority figure over all—right?

Wrong! That sort of pomposity is self-defeating. Such a posture seals the fate of the children. Resistance skyrockets. Such professionals would have no one to blame but themselves for the succession of failures that would most definitely result.

Serving does not mean that I was to take control of the clients and families, either. It meant to empower the families to regain the control. For instance, if a mother needed to make an appointment, I could assume a pompous, self-righteous, and authoritative posture and order her to make the appointment. Or I could put the parent on my back, increasing her sense of helplessness, while initiating and reinforcing a dependent or codependent relationship by making the appointment for her. Or I could walk her through the activity of making the appointment. Which approach might proactively be generalized to future situations?

I wasn't there to reinforce or build walls no one could penetrate. I was there to bring down walls that often were already firmly in place.

We need to be receptive to the thoughts and feelings of the people who are in our care. We need to be able to retract statements when we discover we have made an error in something we've said, and to acknowledge when we've made a mistake. Such an admission lets people know we're able to forgive the errors and mistakes of others. We need to accept counsel and advice from our colleagues and mentors when we have found ours isn't the best way, and to learn how to ask for and to accept counsel if we expect others to take counsel from us.

We need to be reflective, resilient, and flexible in following through with our plans. At the same time, we need to be kind, firm, and consistent. When we think of troubled children, of adults who were abused as children, and of adults who are being (or feeling) abused in the present, it is easier to think of them as survivors. Such a label gives us a bit more of an edge than when we think of them as the warriors that they are.

To be a warrior, there has to be a war. When we speak of "survivors," we are implying the war and the struggle are over when, for some, it has only just begun. For other families of troubled children, the war has been going on for three or more generations. All three generations often are in the home at the same time.

Our greatest challenge is to be clear—and then to make it clear to the adults and children—whose side we are on in that war. I needed to see that the adults and the children were on the same side and that I wanted to be invited to join them.

We can't connect with guardians and professionals by undermining, condemning, and fault finding, the way that counselor did in my office that morning. We need to connect in empowering ways. We need to ensure the necessary resources are made available to them. We can't continue to put the burden of dealing with troubled children on the shoulders of guardians and teachers without giving them the means to nurture and educate them.

We aren't so far apart that we can't feel a child's pain. We need to hear their silent cries, and then we need to teach them that they have a right to smile, laugh, and sing. They need to know they do belong, right here, with you and me.

In our approach to troubled kids and their families, as well as to all the professionals involved in their care, we need to look for, recognize, and appreciate our similarities even as we learn to accept and celebrate our differences. We can try to look the other way. We can try to escape and say it isn't our problem if people can't live in healthy and productive ways—but when we do, we lose.

We have to realize that, when we turn our backs and close our eyes to the darkness in their lives, we also shut ourselves off and apart from their light. We lose what they have to give. We need to protect and embrace the troubled ones with all of our might and wisdom.

We need to address and engage the entire family system of the troubled child. Many guardians suffer from severe depression or other mental disorders that have gone undiagnosed and untreated. It is also true that in an attempt to cope with daily stress and obligations, some guardians resort to alcohol and street drugs to get them through the worst of it. Drugs and alcohol are used as a form of self-medication to help them escape or manage what seems to them to be insurmountable levels of stress.

What I want to do is to challenge the reader to transcend the tendency to negatively judge and condemn that population and instead focus on reducing the stress. We can't connect if we condemn the guardians of troubled kids, no matter how unsettling their life situations. We must connect, or we will continue to contend with them and their children in our communities, on our roads, and in our schools. It would be dangerous to turn our backs on them. It would only increase our own stress in the long run.

We need to find ways to connect that empower and heal them, for our own sake and for the safety of our community and schools, if for no other reason. We need to develop and exercise our empowering skills even when no one is looking. Left to our own devices, we can easily slip back into our conditioned way of interpreting and responding to difficult situations and people.

We need to learn and practice positive actions instead of negative reactions as we observe and examine ourselves daily. We need to consciously and deliberately identify and discard our own biases and ineffective practices. If we don't, they will continue to contaminate and severely compromise our relationships with troubled children and their families. We will only compound the trouble experienced by troubled kids.

We need to raise our own standards of being, and then we need to be ever mindful that we are living up to and operating from those higher standards. We must monitor ourselves and each other. We, as guardians and professionals, must be forever growing, reaching, learning, giving, and being the best of ourselves even as we make ourselves well. We must balance the joys and sorrows of daily living and strive for balance in our own lives if we are to effect that balance in the lives of troubled children.

We need to know how to think and act independent of others and to be aware of our own faults and limitations as well as of all of our strengths. We need to know how to empower ourselves. We need to actively strive for balance in our own lives in order to effect that balance in the lives of the children and their families.

If we don't we will be approaching the challenges we face with only a fragment of our being. As we work on making ourselves whole, we can then be whole and holistic in our approach to these children and those who care for them.

We need to be receptive to change: flexible, reflective, and resilient in our thinking, postures, and attitudes. It isn't necessary to moralize or preach, but rather observe and listen with an open mind and heart, and then model, guide, and teach.

We need not fear or shrink from an escalation of temperament. Nor does it serve us to overreact emotionally to an escalation of temperament. Instead, we need to learn how to de-escalate temperament with concern, understanding, clarity, and intelligence.

We need to be mindful of the distinctions between opinions and facts. We must ask whether it is the event that is disturbing us, or our perceptions and postures about that event.

We should be familiar with and practice the healing power of deep breaths and other relaxation techniques. When we know how to pamper ourselves, we can then encourage self-pampering in others.

We shouldn't see ourselves as God, or in any way superior to those we serve. We shouldn't seek respect, appreciation, or congratulations for being whole and positive. We don't need to be regarded as heroes, and we don't need to judge or place ourselves on a pedestal above troubled kids and their families.

We need to know how to serve and to be served. We need to know how to love and to be loved. We need to know the power of self-love and self-acceptance and how to foster both in our interactions with others. At the same time, we need to remain mindful of the debilitating power of self-loathing and rejection, humiliation, and shame.

We need to embrace love and life, and then encourage the same in all of our relationships.

We need to understand the dynamics of the dysfunctional family systems these children experience. Then, we need to recognize the impact those dynamics have on their emotional development and behavior. This understanding requires that we force ourselves to look behind closed doors. Only then will we see and begin to understand the fear and pain behind these children's rage and resistance. As soon as we begin to see what they know and what, for them, is factual, we will know what to do. Our approach will be more objective and less subjective. It will be harder for us to take their acting-out behaviors personally. On the contrary, we will become more adept at responding to them on a personal level, in a much more positive way.

Troubled kids and their guardians know what it is to hurt and to be afraid. They have learned to fear being touched, being alone, being in the dark, or of just being seen or heard. Some are deathly afraid of being held. They know what it is to be afraid of their own dreams and are often afraid to sleep.

Many have been insulted with such crude and debasing words that they fear the sound of their own name and even their own reflection. Others have learned to fear their own father or mother and sometimes both of them. Some have learned to fear their own siblings and other extended family members and significant others who have been given the misguided authority to beat them. Such children learn to fear all men or all women.

I have known troubled children to fear that someone in their family environment could one day lose control and seriously hurt or even kill them. Some of these little ones learn to be afraid to move a muscle or to speak. They are deathly afraid to fail or even to make the slightest mistake. Many have learned to be afraid to cry, because if they do, they will be slapped, kicked, pushed, or picked up and thrown. Some are just as afraid to laugh or to make a noise of any kind.

Countless children grow up afraid to feel anything. Some are afraid of their own thoughts and self-talk almost as much as they fear the voices of their caregivers. Many troubled children feel rejected even when no one is rejecting them. They experience a deep sense of loss and grief for no apparent reason.

While some have learned to be totally withdrawn and numb, others frequently express extreme ranges of emotion.

Troubled children are distanced, humiliated, and ashamed when they do something wrong and are often repeatedly blamed for something they did not do. Many of them have also learned how it feels to be blamed, over and over again, for something they did do wrong and to never be forgiven. They know how it feels to be forgotten, ignored, and abandoned.

Children who are repeatedly put down feel that everyone else is better and more lovable than they are. They begin to feel and believe that they will never fit in. Some learn to feel significantly smaller than their opponent, and then they grow up always seeing everyone else as being bigger, more likable, more competent, or more gifted than they are, even when they actually are taller, more likable, more competent, or gifted than anyone else in the room.

They know what it's like to never be trusted. They've learned to never be able to trust anyone and to repeatedly trust someone who was untrustworthy from the start. They know how it feels to be little and have no one to rely on, to be lied to repeatedly, and to be betrayed by their guardians.

Some children live in such volatile atmospheres that they constantly fear for the lives of their siblings or for the life of their parent. They learn to fear for their own life in the hands of a parent or guardian. Many children learn to pretend it doesn't hurt when they have been mentally, emotionally, or physically abused. They learn to pretend everything is okay. Most troubled children know how it feels to have to smile when they want to cry and to silently cry when everyone around them is having a good time. They know how it feels to resent the gaiety of others as they feel repeatedly left out. Too many know how it feels to be called the bastard child.

Children who have been sexually abused often are afraid of their own nakedness. Many children have learned to fear the experience of pleasure and even the slightest discomfort or sensations of any kind. Sexually abused children are quite often confused about the difference between parental and sexual love. They have been "talked dirty" to by someone who has power and authority over them and subjected to the sexual advances and innuendo of one who scares and even repulses them. Many have experienced sexual sensations at the discretion of someone who has beaten them and threatened to kill them, over and over again.

Many troubled children have learned most or all of such things—and more—by the time they have reached the age of three or four. Some have grown up to be guardians or professionals now.

It is true that we have a right to our own way of thinking and to believe what we want to believe. But it is my firm belief that those who defend biases, prejudices, and ineffective practices do not belong with troubled kids. Such professionals are in the wrong profession if they won't even consider a more progressive and effective way of managing these children, in my opinion.

Most professionals enter the workforce with a good heart, but then lose heart after repeated poor success rates resulting from a lack of training, experience, and their own biases and prejudices. Moreover, they may be excellent scholars of counseling and education but lack the insight, character, and skills they need in order to work effectively with troubled children and their families.

A significant number of troubled children have been rescued from dysfunctional family systems only to be thrown into the hands of guardians who haven't a clue how to heal and help them. Their intent is to manage them instead. I encountered this, time and again, when working as a home intervention therapist with children in foster care. My work with Tiara, described in the next chapter, is, I'm sad to say, only one of the many examples I could give.

Chapter Three

Tiara and Jamal

Tiara was seven and her brother, Jamal, was six when the Department of Children and Families removed them from their home and placed them in foster care. It had been reported that they had been physically abused and neglected. What's more, their mother, Tamara, had subsequently failed to follow through on any of the sanctions she was to complete in order for her children to be returned to her.

By the time they were assigned to me, the children had been separated from their mother for over a year and had been in their fifth foster home for only three months. During my first meeting with the foster parent, she told me that the children's behavior could not be stabilized because their mother would fail to show up for her scheduled visitations. No matter how well they had adjusted, up to the day of that appointment, the mother's failure to show up would set them back to square one. Foster parents would get so exasperated with the mother and the reactive behaviors of the children that they would request the department place the children somewhere else.

The mother not only failed to show up for her visits, she also continued using drugs, remained in and out of a relationship with a drug addict, and neglected to secure employment and suitable housing.

I was assigned to be the bridge between the mother and her children and to assist her in following through in a way that met the standards of the Department of Children and Family Services. At the same time, I was tasked to devise behavior management goals and objectives that would improve the children's behavior at home and at school, whether the mother followed through or not with her sanctions and visitation privileges. I took this on with a light heart, as I had been able to effect positive outcomes in similar situations in the past. But my heart grew heavy as I came to see that it wasn't only the mother and children that required immediate intervention. This hit me on the first day of introductions to the foster parent and the children.

I recall sitting at the table in the kitchen with the foster parent. We had just finished the intake packet and were waiting for the children to come home from school. The foster parent was sitting in a chair at the end of the table, straight across the hall from the front door. From where I was sitting, I could also see the front door on the opposite wall of the living room.

It wasn't long before the door opened and in bounced a little girl all smiles and exuberance. She bounced over to the foster parent, climbed up in her lap, and nestled her nose in the foster mother's neck as she received a big hug and was asked how her day went. I took in a deep sigh and felt so good to see how comfortable and loving the welcome home was for this sweet little child. I also noticed how much care had been taken in getting her ready for school. Her hair was braided and decorated with beautiful butterfly barrettes. Her skirt and blouse matched and had little Winnie the Pooh characters on the pockets. She had pretty red patent leather buckle shoes that looked so shiny and new.

I smiled as I watched her settle in the foster mother's lap and then listened to them giggle and tease and tickle each other. I thought to myself, *There isn't a treatment plan in the world that could match the healing power of this moment. She will have this experience to recall and reflect on throughout the rest of her days, no matter what happens.*

But then the front door slowly opened, again. Around the edge of the door peeked another little girl about the same size and age as the one I had been watching, and I realized the first little girl was the mother's natural child. I could see at once that the second little girl's hair hadn't been brushed. There were no barrettes. She had on a T-shirt that was too large for her and a faded, frayed pair of pants. Her tennis shoes were dirty. One was untied and the other was missing a lace.

Before she could get all the way in the door, the foster mother barked, "Don't stand there with the door open! Where is your brother?"

The little girl jumped, so frightened by the foster parent's tone that she dropped her book bag. Several colored papers fell to the floor. Her brother pushed past her, stepping on them. She pushed him to get off of them and then bent down to pick up the mess. She was frantically trying to gather them up while pushing them out of the way with her foot so she could get the door shut.

The foster parent pressed her lips together, shook her head, and said, "Now take them to your room and get back out here. This lady is here to see you."

There were no hugs or smiles for either one of them.

Troubled children are often seen as being out of control at home and at school. External controls in the form of negative consequences are created to make sure they are doing exactly what they are supposed to be doing—and to keep them from disturbing others. It is thought that since they have come from such dysfunctional families, they need constant reminding and correction in order to keep them from turning out like their parents. The children are expected to manage themselves, and severe consequences are implemented if they don't learn how to manage themselves, *right now*. The more dysfunctional their family systems were, the harsher the reprimands.

When the focus is on the problematic behaviors, there is little recognition—and too much reinforcement—of the emotional behaviors that are actually making the children act the way they do. When the emphasis is on implementing such external controls, children are less likely to develop their own internal controls. There is even less awareness of the negative messages learned and repeated in the self-talk and mental tapes that fuel the toxic emotions many of these children feel.

I tell troubled children and their guardians, while placing my hand on my heart center, that when they feel better *in here,* they will act better and do better at home and at school. That simple gesture has been the secret to my success with troubled children and their families. It is the gesture I have used to connect with even the most difficult children and guardians.

As I took in the particulars of this foster parent's relationship with these children, I knew what I had to do. My first goal would be to encourage nurturance between the foster parent and the foster children. The contrast between how the foster mother received her natural child and the way she treated the foster children could only cause a divide between them and severely compromise the self-esteem and self-worth of the foster children. In order to reduce the negative effects of their past and current relationship with their natural parent, I would need to encourage an atmosphere of nurturance and loving acceptance in their present environment.

Troubled children are used to hearing how they are affecting others. When we focus instead on how they feel in their heart center, we are validating their pain and their conviction that they have a right to feel better. When they feel better, they change their behavior.

It is possible to create enough fear in the child to make the child control her behavior when the professionals and guardians are in the room. We can accomplish this, if we get an early start, much in the same way as we might train a dog. The child can learn to bury her pain, anger, self-loathing, fears, and negative opinions about the people who have reigned over her. She can learn to put on a smile and to comply with our rules and regulations.

Troubled children do know right from wrong. They can be forced to act on what they know without revealing their true emotions. But what happens when we are not in the room? What happens, a few years down the road, when the children hit puberty—or later, when they are out on their own? How will they then relate to their own children, except by example of everything we taught them?

Troubled children need to feel safe and sound. And, just as importantly, they need to feel that they do belong to us, in that home or classroom, as much as anyone else. They need to feel loved, and they need to know that their opinions and feelings are important even when they are "bad" opinions and "bad" feelings.

Many guardians and teachers have asked me, "How am I supposed to love or even like him when he acts like that?"

My response is, "If you can't feel it, fake it. Every time you feel the urge to push, pull instead."

We need to be consistent in positive and empowering ways. It sounds so easy, but it isn't. When children act out or withdraw, guardians and professionals feel manipulated—and no one likes to be manipulated. In an attempt to not feel manipulated, we fall into power struggles with the injured and troubled child. Invariably, when adults and children engage in power struggles, the tension builds, the volume increases, and emotional reactions take the place of creative action. We allow ourselves to be drawn into responding with a negative reaction.

What is the result? A pattern of toxic interactive communication develops in that relationship. The children soon feel just as unsafe and as unsound with us as they have with the other adults in their lives. These negative events trigger all of the fears and rage that were felt in recent and remote crisis situations at home or in the classroom. We suddenly find ourselves facing a raging monster. Or we find the children have withdrawn so far inside themselves that no one can reach or budge them.

In either case, the children and everyone who encounters them are set up for a series of negative events.

Power struggles happen most often when the adult has taken the child's rage or withdrawal personally. The disappointment and hopelessness in the child is felt as anger directed at the adult. The adult's reaction becomes more and more defensive. The adult begins to be angry at the child. It's as if the adult is saying to the troubled child (with their own facial expressions and body language, if not under their breath), "I can loathe you with far more cause than you can loathe me, you little brat!"

Few professionals and guardians would actually express such vehemence. This we know is true. But I am writing this for the ones who do. They are just down the hall and around the block from you. There are adults who use the foulest language to intimidate and coerce a child into immediate compliance.

In response to the withdrawn child, I have actually heard adults yell, "Go somewhere else if you want to feel sorry for yourself!"

"Get out of my sight!"

"Go ahead and enjoy your pity party."

"I wouldn't touch you with a ten-foot pole."

"Go to your room! You are not going to sit here and sulk."

To the troubled child who breaks down and cries in response to the meanness of others and problems in his life, I have heard adults yell, "Shut your mouth, or I'll shove my foot so far up your butt your head will spin!"

When that didn't shut the child up, I have heard them yell, "I'll give you something to cry about!"

Troubled children have plenty to cry about. Let's give them something to smile about instead, from deep down inside ourselves.

My work with that family continues to be one of the highlights of my counseling career. I met Tamara, the mother, and found out that she had been devastated by the loss of her children and a relationship with a drug addict. He had been caught cheating on her multiple times until he finally moved in with another woman he had gotten pregnant. She felt she wasn't prepared to be a good enough mother and couldn't live with the guilt and regret she had already felt about the life she had given her children prior to their removal from her home. She felt that she was worthless and that the children were better off forgetting her and living without her.

I saw her differently. Had she been worthless, wouldn't she have been indifferent about the life she had given her children? Might she even have fought to have them back so she could milk the state for the welfare checks they would have allowed her to receive, regardless of the quality of life she could offer them? I saw a woman who loved her children so much that she could let them go, despite the debilitating depth of sorrow their absence from her home caused her to feel.

I challenged her to identify the thoughts and negative self-talk that prevented her from doing the things she needed to do to get her children back. I helped her to acknowledge the strengths she had inside herself that had helped her to overcome obstacles in the past. I was able to educate her on how the drugs and alcohol she was using contributed to the mental, emotional, and physical pain that kept her from functioning.

During the first eight weeks, we did three sessions a week. I split my time with her and her children. The time spent with her in the beginning was used to challenge her despondency, substance abuse, and hopelessness. She had given up. I told her, in no uncertain terms, that no one gives up on my watch.

On days when she would feel too ill to participate in counseling, I would literally pull her out of bed, stand her on her feet, and order her to come outside with me, to get some air. She would reluctantly agree, first to accompany me to the end of her street, but soon, she was willing to take a ride to the Salvation Army. There she and I picked out a couple of dresses that were just her size and shoes to match and capris and blouses and jeans. Once she was able to see herself dressed up with her hair brushed, she was ready to check into a detox center. I visited her there every day to talk about her discharge plans.

I kept the children abreast of the approach I was taking with their mom and let them know that she wanted to be well and strong before she saw them again. They seemed to understand and waited with the hope that this time she really would come around. By explaining her condition in age-appropriate terms, I was able to give them a more objective understanding of what had kept her away. Until then, their understanding had been subjective. They had taken her absence and failure to follow the required sanctions personally. They had felt she didn't value them enough to follow through. Now they knew that she did value them and that she wanted very much to earn her right to have them back at home.

Part of her sanctions had to do with finding employment. That was hard for her, as she had dropped out of high school. To help her, I spent hours with her on weekends when my own children had events or activities outside the home to occupy them, and on weekday mornings after my children left for school, before I was due to show up at my counseling center. I took her to yoga classes so she could learn the art of meditation, yoga, and relaxation. We spent many afternoons and mornings reviewing material from a GED manual until she scored high enough on the practice tests to take the real test for her GED.

Even before she took the test, I took her to the local community college for aptitude tests to help her choose a course of action that could help her to gain confidence in pursuing an associate's degree. According to the aptitude tests, she would do well in customer service, medical billing, or even a nursing program. Because of her propensity for illegal drugs, we agreed that she should probably avoid the medical field. Instead she started thinking about becoming a yoga instructor.

We looked into what it would take for her to become a yoga instructor and found a place where she could actually work as a yoga instructor assistant. She stayed in outpatient drug rehabilitation and did so well in her new position that she began to receive referrals from clients.

The initial visits with her children began three weeks into my intervention with her. The visits were short at first. The children met with her for an ice cream at the local ice cream parlor twice a week. After a few weeks, we arranged picnics and little excursions to the park, the riverbank, and finally a whole day at the zoo with the foster mother and her daughter. That was the day I surprised her with the papers she needed to sign, in order to have her children returned to her home.

She was surprised and thrilled, as were both her children. They all agreed to continue receiving my services for the time it took her to adjust to having them returned to the home. The foster mother and daughter expressed elation for the mother and children but then cried a little, saying how much they would miss them. It was a very good day.

I invite the reader to come behind the scenes, to meet some more troubled children and the adults in their lives that I have had the privilege to meet face to face and eye to eye. As you will see in the chapters that follow, the work that is done during those first few sessions sets the stage and pace—not just for the treatment phase, but also for the entire healing process that continues once my work is done.

In these chapters, I demonstrate how I connect with the guardians and professionals involved in the lives of each of seven troubled children. I identify the underlying issues that need to be addressed, while identifying and reinforcing the strengths and positives that already exist. I show how to use those strengths and positives to make the changes that need to take place.

I struggle at times to hold myself to the standards that I believe are essential in forming right relations with those I serve. As I enter each home or classroom, I am confronted by my own limitations and tendencies that could, without astute self-checking, sabotage my intervention.

After reading this book, you might find it easier to identify troubled children such as Billy, Amy Lynn, and Kevin and to reach out to the adults in their lives as I did with Tamara. My hope is that you will, and that whenever you are close enough to feel the pain behind their rage or to hear their silent cries, you might reach out and pull them in to a place where they can feel safe and sound. Only then will they share with you the shattering secrets they hold. If you allow yourself to listen, if even to just one, with an open heart and an inquiring mind, you will know how to respond in a way that will make a difference in the life of a troubled child.

Chapter Four

Ishmael—Part One

Ishmael, aged seven, had behaved as a bully and a terror all morning, from the first moment he got on the school bus. By the time the first bell rang, he had been warned twice to keep his hands to himself. He had pushed one boy down who had accidentally stepped on his foot rushing to get the only choice seat left in the back of the bus. Later he almost hit a second boy, who was determined to be first in line at the water fountain.

Soon after the second bell, the teacher managed to get everyone seated and working on an assignment. And off he went again. This time she texted me with her telephone number followed by 911.

Ishmael had already been referred by his school to the community-based mental health agency where I was employed as a home- and school-based therapist. He was to receive individual and family counseling because his teacher wanted him to be removed from her class and placed in special education. In order to make that happen, she had to document that other avenues such as behavior management, teacher parent conferences, and counseling had been tried and failed.

I was to go in and provide the documentation that would prove the counseling component was as unsuccessful as everything else and that the only recourse was to transfer him to the special education wing immediately. I was to be no more than a gesture or a pawn in that endeavor.

His teacher wanted me to get started as soon as possible so that there would be no delay in getting him out of her class. I was not to rock the boat or in any way interfere in that process. The teacher's intention for the referral was not so that I could improve the situation; the only improvement she could envision was for him to be out of that classroom—and the sooner the better.

All of this had been explained to me in a manner that implied that surely I understood the reasons and would in no way question the emergent aspect of the situation. Clearly, I was not to complicate that process. She delivered the same message to me repeatedly: all I had to do was to prove, through my collateral documentation, that the counseling was unsuccessful and that the referral was the only viable solution left. If I could accomplish that, I would be a cherished member of her team, and our agency stood to receive even more referrals from her, since there were others who warranted transfers, in her opinion.

Once the school had submitted the referral to our agency, a case manager contacted the mother and gave her an appointment day and time to show up at the agency. She would need to sign authorizations for treatment and release of information forms that would allow the agency and the school to exchange information that would facilitate and expedite his transfer. I made a point of meeting the mother at that appointment, so that I could provide her with my number and encourage her to call me if anything should come up between the intake and our first counseling session.

Once I had the authorizations and release of information forms in hand, I went directly to the school to introduce myself to his teacher and to leave my number with her, as well.

I had to tell both of them, apologetically, that it could be a week or so before I could begin to work with Ishmael, as I had more than the recommended number of children already on my case load. The mother seemed relieved; she didn't know how she was going to fit the counseling into her schedule anyway.

The teacher acted as if she was extremely annoyed about the delay. She showed me the paperwork she had completed for the transfer. He had finally been tested by the school psychologist and duly labeled "emotionally disturbed." She thought that should have been sufficient evidence of the need for his immediate transfer, but there was the small matter of the counseling requirement. That was the one missing piece, the one component she had overlooked. To her it was simply a formality that she had to demonstrate on paper in order to push the transfer through. The idea that I wouldn't be able to start for a week or two unnerved her to no end. In her mind, it was ludicrous that his transfer should be held up at all, and now she was hearing it would be a while before I could even get started.

"Isn't there someone else who could get started with him?" the teacher asked, rather emphatically.

I had to tell her no. Unfortunately, most of my associates had the same number on their caseloads. We were pushing sixty to seventy hours into our forty-hour salaried work weeks just to service them.

She continued to complain that there had been one delay after another. It had taken several months to get the required psychological testing done. The request for that appointment had been sent out to the psychologist a little more than half way through the last school year. And yet, he didn't get tested until three months into the current year.

All I could do was provide her with my number and let her know that I would make myself available to her, should he act out at all between then and our first actual session. She settled for this; at least it was a promise that I would be there to collaterally document each and every incident from the get-go.

I was disappointed that it didn't seem to matter to her whether or not I would have time to do any real counseling with him at home or at school. While I noted this, I didn't address it. The fact that it served her purposes to text me at every turn served my purposes as well. I wanted to be abreast of any problems that might factor into his treatment plan, as well as any disciplinary measures the school might take in the interim.

As it turned out, that "interim" was to be less than I thought. I was called by his mother, Lydia, an hour before I was texted by his teacher—the very next morning. I called the mother's number immediately. She answered the phone screaming hysterically that I had to come over to her house as soon as possible. I said I would come right away but asked her to tell me, first, if she was all right and to describe what was wrong.

She told me that she and her husband had fought during the night. Now he was gone, and the police were after him, and she had to go to work. The car wouldn't start and she had no way to get the baby to day care or herself to work, and if she missed a day she would get fired. She didn't know what to do.

I told her I would be right over and hung up.

As soon as I got there, she sputtered another tangential account of the fight and Ishmael's role in it, the words she had with him before he left for school, and all the events that led up to the fight that had begun the night before. Ishmael's father had demanded that she give him some money for crack. She couldn't, as she barely had enough to pay the rent.

"He's a good man, but when he drinks and hangs around his brothers, he gets to smoking that crack," she said. "He gets so nasty. I can't stop him. When I try he just gets mad. I never should have started up with him. I know better, but what was I supposed to do? I can't give him the rent. He's already used up everything I had to buy food. I have to work. I could lose my job and him, and then where would I be? I get so I just don't care anymore. When I try I get this." She put her hand up to the bruises under her eye.

She was getting the baby up and dressed as she spoke to me. I just followed her around the house and let her go on about the fight. I couldn't help but notice how barren and cold her house felt. Hers was the only bed with a mattress. Ishmael's bed had two thin blankets that were spread over coil bed springs. No pillows. The baby had a crib, though, that stood, in an otherwise bare room, at the end of the hall opposite the bathroom. The whole house was dark except for the living room, where the windows faced east. There weren't any curtains.

"Lydia, how are you going to work today? You've got that huge bruise under your eye and your mouth is all swollen."

By this time, the baby was on the floor playing with a spoon she had found near where her mother had put her down. Lydia dropped herself into the couch. She just shook her head and answered, "Lord, I don't know."

"He will be picked up eventually and put in jail for doing this to you. This is domestic violence, and it's against the law," I said.

"Yeah, and he'll get his mother to bail him out. She did that for him before."

"He has been arrested for this before?"

"No. He was arrested for a DUI. It was a while ago."

"Do you want me to help you get a restraining order against him?"

"A what?"

"A restraining order. You can go to the Sheriff's Department and tell them that he did this to you and you want a court order that will keep him away. Once you have that, you can have him arrested for showing up here again. You can't keep letting him do this to you and the kids."

She shook her head. "He's not always like this. He's a good man. He doesn't do this unless he's been drinking. He's just not himself when he gets to drinking. If he'd just stop drinking!"

She barely got the last few words out before she dropped her head into her hands and started to cry. Her whole body shook as she cried. I sat there in silence until she was able to gain her composure. And then I said, "This isn't just about his drinking and drug use. He's violent. You have to draw the line there. There can be no violence in this house. Not with you, and most certainly not with your two precious children in here. You have to make that clear. There can be no more violence in here."

"I pushed him to that. He wouldn't have gotten violent if I hadn't run my mouth. I just get so mad I can't stop myself. I said things I shouldn't have, and he kept telling me to shut up. But the more he told me to shut up, the more I had to say. It's just I, he—Lord, I don't know. I know better than to get into it with him when he's been drinking."

"So what are you saying?" I challenged her. "Are you saying you should have given him the rent money? You could have just handed over the rent money and he would have been on his way and none of this would have happened?"

She nodded, missing the sarcasm in my voice.

"Lydia, you couldn't give him the rent money," I said. "This is not your fault. The fact that he doesn't control his temper and behave rationally when he drinks is his problem. You are not responsible for that. You are responsible for keeping a roof over the heads of your kids and for keeping food in the house. He expects you to be as irresponsible as he is. If you refuse, he will beat you up? Where's that at? What kind of a deal is that? Those aren't your terms; those are his terms. You are doing all the work and getting all the grief."

She just shrugged.

"You can't have somebody around that behaves like that," I continued. "You and the kids are better off without him. You need to get him out and keep him out. It comes down to him or the children—you have to make a choice between exposing them to violence and the risk of getting severely traumatized, or getting rid of him. I'd get rid of him if I were you. You don't need this. You need to get a restraining order against him. Didn't the police tell you that you could get a restraining order for when he gets out of jail?"

"I can't put my baby's daddy back in jail. How would they feel, having to tell their friends that their dad is in jail? What would they think of me if I did that?"

"Lydia, he will be informed of the restraining order. If he comes around in spite of that order, he is putting himself in jail."

I looked over at her and let my words ring in my own ears, as I watched her fold herself up in her arms, rocking back and forth, as if she were trying to rock out the overwhelming sense of hopelessness she felt. As she saw it, no matter what she did, it wouldn't be good.

"I understand what you are saying about them having to tell their friends that their dad is in jail. That is hard. It would be horrible for their self-esteem. But there are worse things. Living in these conditions is a lot worse. Living in a violent environment is no good for any of you. Someone could get seriously hurt. How would they explain that to their friends? He needs to learn that violence isn't allowed around you and your kids, and he needs to learn that today. He cannot continue to get away with this kind of behavior. You have a right to stand up for yourself and to draw the line. You have the right to say, 'No more violence!'"

"Yeah right! If I said that to him, he would punch me out. Anyway, he doesn't like to fight with me. He'll be sorry. We'll make up and everything will be okay."

She was too enmeshed in their relationship to see that everything would not be okay. Not for long, anyway. I continued to challenge her. "It'll be okay for how long? Until he drinks and uses drugs again. You know that as well as I do. How often does he drink?"

"He's trying to stop, but he gets upset with the temp service. He waits in line all day, sometimes two and three days in a row, without getting any work. He gets upset and gives up."

"Temp service? What's that?"

"He goes down to the employment office and stands in line all day waiting for a temporary job. Sometimes a job can last a few weeks. Most of the time, they just need someone for a few hours. They pile them all up in the back of a truck and take them off to a site where they can pick up a few bucks. He hates it. Whether he gets a job or not, he can't make enough to provide for us. He says he feels as if he's no better than a prisoner in a work camp. They treat them all as if they were bums. They don't treat them with any respect. They're supposed to bow down with their 'yes sirs' and 'no sirs' all day and then take their puny wages and go home."

"I see," I said pensively. There I was, crusading for the rights of this woman, impetuously waving the flag against domestic violence in her face. I was demanding that she get a restraining order against her husband to keep him out of there once and for all. I had been pushing her to have the jerk thrown in jail.

At the same time, I was struggling with the thoughts in the back of my mind. I was seeing her as being fifty percent responsible for the way he treated her—not because, as she thought, she provoked him, but because she kept letting him treat her that way. While I hadn't voiced those thoughts, I have to admit I thought them. In fact, I was getting as frustrated with her as I had become with him. There were moments early on, during her defense of him, when I thought of throwing my hands up and bowing out of the whole situation. The only reason I stuck to my guns in the beginning was because I didn't want to leave her or the kids at risk for more violence in the home.

But now I was confronted with my own intolerance of violent people and the people who allow themselves to be repeatedly victimized by them. And then, when they make excuses for them? Oh! I had to admit, at least to myself, it had made me cringe.

That self-awareness wasn't complimentary, but it was something I needed to struggle with, as I struggled with their issues. If I didn't, there would be no way I could influence positive changes in that family system. If I continued to indulge in my self-righteous discourse and gut reaction to the situation, using adamant and scolding tones, I would alienate them—and inadvertently increase the tension between them. They would then play that tension out on each other and the kids in my absence.

My first and expressed reaction was, in part, a result of the knowledge I had gained about alcoholics, drug addicts, and domestic violence. This knowledge came from textbooks and my own professional training. The insight revealed in my second thoughts, though, came from what I had accumulated in my attempt to integrate and implement that knowledge with actual experience during the course of my interventions with families.

What I learned in the field was that most couples do not split up when the courts or the Department of Children and Families split them up. They just become more covert. More times than not, the spouses or partners and the kids learn to lie and hide the fact that the estranged one is still in the home. Not only are they still in the home, but they are often vengeful against the one or ones who told on them. Consequently, in our attempt to protect the innocent, we put them at a higher risk for even more verbal and physical oppression and violence. This phenomenon has been proven to me again and again by children who have given me information for the Telling Wheel that I introduced in Chapter Two.

As righteous as my original arguments might have sounded on the surface, I knew from that experience with families of troubled children that I had taken the wrong approach to this from the start. I needed to backtrack now and take a different course. In order to keep sight of my goals, I needed to connect with the whole family. To do that, I had to get off my high horse.

I looked up at her and said, "I'm not sure we can prevent him from going to jail. I do understand what you are saying, though. It will be another blow to Ishmael's self-esteem, but it doesn't have to be a bad thing. I'd be willing to do whatever I can to help turn it into a good thing if the two of you would agree to participate in the counseling."

"He won't! He thinks you are all quacks. He wouldn't have anything to do with it. He already told me that."

"Well, we have a little leverage now. What if I were to appear at his hearing and ask the judge to set aside the order for his detention for as long as he is participating in counseling for anger management, domestic violence, and substance abuse?"

Lydia's eyes widened and a big smile spread across her face.

"I have seen judges do this in the past," I went on. "They give the defendant the option of treatment or detention. Treatment would have to include weekly anger management sessions, Alcoholics Anonymous or Narcotics Anonymous meetings, and domestic violence and family counseling."

"Sounds great, but he won't do it. He'll say he will but he won't show up. He doesn't think he has a problem."

"That might be true. I've worked as a crisis intervention therapist at a crisis stabilization unit where we also admitted addicts and alcoholics to a substance abuse program. Many of them were admitted involuntarily there, at the request of their families or employers. Most of them came in with the same lack of self-awareness, insight, and education about drugs and alcohol. Not all of them admitted that they had a problem. Many felt they had been victimized by their families, employers, and the judge who signed the order."

She nodded, as if that was her story too.

"The encouraging thing is that, when they get in there and encounter the other people who came in with the same attitude, they learn very quickly that it won't fly. Just as the saying goes, 'You can't con a con,' an alcoholic can't con an alcoholic in recovery very well, either. They break through their denial as they hear of the denial of others. They start to see a way through that denial once they begin to hear the stories of how others have broken through their denial. They begin to gain insight and self-awareness by listening to the stories of others who have demonstrated the same lack of insight he has demonstrated. He would see himself in their stories, right up to the part where they realize they have had a problem with drugs and alcohol."

"Yeah?"

"Yes. Over time he'll begin to see himself as having a problem—and then the work begins. Now some fail; this is also true. But we can give him the benefit of the doubt and stand by him until he shows us that it isn't going to work for him. I'd say it's worth a try. What do you think?"

Lydia lowered her eyes and sighed. "He'd probably go and then drink after the sessions."

"No, no, no, that won't happen. Well, it could happen, but not two times."

"Why do you say that?"

"I'll ask the judge to order random drug and alcohol screens. If he is caught with dirty urine, the whole program changes. He'll either be ordered to jail or to a treatment center where he can't access drugs and alcohol for an extended period of time. It would also be stipulated that if there has been even the slightest incidence of violence in here, he will automatically go to jail and await a hearing to answer the charges of assault and battery. We have the upper hand now. He just might get well in spite of himself if we team up here and give him that opportunity. What do you say?"

"I don't know. Do you really think it will work?"

"I think it's worth a try. I see it as his only option. It needs to be presented to him as his only option, if he wants to stay involved with you and the children. I understand this will be hard for you to do. I need you to try to understand that he has to see this as his only option. Even if you don't feel you have the desire or the strength to kick him out for good, you have to make him understand that he will be kicked out if he doesn't get some help. The only way you're going to be able to do that is to keep him out until he gets help."

"I'm not sure what you mean?"

"The judge will probably be more receptive to a plan that orders him to complete counseling in anger management and domestic violence along with documented attendance in AA or NA, as a stipulation and condition of his return to your home. He would be put on probation, and if he comes into your home before the judge allows him to, he'll be picked up and arrested for a violation of probation. If he misses a meeting or session, he would be charged with a violation of probation also. This charge would be added to his other charges. He would have to serve the time for all the charges sequentially. He could find himself in jail or prison for quite some time."

"I don't want him in jail."

"But he's headed for jail anyway—he's been violent with you, and there is a law against domestic violence. He already broke that law. The states attorney already has and will exercise the power to enforce that law. It would be up to him and the judge as to how that law will be enforced. If you're willing and able to cooperate with me, I'll meet with his public defender and ask that he or she petition the judge to consider treatment as an integral part of his sentencing rather than incarceration. He would be given the choice of treatment or punishment. Public defenders do this frequently, and most judges will order it. I'll simply make sure that those options are made available to him, in this instance, if that's what you want me to do. It's up to you."

At that point in the discussion, I was able to show her that she wasn't as powerless as she had been feeling up to now. She could take control and exercise that control in a way that would improve her whole situation. I was also telling her that she wasn't facing this alone anymore. She had a network that included me, the public defender, the states attorney, the judge, and his probation officer.

"So what do I do?"

"Three things: one, you stay out of the way and let him get arrested. Two, you tell him about me and give him my card. Let him know that I'm willing to speak to his public defender. One will be appointed to him at his arraignment. If he's interested, he has to call me. I won't accept any messages from you regarding his treatment. He'll have to contact me himself, and then he'll have to sign a release of information form so that I'm at liberty to speak to his public defender and the judge without breaching confidentiality. Three, you'll need to go to Al-Anon one or more times a week. You have some healing to do as well. You have developed a co-dependent relationship with him that will sabotage his treatment if you don't get some help."

"Co-dependent? I don't drink."

"Yes. That term is misleading. A co-dependent has been blinded by and caught up in the denial system of the alcoholic and drug addict. A co-dependent takes up the slack the addict leaves behind in the wake of his addiction, which means the co-dependent is shielding the addict from the fall and consequences of the irresponsible behavior that follows addictive use of drugs and alcohol. The addict gets sicker and sicker, and the co-dependent gets busier and busier cleaning up and picking up the pieces.

"Co-dependents cover up for addicts in every way possible. They even go so far as to take the blame for the dependency, as I heard you do earlier in this conversation."

Lydia blushed as I said this and, in a fleeting moment of insight, she could see that I was right. She definitely had been covering up for him and taking the blame for his addiction and violent behavior. A large part of her believed she was responsible for what had happened the night before and believed that if she had acted differently or been more successful at making things nice for him, he wouldn't have gotten drunk or resorted to using crack.

"Melody Beattie wrote a book called *Co-Dependent No More*. I suggest you read that book and go to Al-Anon meetings in addition to participating in the family counseling you and I are now doing."

"What's Al-Anon?"

"Al-Anon is a support group of people who have been or are currently in relationships with addicts and alcoholics. The group operates on premises borrowed from the twelve-step program of AA. Al-Anons know what you're going through. They know the level of pain and frustration people living with chemically dependents are experiencing. They know how helpless and powerless you've been made to feel in trying to keep your home and relationship intact despite his addictive behavior. They know how your attempt to keep everything looking good enables him and makes him sicker and sicker. They know how your efforts to make things okay actually propels him closer to the inevitability of an early death. They know how mortifying addiction is—not just for the addict, but for everyone with whom he interacts."

"That's for sure." She heaved a big sigh.

"They know how serious his condition is and how important his recovery would be for him and his family. They don't judge; they gather to empower and teach each other. It could be a way for you to learn about addiction and co-dependency. And it can give you the strength and the awareness you need to begin to heal yourself. You'll have to begin to work on healing yourself before you can help him and your children."

"I'm not comfortable in groups of people. It sounds good, but I don't like talking to a bunch of people about my problems. I mean, I'm sure it's good for some people but…" She shuddered. "I can't do that. It would be too weird. Besides, when would I go? What would I do with the kids?"

"I'm sure there will be others there who don't feel so comfortable in groups either, but Al-Anon works. It really does. People who live with addicts are isolated from other people, and that isn't good either. I think it would be good for you to do this, whether he chooses treatment for himself or not. I'll help you get there if you'll agree to check it out. I mean, if you go to a couple meetings and then decide it isn't for you, I'll drop it. But at least if you go, you'll be in a position to make an informed decision about whether or not it'll work for you. Right now it sounds scary, but you just might be surprised. Won't you at least check it out?"

She shrugged again, and I decided to press a little more. "Come on! We're expecting him to go to AA. He probably feels the same way about groups as you do, and yet we aren't giving him a choice. Besides, if he sees that you're trying to deal with the problem, it'll be harder for him to deny that there is a problem. You could actually help him by helping yourself. Let's do it! I'm going to be coming around two and three times a week. We could schedule some of our time together so that I'm available to get you there and then to do my therapy with the kids while you're at the first few meetings. After that, you should be able to connect with someone at the meeting who would be willing to give you a ride. How about it?"

She surrendered. I had presented enough of an argument that she gave in and agreed to check it out, reluctantly and with absolutely no enthusiasm, but that was enough for me. Then, after a brief period of reflection, Lydia expressed more doubt. "I wonder what he'll say about it? It'll probably make him mad. He doesn't like me going anywhere or doing anything except work or being here with the kids."

"He probably won't like the idea. But, again, we can make that part of our deal with him. Remember, you have the upper hand right now. You're calling the shots. We'll include this in the treatment plan that I'll offer to present to the judge on his behalf. We have leverage here, and I want to maximize it to the highest degree. He got to play tough guy last night. Now he has to reckon with the likes of me." I laughed a little and then added, "He's met his match!"

Lydia laughed a little too. It was good to see that her disposition had come a long way from rocking out the hopelessness she had felt while folded up in a defenseless ball, earlier in the session.

"Okay, it's decided. I'll go by the school and see how Ishmael is doing. He must be feeling awful after last night. Keep my number handy and text me if your husband should show up before the police catch up with him. The best thing you could do, to get this ball rolling, is find out where he is and see to it that the police get to him before he has a chance to come back."

Lydia squirmed a bit and exhibited some ambivalence about being the one to turn him in to the police. She probably still had some hopes of waking up from this nightmare in his arms or of kissing and making up, as they had done time and again. I pointed this out to her. She laughed nervously before agreeing to do what she had to do to keep him from showing up uninvited.

I let her know that I would be available by text anytime and that I would be showing up at least two and three times a week for counseling sessions. I also told her that I would be going to the school to see Ishmael and that he would be the focus of the counseling I would be doing with them.

Just as I finished that last sentence, my phone rang. I recognized the number as his school. I looked up at her and exclaimed, "Uh-oh. Something must be going down with Ishmael. She put a 911 in after the number. This can't be good. I better get over there."

I stood up quickly to go. She got up and thanked me for all of my help. I reminded her that I would be waiting for the text from her that would indicate either her husband had been arrested or he had returned home.

I then drove to Ishmael's school, as fast as I could, without breaking any laws. I entered the building, got his room number from the front desk, and appeared at his classroom door—in nine minutes flat.

Chapter Five

Ishmael—Part Two

Immediately upon entering Ishmael's classroom, I could see that his teacher was terribly flustered and upset. Ishmael didn't look happy either, sitting apart from the others, in the back of the room. His arms were folded and his head was down on his desk.

His teacher said, "He is to stay there for the rest of the day." And then, loud enough for him and everyone else in the room to hear, she justified his consequence further, saying, "He got so angry while doing his work that he threw his books on the floor, tipped his desk over, and then picked up his chair and threatened to throw it at me."

It was time for recess, and the teacher was lining the class up at the door. Her aide was going to remain in the doorway of the class to keep an eye on him until I arrived, but now that I was there, the teacher told the aide she could join her outside while I stayed in the room with Ishmael.

I politely declined, saying, "I'd rather have a minute with you before speaking with him, if that would be all right?"

The teacher grunted a bit under her breath and then reassigned the aide to Ishmael. Without a formal gesture or invitation from his teacher, I followed her outside, keeping sufficient distance for her to see that the class had found things to do on the playground. I then walked up to her and asked her to tell me again what had happened. My intention, at that moment, was to give her a chance to decompress and vent without upsetting the rest of her class or further embarrassing the culprit.

I could tell by her tone and carefully chosen words that she had little faith in what anybody would be able to do with Ishmael. She was determined to get the principal to make an exception and allow her to send him to the special education wing as soon as the lunch bell rang. Since he had only threatened to throw things, she couldn't have him suspended.

Then in a defensive tone she added, "What good would that do anyway? He'd still be back." By her mood and tone it would have been easy to think she was a big part of his problem.

My word, what vehemence! I said to myself.

"Any child of mine who behaved in that way would have had his due," she went on to say, "let me tell you!"

I was careful not to disagree with her. I used a sympathetic and concerned tone. I didn't want to give her the impression that I was judging her and taking his side. Had I been in her shoes, with the same level of responsibility on my shoulders that she carried for each of the thirty children in her class, I might have been just as exasperated if not downright fed up with such behavior.

I did recognize the gravity of the situation. I wanted her to know that I understood that he should be held accountable for his own behavior. But I also wanted to enlighten her on what was behind it all. I believed that if she had known why he was so disturbed, her reaction would have been different. She wouldn't have been at such a loss in figuring out what to do with him. I believed that information would trigger an increase in her intelligent responses and objectivity and that an increase in her objectivity would decrease the subjective emotional reactivity that I could feel in the atmosphere. I also wanted her to know that she wasn't alone in her efforts with him, because I was there now to intervene.

I leaned in close to her ear so that none of the children could hear me and said, "His behavior is very symptomatic. His family should have received services long before he got so out of hand." By saying that and without minimizing what he had done, I directed the focus of the problem onto his entire family system and to the delays in seeking outside intervention that should have been in place long before he reached the second grade. In doing that, I hoped to relieve her of any sense of guilt, failure, or hopelessness she might have been feeling.

She wasn't so easily calmed. She turned, looked at me squarely in the face, pursed her lips—looking as if she would like to slap me—and hissed, "Symptomatic? Symptomatic of what?"

Here again, his behavior was seen as the problem and not as it should have been perceived: as a symptom of a much greater problem brewing within the dynamics of his actual home life situation.

Teachers for the most part want to be successful with each individual student in their classes. When they meet with failure, it is devastating. They have an enormous responsibility, having to protect every child in their class from those children who are acting out in aggressive ways. How can they protect the other children without setting the destructive ones apart? At the same time, how can they effectively teach the disruptive ones to be an integral part of the group when they have been set outside the group, in response to their disruptive behavior?

These were the issues I hoped to be able to address.

I searched her face for some sign of the compassion I knew she had. In that moment, there was no such sign. I had to settle for what I did have; her full attention and eye contact. I took in a deep, slow breath, and said, "Ishmael's mother signed a Release of Information form so that I would be able to discuss some of the details of what it was like for him at his house, all through the night last night. It must have felt like a living nightmare to him." While it would have been a breach of confidentiality to disclose the details of what it had been like at his house the night before, without the Release of Information form that Ishmael's mother had signed for me, I could disclose what had happened to him and how he might have felt. I spoke softly, almost in a whisper, emphasizing the secretive nature of the information. I wanted her to realize I was taking her into my confidence, with enough information to help her to understand and deal better with his behavior.

"I just came from his house, where I have been talking to his mother. She had texted me frantically, a little before seven this morning."

That information actually carried more of an impact than it might have suggested on the surface. What I was saying to her was that my information was firsthand and that it was about an actual event. I was able to shift her focus to what may have triggered the outward, disruptive behavior he had demonstrated.

I hoped for the sake of that little boy, who now appeared so completely deflated and dejected in the back of the room, that she would consider taking a different approach with him. Furthermore, the fact that not only had I received and responded to a text, but I had actually gone to his house at that hour, gave me a degree of credibility that might otherwise have taken some time to prove.

I didn't offer any more information. I just stood there waiting and watching the children play. She appeared to be processing what I had said. Without any further prompt from me, she might have begun to realize that the cast of characters, in what had been a tragic play, extended beyond herself and Ishmael—and even further beyond herself, Ishmael, and me. I wanted her to see that there was more to what had transpired today and last night than what had met the eye.

Whether it was her curiosity or her conscience, or a combination of the two that got to her, I couldn't tell. I hoped it was more of the latter. She had been as flustered and as angry as she could be at a seven-year-old boy. Somehow he had gotten her goat and had caused her to reach a level of exasperation that she could barely control.

As I guided her toward a more objective and much less subjective examination of events, she was able to relax a little. Perhaps now she could see that he wasn't bigger than her and everyone else in the room, as he may have appeared to her just moments ago. In fact, if there were circumstances that might have explained his behavior, he might not be as big as he may have looked to her, right now, over there at the desk in the back of the room. I can't say for sure if these thoughts entered her mind, but it seemed as though they might have by the way her face fell and her eyes softened.

"What happened?" she asked. It was almost as if she were saying, "Tell me someone hadn't hurt him."

Ah! Now I had her humanity. And in that great state of wholeness when one's mind, heart, and soul are called to arms, she no longer stood before me, vengeful and ready to pounce on every word that came out of my mouth. Nor was she the fragmented and torn victim of this seven-year-old monster that just a few moments ago had her by the throat so tight she could hardly speak or swallow. No, now I had her whole integrated being, recoiling and receptive to hearing that there may have been some substantive rationale behind the torment he was expressing earlier that morning.

In response to her question, I took in another slow, deep breath with my eyes downcast, nodding as I whispered, "Something terrible and terrifying happened to him."

In that moment, our mutual humility brought us together, shoulder to shoulder and, eye to eye. We were no longer the corporal and the private. We were two professionals drawing from the better parts of each other to examine and deal with information that could clarify a very difficult situation. With that clarity, we could actually rise to the task of joining forces, setting in motion whatever was necessary to make things better for him, his teacher, and the other kids in his class—at least for the rest of today.

She invited me to sit with her at the picnic table and asked her aide to take over for a few minutes. As soon as we were both seated, I leaned in to engage her full attention, and then I began to describe his part in the drama that had occurred in his house the night before.

"I can tell you that he was so frightened that he spent the night in the back of his closet, rocking and cuddling his baby sister and that he went out into the night to a neighbor's house to call 911, because he felt he had to protect himself, his baby sister, and his mother. It breaks my heart to think that a little boy who would be so brave as to run out into the night to get help, without any concern for his own safety, would be sitting in such a pool of humiliation now." I let her mull over what little information I had just revealed to her, and then I continued to relay the story Ishmael had shared with his mother earlier that morning.

"Ishmael told his mother that the yelling between her and his father awakened his baby sister. When she started to cry, he got so scared for her that he climbed out of his bed, opened his door, and slid along the wall in the dark to her room, to get her. He knew if he didn't get in there first and stop her from crying, his father would go in there and beat her with his belt. His mother then confirmed that he does that a lot to both of them when he gets drunk at night. His baby sister quieted down when he lifted her out of her crib. Holding her in his arms, he then felt his way along the wall and back down the hall, to his room, and quietly shut his door behind him, so that his dad wouldn't hear them.

"He became more and more frightened as his parents' curses and epithets got louder. All of a sudden, he heard a door slam shut—and then he heard his father shout that he was going to kick it in. He heard his mother scream and a window break, all at the same time. Ishmael got so scared that his father would hurt his mother, or burst in and start in on him and his sister, that he stuck his sister in the back of his closet and climbed out of his bedroom window to get help from his neighbor's house.

"The neighbor called the police and then tried to persuade Ishmael to stay with him to be safe, but he was too scared for his little sister and refused to stay. He was in a hurry to get back with her. When the neighbor said he would go back with him, Ishmael cried that it would only get his dad even madder before the police could get there. He made him promise that he wouldn't. The neighbor argued that he could protect him, but Ishmael was so scared and in such a panic over the idea that the neighbor finally gave in and promised not to come.

"When he got back to his room, Ishmael climbed into the closet beside his baby sister, who had fallen asleep where he left her. He scooped her up and held her in his arms on the floor, in the far back corner of his closet. There he watched and waited anxiously for the police, until he couldn't stay awake anymore. He was still in there on the floor when his mother went in to get him up for school. No one from the Sheriff's Department came until after daybreak."

The teacher looked up at me, and I could see tears were beginning to well up in her eyes. She said, "They never do. They don't want to go into those projects in the middle of the night. They always wait until daylight." I didn't argue with her, although I didn't agree. I was very proud of our local police force for their swift responses to claims of domestic violence, but this was not the time to get into an argument with her about that.

"When the police did come," I continued, "Ishmael's father dashed out the back door and couldn't be found. Although the fight was over by then, his daddy knew he would be arrested because Lydia had bruises on her face and a bloody swollen lip.

"By the time Ishmael had to go to school, the police hadn't caught up with his father. He didn't know if they ever would catch him. He didn't know what his dad would do about him running to his neighbor for help. His mother had told him she wouldn't let him come back and that he shouldn't worry about it, but Ishmael had heard her say that lots of times. He stopped believing that she meant it.

"He told his mom that the neighbor had called 911 and that he was really mad at the police for not coming right away. She then said he told her, in very definite terms, that if his daddy came back and hurt her again, he would hurt him. His mother said she scolded him for talking such nonsense and then told him to get ready for school. She said she should have kept him home until he had calmed down, but then, she didn't know if there would be more fighting before she left for work."

I paused and gave her a moment to reflect on what had been shared with her. I looked over at Ishmael; I could see him through the door of the classroom, and I guessed how he must be feeling now. I then turned to his teacher and shared with her my thoughts on that very subject.

"Ishmael is upset for lots of reasons. He is tired. He is angry at the police and at his mother and father. He is worried for his sister, who is home alone with them. He knows he can't go back to watch out for her until the school bell rings. He is feeling as scared and stuck as a defenseless creature in a cage. He can't think about arithmetic today."

I saw more tears well up in her eyes as I continued to share my thoughts with her. "Some might say he should be referred to a psychiatrist to get some Ritalin. Others might agree that he should be put in special education classes so he can be with other boys and girls whose home lives are the same, but I adamantly disagree. Troubled children like Ishmael are smart and sensitive. They are warriors, not survivors yet. They are the small wonders of the world, and they have so much to give.

"We can condemn this child for the behavior of the people governing him at home. We can focus on all the bad images brought to mind in recounting the behavior of his parents the night before. Or, we can focus on how brave he was to go out into the night, how scared he must have been to leave the safety of his room, to edge his way along the wall, all the way down the hall, in the dark, to rescue his baby sister, while his mother and father were throwing things and screaming at each other, louder and louder, in the next room. I let myself imagine how he felt as he sacrificed himself to rescue her from their father and how he must have trembled as he cuddled her in his arms, sitting on the floor in the back of his closet, throughout the night."

Now that she had softened and shown how touched she was by the story of his bravery and selflessness the night before, I asked her, again, to delay her referral to special education classes, encouraging her to think about how that action could set off a chain reaction that could impact him in profoundly negative ways for the rest of his life. I let her know that I felt such a referral would be a terrible mistake.

I argued as persuasively as I could, "It would be as if we were saying, 'Because of your abusive home life, you don't belong with the rest of us. You must be with your own kind. We won't put up with you. We won't help you control your behavior by pulling you in to where you feel safe and sound. We won't join forces to help you feel as if you are one of us and that you are where you belong.' Instead we would be saying, 'You don't belong here. You belong in a group where no one feels safe, half the time. We will not put up with your anger and your pain. Go away and influence your own kind with your behavior. We don't want it here!'"

I then said, gravely, "Such sentiments may seem justified in the narrow view of that incident today in your classroom. But have we solved the problem by putting him in a class with children who are so disruptive that he won't be able to learn? By isolating the behavior to one hall or wing of the school, have we isolated it, at all, from the other kids in his class and neighborhood? More important, have we done anything to reduce the pain and rage behind it all? No! It is here, fueling toxic reactive behaviors in children in our streets, markets, shopping malls, schools, churches, and neighborhoods. And it seems to be getting worse, despite these 'special' classes, every year."

She nodded and listened without objecting, so I continued.

"Our tendency to escape what we could embrace, to push away when we could pull these children in, is a big mistake, in my view. It is blatantly evident in the press that crime rates involving our young have escalated, despite the commencement of these programs. We are accomplishing the opposite of our intent by creating such factions. By endorsing them, we are undermining and corrupting society.

"We need to dissolve rather than reinforce the mindset of 'Us and Them.' We need to teach parents and teachers how to help troubled children heal and grow in the mainstream."

His teacher looked up at me with tears again welling in her eyes. She shook her head and, with a somewhat defeated posture and tone, she said, "You are so right. But even when we do ask for help with them, we are told there aren't enough counselors to go around."

I agreed with her and added, "We could allow more college students, majoring in education, psychology, and sociology, to intern as teacher's assistants and counselors. We could help cover tuition costs for professionals with life experience, holding degrees in special fields, to become certified in education. We could offer parenting classes, substance abuse treatment, and more home- and school-based counseling programs on the school grounds. It is remarkable that even as the numbers of crimes among the young increase, we have limited the funds, even to the point of closing down many such home- and school-based programs for lack of funding."

I wanted her to understand that I was on her side and, although I had a different solution in mind, I did see that hers was a real problem that could not be minimized or dismissed. "We do need to address and resolve the behavior management issues in our schools. We need to fund school- and home-based programs sufficiently in order to hire the number of counselors that it would take to actually make a difference in the lives of these children, so that teachers don't have to wait to get help managing them.

"Too frequently, the tax payer's money is being used to ignite the timbers of another form of segregation by isolating troubled children in special education classes, juvenile detention centers, residential programs, and prisons. We are losing more than our hard-earned money: we are putting ourselves in danger of losing precious peace of mind, even in our most affluent communities."

I reached my hand across the picnic table to her in a gesture of empathy and support, as I asked her to delay her referral to special education. She did agree to delay it. I told her I would be working intensively with her, his family, and with Ishmael. I asked that she wait to see if things changed for the better. Most often I have had to warn parents, guardians, and teachers that things would get worse before they got better, but in this situation I could not imagine worse.

"There is no magic wand," I said. "The fruits of our efforts today will be realized over time, long after I am gone. Treatment is a process, not an event. It's not my job to change anything or anyone. It was my job to put the machinery and tools in place for change to occur, over time.

My goal was to take the back seat and to remind or teach the guardians and teachers how to drive. I wanted those who knew how to drive to refresh their driving skills. But I also wanted them to learn to take the most scenic roads. It was never my intention to make them suffer through the treatment process. I wanted it to be enlightening and fun.

I was very pleased with the outcome of my intervention with Ishmael. His teacher did agree to work with me. His dad satisfied the court order for anger management and domestic violence counseling. He attended AA several times a week, even after he was allowed back in the home. I was able to help him get into some classes where he could get the mechanics training he needed to get a good job with a local auto shop. He was able to land that job in the middle of his first semester at the local community college. His boss told him he was good enough to learn the rest there if he wanted to work full time. He started out earning twice what he had ever earned before.

His mother was equally committed to her Al-Anon meetings. She attended a co-dependency support group and made new friends. One friend introduced her to her boss, who hired her for a position that allowed for her to have a flexible schedule.

Ishmael spent many afternoons with me. As a backdrop for our individual sessions, we got into doing things that helped him see the brighter side of life. We took a field trip to an ostrich farm. The ostriches made us laugh as they followed us back and forth, running and walking along their side of the fence.

I let him talk about the way he felt when his parents had their fights. He expressed the deep disappointment he had been made to feel and the weight of powerlessness that swelled in him when he found he couldn't stop them, no matter how hard he tried. He had been made to feel so small and vulnerable. I challenged him to see how strong he had been the whole time, and how big he looked to me when he reached out to help his sister in the midst of the storm of violence going on that night.

We went to the museum and saw the dinosaurs. We picnicked at the pond and fed the ducks for hours. We checked books out of the library that would help us identify local vegetation and wildlife. We'd then go to the national park and see if we could find any of them. It was every bit as exciting as any other treasure hunt would have been. We'd sit on the riverbank sometimes and pretend to wait for Tom Sawyer to come around the bend. We had plans for where we'd go if he ever did come. Somehow we always felt he really would, this time. But sooner or later we'd give up and eat our picnic lunch without him.

Years later, he ran up to me in a local department store, calling out to his mother that I was there. In a flood of exuberant words, he told me that she and his dad were both working at higher paying jobs and that everything had changed for the better. He was on the honor roll and was one of the best football running backs his school had ever had. He gave me a great big hug and said he owed it all to me.

"Me?" I chided. "What do you mean? I don't know the first thing about football. You did this all by yourself. I might have just cleared the way a little, a long time ago, but look at you! Look at what you have made of yourself!"

I beamed ear to ear all the way home after that encounter, saying, "Wow!" to myself, over and over.

Chapter Six

Angela

Sometimes it was helpful to think of how it must have been for the more intimidating adults when they were kids. I was able to extend a little more compassion, patience, and understanding to them when I did. I would think of them this way especially if a guardian or teacher was extremely big and mean. I would speculate that they were quite possibly treated in much the same way, when they were little, as they were treating their own little ones now. I would then picture them in knee socks and shorts, trying to get somebody in the house to get them a drink of water. I let myself imagine how it must have hurt to get popped in the mouth for speaking out of turn, or slammed in the back of the head by somebody's hand just for being small and "stupid."

In keeping with that perspective, I was able to keep an open mind and to refrain from jumping to conclusions about anyone, no matter what their size and disposition. While I tried to take in all the information given to me in my left ear, I kept my right ear open for the other side of the story.

And there always was another side to the story that was, more often than not, just as intriguing and plausible—if not downright believable—as the first account. Without this deliberate attempt to keep an open mind, I found it easy to make the wrong assumptions or to jump to the wrong conclusions. My work with Angela is a great example of how easily I could have jumped to all the wrong conclusions.

Angela, aged seventeen, lived in the projects with her biological parents and was having trouble with her attendance, grades, and behavior in school. When I tried to work with her, she was extremely resistant. She wouldn't talk about her family. She denied that there were any problems at home.

Her parents were equally mute. They didn't air their dirty laundry in public and resented the school's referral and having to allow outside intervention.

"Everything is fine at home. The problem at school must be with the teachers," her mother said.

In light of their resistance, I was surprised to receive a call from Angela a little after midnight on New Year's Eve. Her voice quivered and trembled as she told me about the fight she and her mother were having with her father. I could hear dishes hitting the walls and floor in the background. She cried as she told me they were throwing things and yelling at each other, and that she was going to call the police.

I asked her to put her father on the phone. She did.

I could easily have escalated the ruckus had I assumed he was at fault or had I been the least bit authoritative or judgmental. Instead, I took an investigative approach and asked him if he felt he was being ganged up on. He said yes, indeed, he did. I asked how he would feel if I were to come over there and talk with him alone outside.

He was shocked. "You're going to come here in the middle of the night?"

I said, "I can be there in just a few minutes."

He was silent for a moment and then said, "Sure! I'll wait for you out by the entrance."

After I made him promise that he would go outside, to the end of his road, I asked him to put Angela back on the phone. I told her of my plan and then told her to call 911 if things got out of hand before I got there. Now this was a paradoxical maneuver that I wouldn't recommend to everyone, but it was surprisingly successful.

Angela's dad had a lot to talk about, and I was able to keep my mind open—despite the picture painted by the daughter that he was the villain. He felt powerless in that family. He worked two jobs to keep them in shoes and clothes and a roof over their heads. But he wasn't allowed to participate in the parenting of his daughter or in any of the big decisions about any of his children's welfare. What's more, although he had two young sons, his two daughters were grown. Angela, the youngest daughter, was seventeen, in her senior year in high school, and the only daughter still at home.

He had fostered and enjoyed a very close relationship with both of his daughters and now one was already out of the home while the other was close behind. Detaching was very hard for him. It made him hold on so tight that both girls had fought him to get away. They pulled every kind of travesty they could to prove that he was losing his hold. They saw their father as being too rigid, strict, and protective. They no longer felt his love for them or their love for him.

In pulling away from him, they had resisted any form of authority and butted against every boundary at home and at school, like a goat butting against a fence.

The mother had always sided with the girls. She understood their need to be recognized as having grown up. Between her and the daughters, the father felt he didn't have a leg to stand on.

The argument that night commenced when he caught Angela coming home from a New Year's Eve dance "with nothing on." This was, of course, an exaggeration, which I was able to get him to admit. She had on a long satin skirt and sequined top. It was an elegant formal New Year's Eve outfit, and she looked absolutely gorgeous in it. While I understood a father's concern about his daughter going out in what could have been viewed as a provocative outfit that made her look older than her actual age, it wasn't out of step at all with what the girls were wearing to a formal dance.

He wasn't trying to be mean; instead, he was looking out for her in an overly protective way. I certainly didn't want to hold that against him, and I was happy I hadn't jumped to conclusions or advised her on the phone to hurry and call the police. It might have turned out that he was a threat to them, but I wanted to at least be in a position to make that decision for myself. I felt lucky to have had a chance to talk to him.

My receptivity and reflective listening caught him off guard. He talked to me openly for over an hour, shifting from sighs of exasperation to tears. As we drove back to his place from the entrance, I teased, "So, it's been a while since you were understood in that clan of ruthless females, huh?"

He laughed heartily and then agreed to work with me in family sessions to bridge the communication gap between him and his wife and daughter.

I have learned to approach situations with an open, investigative, and non-judgmental mind. Were I to approach them with a narrow or closed mind, I wouldn't get so much as a foot in the door, twice. If we know it all and question nothing, nothing will be revealed or confirmed. If we inquire from a holier-than- thou judgment seat, we will find ourselves, and the throne we're sitting on, out on the street in a heartbeat.

Professionals only increase resistance when they approach families with such a pompous attitude I applaud the families for standing their ground and for tossing the charlatans out. And I apologize profusely for their self-proclaimed holier-than-thou posturing and attitudes. In the chapters that follow, I demonstrate how to alleviate the level of frustration guardians express, and I introduce the insight, strategies, skills, and techniques I used to guide them to a successful outcome.

Chapter Seven

KATY—PART I

A representative knocked on the door of my office at the Crisis Stabilization Unit (CSU) and announced, "There's a mother out here who wants you to get a psychiatrist in here to see her daughter or to have her admitted to the CSU."

"For what? Did she say?"

"No, but she looks upset."

I went out to introduce myself to the mother, who told me her name was Gretchen. Before I could tell her my name, she demanded that I allow her to admit her daughter into the Crisis Stabilization Unit.

"Where is she?"

"She's in there." I looked to where she was pointing. She had shut the six-year-old child into one of the screening rooms, where I could see her jumping up and down so that her smiling face disappeared and reappeared in the window of the door. Her mother wasn't smiling.

"Why don't you tell me what's been going on," I said.

"She's been showing her butt! She won't listen to what I say, and she terrorizes my babies. And then, when I try to discipline her, she throws a temper tantrum, destroys everything in the room, bangs herself on the wall, throws herself down on the floor and screams and yells. She's completely out of control. I've got to get some help. I want to see a psychiatrist."

"We do have a doctor on call, but let's talk for a few minutes and see if I can get her to tell me why she's so angry and upset."

"There's nothing to talk about. I want to talk to a psychiatrist. The medicine her regular doctor gave her for ADHD isn't working. I want to sign her into the CSU and get back home to my family. She needs some medication and counseling or something that will stop her behavior. I can't—I've tried everything."

"I'll talk to her if you'd like. I'll do a full assessment and determine if she meets criteria for admission."

"There's nothing to talk about," she insisted. "I'm ready to sign her in. I have small children at home, and I don't have time to hang around here. I have no problem signing her in, and I'm not taking her home. I can't have her at home where she ruins everything for everyone else. I've had enough!"

I explained to the mother, to be admitted voluntarily, the child would have to meet specific criteria, and then, she would have to participate in a private hearing so we could determine her willingness to sign herself in to the CSU.

"What do you mean? What criteria?" she demanded.

"The child must be a danger to herself or others."

The mother's body language suggested that she might be a danger to me and her daughter if the daughter wasn't admitted immediately. It was evident that the daughter had pushed Gretchen to the point where she couldn't be certain she would be able to control herself in managing the child without hauling off and smacking her—or worse. Unfortunately, that reason alone wasn't good cause for an involuntary admission of the child, although I must admit thinking that Gretchen might meet the criteria herself, if she didn't find a way to calm down.

I wanted the mother to relax and to be ready to participate in the assessment process before we entered the room, so I decided to attempt to do some crises intervention with her right there in the hall. But before I could open my mouth, Gretchen said, rather abruptly, "She's barely six years old. How is she supposed to sign herself in? I'm her guardian!" She was shaking and so angry she could hardly speak.

"I understand how that sounds, but it's the law. Every state has its own procedures and requirements for signing someone into a crisis stabilization unit, whether it's on an involuntary or voluntary basis. In Florida, the child would have to be willing to sign herself in if she were to be admitted on a voluntary basis. You wouldn't be able to sign her in without the child's agreement to be admitted. There would have to be a private hearing that allows the child the opportunity to understand what she is agreeing to, and then she would have to agree, without any coercion, to be admitted. Are you her biological parent?"

"No. She has been with me since August. She's my brother's daughter. He and his wife lost all of their children to the Department of Children and Families, and they finally gave me custody of Katy. They had been abusing the kids."

"You have legally adopted Katy? There has been a termination of parental rights (TPR)?"

"I have guardianship. The adoption is in process."

"Is there a TPR—that is, have the parental rights been terminated by the Department of Children and Families?"

"No. They are in the process of doing that."

"Do you have a court document authorizing you to sign for psychiatric treatment and psychotropic medication?"

"I have a court order authorizing me to seek any medical attention she needs."

"Does it have a clause for mental/nervous or psychiatric treatment and medication?"

"I don't think so."

"Well, unfortunately, without that authorization, stamped and signed by a court, we would need the parents' consent for treatment."

"I'm her guardian! I have the court papers that say I am her guardian."

"I understand, but the state statutes are very specific about that." I let her know that I did sympathize with her, but the statutes were clear: I couldn't accept the child on a voluntary basis without the biological parents' consent for treatment, unless there was a TPR.

"If she is a danger to herself or others, she can be admitted. But we wouldn't be able to treat or medicate her without either a Termination of Parental Rights or a court document that specifies your authority to sign for psychiatric or mental health services. Psychiatric services are not included in the medical authorization for treatment."

"Well, we'll just have to forget it then. Her parents won't sign for her. They don't think there's anything wrong with her. They don't think she needs treatment. Are you telling me that if she were suicidal or homicidal that you wouldn't take her because I don't have those papers?"

"No. We can take her; we just won't be able to treat her. We might be able to get an emergency treatment order to medicate her if necessary, but we would still need those signatures."

"That's ridiculous! What am I supposed to do? I'm not taking her home, so you'd better do something with her."

In some cases a psychiatrist can request an emergency treatment order (ETO) from the court, but even in that case the order is temporary.

I have explained the law to agents of the department after they insist that because the child is a ward of the state, they automatically have the authority to sign. On the contrary—at least in the state of Florida—the law is clear that if they haven't terminated the parents' rights, they don't have the legal authority to sign for psychiatric services. Without that order, the child is admitted without treatment until a psychiatrist goes to the court and gets the order that will allow treatment. Again, this is true even when the child meets the criteria for admission.

It's also true that a parent or guardian can't sign a child into the CSU on a voluntary status, even when rights are firmly documented, without the child's expressed agreement. And that agreement is to be obtained from the child in a private hearing. When a child needs the security of the CSU to prevent harm to himself or others, and that child won't agree to the admission, an involuntary admission contract can be drawn up by a psychiatrist, medical doctor, clinical nurse practitioner, licensed clinical social worker, licensed mental health counselor, or a law enforcement officer.

After explaining the process to Gretchen in a sympathetic manner, I asked her to allow me to see if I could talk with her and Katy and suggest some short-term strategies that would help them make it through the weekend.

"Sure," Gretchen answered sharply. "Maybe if you actually talk to her, you'll see what I'm talking about. I am not taking her home!"

"Well," I said, as I reached for the knob and stepped aside to let her enter the room, "let's see what we can do."

When we entered the screening room, I told Katy my name and asked her to have a seat on the couch for a minute while I talked to her aunt. Katy had settled down by this time, but it was clear she was in no mind to sit down. She stood instead, with her arms folded, her nose up in the air, and a big smirk on her face. She wasn't going to budge.

Gretchen sat down across from me at the table and started to tell me again about the child's behavior. I held up my hand and politely motioned for her to wait. I wanted to observe the child for a few seconds. She agreed, but not without folding her arms in exasperation. "Go ahead!" she huffed. "She loves the attention. She'll do anything for attention."

I observed that the child was being oppositional and defiant. She would not be cajoled or manipulated into participating in the assessment process. She wouldn't take her nose out of the air to answer any questions. The more I asked her, the higher she'd stick up her nose. She wouldn't even tell me her name.

"Her name is Katy," Gretchen said, interrupting my attempts to get Katy to communicate. She turned a mean face toward Katy and scolded her. "Katy! Stop being such a show-off. Sit down and tell her why you're here."

"She's okay," I said. "If it's all right with you, I don't mind if she wants to stand." I asked the aunt to agree so that I didn't initiate a triangulation by undermining her authority.

Gretchen threw up her hands in a helpless gesture. "Katy is just going to do whatever she wants to do anyway. She never listens. I can't get her to do anything I ask."

"Tell me why she is here. What happened tonight?" I focused my attention on the guardian while watching the child out of the corner of my eye. The shift in my focus caused her to shift her feet a little bit. The smile shrank slightly on her face. Her eyes opened wider.

"Like I said in the hall, she was showing her butt."

"What started it? What happened?"

"She's been acting out all day. At first, I put her in time out, but she kept turning her head around to chide and tease her brother."

"You didn't have to pull my hair or pop me in the mouth," the child whimpered, and then threw herself on the couch.

"That's another thing," Gretchen moaned. "She pinches and bruises herself and then says, 'See! Now I have proof.' She tells everyone I'm abusing her."

"You did pull my hair!" The child looked over at me and said, "And she smooshed my face into the wall, too."

"I did not pull your hair," Gretchen argued. "I was holding your hair and you moved your head. You pushed your own face into the wall."

"Uh huh! I called my brother a baby, and you came up and pushed my head so my face hit the wall."

Gretchen turned to me and rolled her eyes. "She always says I'm abusing her. She does it to herself and then says she's going to show people the bruises and get me in trouble."

Both the child and the guardian may very well have been telling the truth. I was told a few days later, by the child's guardian ad litem, that the child had a history of bruising herself to get the aunt in trouble. In fact, she had done it right in front of her, on one occasion. What I said to the guardian ad litem was, "I wasn't there. The child is saying one thing and the guardian is saying another. I can't say, factually, which one is telling the truth, because I wasn't there. Each story is equally plausible. The child has bruised herself. Now that you've told me you've seen this, I believe it's true that she did it on that one occasion. But that doesn't mean the guardian didn't get so exasperated that she pulled her hair and pushed her face against the wall, in the instance we were discussing in the CSU."

Throughout this interview, Katy did everything she could to test my patience. She danced, twirled, shouted, cried, and ignored me whenever I put a question to her. Through all of that, I was able to get a picture of what she was going through at home.

Her uncle had said he no longer wanted her at his house; he wanted her to stay at the CSU for the rest of her life. Katy reminded Gretchen of this, and she didn't deny it. Instead, she qualified it.

"Well, what does she expect?" she said to me. "She's been acting out all day. The time-out incident was just the beginning. It snowballed from there." Gretchen turned to Katy and demanded, "Tell her what you did just before we left the house."

Katy just stared at her and folded her arms on her chest. Gretchen continued, "I have a three-year-old little girl and an eighteen-month-old little boy. I had just gotten them both to sleep when she decided she wanted a snack. When I told her no, she got mad and ran down the hall to their room.

She slapped the baby, Adam, and woke him up and then ran to Sasha's room and hit her. We have literally had to hold her down and restrain her to keep her from hurting anyone."

I nodded, and Gretchen continued. "She's out of control at school too. They've done everything to help me with her, but nothing helps. I do everything the behavior management specialist tells me to do, to the letter. It doesn't work with her. She gets counseling at school. She has a guardian ad litem that lets me call her all hours of the night for help in figuring out what to do. She's on Ritalin and Clonopin, prescribed by her primary care physician, but that doesn't help—she's getting worse! They say she has ADHD, but none of the medicines are working. I don't believe the ADHD diagnosis. She just likes to show her butt. She knows right from wrong and enjoys stirring everybody up. She likes the attention. She does this dirty dancing thing, too."

That was the child's cue. She jumped up off the couch and said, "Yeah, see?" She then proceeded to bend her knees, drop, move, and thrust her hips in a wide circle with a big smile on her face.

I asked Gretchen if there had been any allegations of sexual abuse.

"Yes. There had been, but they weren't confirmed. Her parents were on drugs and were drunk all the time. They were arrested and jailed over and over again for domestic violence. The children were left alone at the house overnight. They didn't bathe. They never kept any food in the house. On top of that, she kept getting pregnant. We stepped in when the department finally took away her last two children. Katy has been in foster care since she was four years old. By the time we stepped in, Katy had been in fifteen different foster homes. They kept shoving her out because of her behavior."

"Does she have older brothers or sisters?"

"Yes. She has two older sisters and two younger brothers, but they went to live with their various fathers' families." Gretchen then explained that she was Katy's paternal aunt but that Katy calls her "mommy." She also disclosed that she was twenty-eight years old when she got custody of Katy, only five months prior to this interview.

I turned toward Katy and asked sympathetically, "You were taken from your mommy when you were four years old? Do you remember what it was like at your house, with your mommy and daddy? Are you angry about some of the things that happened?"

She looked at me from the couch, where she was now sprawled out with her arms folded on her chest. It appeared as a gesture of resignation, as if she were thinking, *No one knows or cares what I have to say, so why say anything?* I began to consider her, in the light, of the information I had just received.

She was the third born. Since there were two older and two younger siblings, she was the middle child. She had been raised in an environment of drugs, alcohol, and domestic violence. There were allegations of sexual abuse, which could be reflected now in her inappropriate sexual acting-out behavior. Even without the latter, she had plenty of reasons to be hurting and angry. She had not only been exposed to a dysfunctional and violent family system, but she had also lost her mother, father, and four siblings. On top of that, she had a history of multiple foster care placements. Now her paternal aunt, who had two young children of her own to care for, was adopting her because no one else in the family would.

Gretchen was being so harsh with her that Katy couldn't express her thoughts and feelings except in behaviors that disturbed everyone else—in the way that she herself was disturbed. It was as if she were thinking, *If they can't know and don't care, then at least let them feel the same pain and anguish. It's only fair.* I smiled at her as if I agreed.

The aunt's two children were eighteen months and three years old. They were most likely being coddled as babies are meant to be coddled. I sensed that Katy was expected to be beyond that now.

It was clear to me that the aunt could manage her better if she would take some of these factors into account. I sensed that she took them into account only to define the child in terms of the old adage, "The acorn doesn't fall far from the tree." The troubled child was being seen as a carbon copy of the parents, as if she had earned the same rap sheet.

I decided to see if I could get the child to demonstrate and verbalize some of these complaints. I repeated my question with a tone that implied it would be to her benefit to answer. "Are you angry about what happened when you were living with your parents?"

"Yep! And I miss my sisters. They loved me better than she does."

"Did your sisters take care of you?"

"Yep. And they were nice to me. She isn't—she hates me."

I turned to the aunt. "Do you hate her?" The aunt would not respond. I repeated the question. Still no response.

The child's face darkened, and a tear formed in the corner of her eye. "See? They hate me."

"Well, what do you expect?" Gretchen said. "Look at how you behave. You know when you are acting out and you know what you are supposed to do, but you refuse to behave. How can we love you when you act out every day?"

The child turned abruptly so that her back was to us and her face was facing the back of the couch. She started to sob very quietly.

"Right!" Gretchen said. "Now she cries like it matters to her. I'll be honest with you—she's done nothing to make us want to keep her in that house. She's going to cause me to lose the other two, just so they won't be subjected to her threats and bullying. She has choices. She's been warned but nothing we say has any effect on her. She knows what she needs to do, but refuses. She doesn't care, so why should we?"

"Are you saying you don't love her? It's an important question. We want the child to feel that we love them but not their behavior."

The child turned toward her aunt and waited for her to answer. Gretchen remained silent.

Some therapists might say that I shouldn't have pursued this discussion in front of the child, or that my approach was too confrontational. I operate from the premise that when things flare up behind closed doors, all kinds of negative sentiments are expressed. Why not tease some of it out, in my presence? I want to hear what is behind the scenes that is causing this child to act out so vehemently. I want to expose why the child is feeling the way she is and why she acts out with such ferocity.

I never know if the child's predicament will ever be understood. I don't know if the guardian will ever have another opportunity to see her part in what is making the child act out. I approach crisis interventions such as this as an educational opportunity for the family that might otherwise never occur. I'm not there to judge but to heal, yet I can't heal when the wounds are concealed. I can't heal when the cause of the wounds is overlooked. They had to be addressed.

I knew that the aunt would respond with defensiveness, but I've learned that the defensive reaction is temporary. The impact of such an undressing opens the way for a better understanding of the dynamics in question. This often leads to a gentler interaction within the family system. Such exposure and disclosure provides the grist for the mill of the guardians' conscience. This guardian needed to open her mind to the child's viewpoint, if she was ever going to learn how to relate to Katy.

Gretchen was asserting that whatever wounds Katy bore, she had for the most part, brought them on herself. Thus she was getting just what she deserved. This was a lie and a travesty! It underestimated the damage done to the child, prior to being removed from the home, during the two years of multiple placements in foster homes, and as a direct result of the atmosphere of her current placement. It put the whole burden on the child to straighten up and act right without any recognition of, or consideration for, the wounds already in place or the wounding going on in the present.

The guardian's assertion that she had had all the behavior management training she needed and that she followed what she had learned to the letter without success makes my case about behavior management. Behavior management, especially in the aunt's "I won't give an inch" drill sergeant manner, doesn't begin to address, never mind resolve, the child's pain and anguish. The child didn't feel wanted or loved in this home. The less she felt wanted and loved, the more she acted out, in a vicious cycle that spiraled up until it was an out-of-control tornado that perpetually spun through their household. The child was then blamed for the destruction left in the wake of that tornado.

One of the main reasons the guardian didn't feel love for the child was that she took personally all of the child's rage and defiance. She felt unappreciated for all of the classes and counseling she had set up for the child. She claimed to have spent more time on this child than on her own two combined, and to no avail.

The point is illustrated in the following excerpts from our interview.

"Do you love her?" I asked Gretchen.

Rather than answer my question, she turned and addressed the child. "Tell her where we went two weeks ago."

Katy wiped her tears and looked at me, as if to say she didn't know what her aunt was talking about.

"Where did we go?" Gretchen demanded.

Still, there was no response from the child. The guardian then turned to me. "We just spent a week at Disney World."

My eyes must have crossed at that point. I was holding my lips tight together so as not to say, "And how does that answer my question?" Instead I asked, "Did she get to go, too?"

"Yes. She went with us."

"Did she behave while she was there?"

"Oh sure! She was getting to do what she wanted. She was very well behaved."

"So, you're saying that when she feels special or is allowed to participate in a special event that she behaves the way you expect her to behave?"

"Of course! She only acts out when she doesn't get her way."

"But she behaves when she feels special?"

The guardian ignored that question and said, "Her behavior is worse than either of the other two, and they are a lot younger than she is. She is more of a baby than either of them. We are constantly after her. If she doesn't get a snack when she wants or when it is time for a bath or to go to bed, it doesn't matter—she refuses to take orders and won't do what she's told. We don't even have to give her an order. She'll start something up out of the blue with one of them without any provocation. She's always picking on them and hitting them for no reason."

In my view, no child acts out without a reason. Their reasons may be camouflaged, but they are there. It was my job to discover the reason so that I could recommend a more creative response. In doing that, I could relieve the guardian and the child of the stress that was mounting in that home.

I couldn't release that child to her guardian without having improved their understanding of what each other was feeling. At the same time, while the child was clearly distressed, she didn't meet the criteria for involuntary or voluntary admission at that moment. I was compelled to do some intensive crisis intervention with both of them.

Chapter Eight

Katy—Part II

"Do you want to know what I think, Katy?"

When I am about to interpret what I have been told or what I have observed, I always try to remember to qualify my interpretation by saying, "This is what I think." I am very careful not to give absolutes.

In asking the child if she wants to know what I think, I am also sharing the power and control with her. Troubled children are used to having to surrender all of the control. They learn to fight for their share. I wouldn't have gotten anywhere with her by feeding into such a power struggle.

She turned to me and whimpered, "What?"

"I think your aunt is too angry to talk about love right now. Have you done things that she gets angry about?" I was careful not to ask if she has done anything to make her aunt angry. No one can make her aunt angry. That is a response the aunt chooses to allow herself.

"Yeah, she's always angry." She looked over at her aunt and said, "And mean!" She pointed her finger at Gretchen and said it again. "You are mean! You are very, very mean!"

"I'm not mean, but I won't stand for your behavior. You are smart and you know right from wrong. As long as you choose to do the wrong things, I will have to correct and discipline you, whether you like it or not. That's all there is to it."

I thought to myself, *If that was all there was to it, we wouldn't be sitting here in the screening area of the CSU.*

I focused on the child again. "Katy, I think anger hides love sometimes. It is there but you can't see it or feel it, because the anger is in the way. I bet if she didn't get angry, you would see and feel her love. You would know that she loves you. What do you think?"

She didn't answer me. Instead she directed a question to her aunt. "Do you?" She then added impatiently, "Well, do you?"

"Katy, if I didn't care about you, I wouldn't have kept you this long." Gretchen turned to me and said, "I signed her up for basketball. I was prepared to take her to practice three times a week. She blew that. She can't go to basketball practice when she's grounded. I have her signed up for Girl Scouts, too, but I don't believe she'll be able to stick with that either. I can't be expected to drive her back and forth to all of her activities when she can't behave when she is home with me."

The aunt was sounding cold and vengeful on the surface. Beneath the surface she probably was feeling that all of her efforts were for naught. Nothing she did had any effect on the child. There also appeared to be a little tit-for-tat going on—"If the child does this to me, I will do that to her. She wants to make me miserable and take away my peace of mind? I'll make her miserable and take away her basketball practice and Girl Scouts. I'll do everything it takes to let her know that two can play this game."

I knew there would be little hope for Katy if her aunt didn't get some counseling for herself as well. "Have you had family counseling?" I asked.

"I told you, I have a behavior management specialist at the school. Her guidance counselor sees her practically every day, and she has a guardian ad litem."

I kept looking at her, waiting for her to answer my question. It was clear to me that the child wasn't the only one who could benefit from counseling.

Evading my question further, Gretchen continued to rant, "She gets plenty of counseling. It's not doing any good. She knows what she has to do, but she chooses not to. That's all there is to it." Again, she put all of the fault and responsibility on the child for the problems in their relationship and in her current family system.

"How often does she see her primary care physician for medication?"

"Every couple of months he renews her prescriptions."

"You don't have a family counselor?"

"No! She takes up too much of my time already. I run back and forth, from home to the school and from work to the school. They call me two or three times a week. I'm going to lose my job if I have to keep running in and out of the office because she wants to act out. When am I supposed to find time for family counseling?"

Gretchen had a point. I empathized with her and acknowledged how I could see she felt she was doing all the work but things were still getting worse.

"Would you be interested in having a counselor come to your home? The same counselor who would also be working with her at school? There are home- and school-based counselors that could come as often as two or three times a week. They schedule appointments after five o'clock for parents who have to work."

"Well, we'll see. I might look into it. Right now I just want a doctor to give her something to keep her from throwing fits and threatening everybody. If she stopped throwing her temper tantrums and demanding all of the attention, we wouldn't need counseling."

"There might be too much anger on both sides for things to progress without family counseling. You have taken on quite a bundle by adopting her and having two young children at home. It has been five months now, and things still aren't as you might have imagined they would be. You've put a lot of energy and time into making things work out, yet she seems to thwart all of your efforts."

I was validating and empowering her by reflecting back to her all of the things she was doing to improve the situation. But she turned her righteous efforts into self-righteous decrees. As I empowered her, she tore down the child.

"Well, I am trying!"

"Yes, you are. Not everyone would have stuck it out this long."

"That's why she's had so many foster care placements. No one would put up with her. She doesn't see that," she added sarcastically. "I could just as easily have given up on her like everyone else who's tried to live with her. I keep trying, but I can't let her destroy the whole family. No one has any peace with her there. We can't even get through dinner without her throwing one of her fits. My husband sees what it's doing to me and to us, and he's had enough of it. I don't know if we can continue. She can't keep on behaving the way she does. I think she wants us to give her up. She doesn't know how close she is to getting her way. It's hard not to get angry when she throws herself on the floor and screams every time we scold her or tell her she can't have something or do something she wants to do."

I wanted to ask Gretchen if she liked anything about the child, but I was afraid she might not have anything to say. I wanted her to tell me how many times she heard herself say "no" in an evening, as opposed to the number of times she said "yes." But I didn't want to add salt to the wound. I had already confronted her; now she needed to vent. She needed some validation for the time and energy she was putting into the situation. She felt frustrated and angry, and the more frustrated and angry she got, the worse the situation got. She knew she was past the point of no return, with no relief in sight. The two of them were butting heads, neither one willing to give an inch.

The worst of it was that, while Gretchen was indeed angry with the child, the child didn't appear to be all that angry with her aunt. She appeared to feel rejected—and hurt by the rejection—but not at all angry. Katy displayed in her tone, body language, and facial expressions that she didn't believe she was being understood or cared for in the way she needed to be understood and cared for.

I tried to explain to the child that a person can't show how much they understand and care for someone when they are angry. No matter how much love there is, the anger is more obvious. If her aunt wasn't angry, Katy would have seen and felt her love.

Gretchen paid close attention to what I was saying to Katy. What she may not have realized was that Katy's anger was there even before she moved in with her aunt's family. At the same time, it was easy for Gretchen to think Katy was the problem. After all, Gretchen wasn't a raving lunatic before the child moved in with them. She remembered being a nice—even sweet—person. All of a sudden she was so frustrated and angry that she couldn't sleep at night. She was snapping at her husband and putting on weight. Even her status at work was being threatened.

The husband saw what all of this was doing to her, and so he put his two cents in—only making matters worse. The child didn't need to be threatened with being thrown out of the home. But it appeared, from their perspective, that Katy was winning the fight. Gretchen couldn't let her win. She wouldn't let her win. Someone simply had to do something.

By now, every member of that house wanted to find a way out. The aunt saw that keeping her or letting her go would have the same result. Either way, she failed. She couldn't fail; she couldn't keep her and she couldn't give her up. She didn't know what to do, and that's why she was at the CSU.

Before I could let them leave, I had to open Gretchen's mind to another way of looking at things. She had to stop taking all of the child's behavior personally. At the same time, she had to see her part in triggering Katy's rage. And she did trigger it. What's more, when she held back affection and refused to nurture the child, she actually added to Katy's rage. In that regard, she was responsible for a portion of the anger the child was acting out. She shouldn't have responded emotionally to the emotional condition of the child. She needed to be educated on how to deal with the child's rage without becoming enraged herself.

If she didn't, the child would continue to act out and the whole family could become emotionally ill.

Gretchen caused Katy to escalate when she responded to Katy's behavior with anger. There definitely was a need for intensive counseling intervention for this family, but Gretchen wouldn't commit to that. I felt compelled to do as much good as possible in the little bit of time I had.

"Gretchen, you're going to burn yourself out," I said. "You've taken on so much. I wish there was more that I could do. You aren't the cause of all of Katy's pain and rage. She was angry long before she moved in with you. I know that you must feel that she is safe now and that she should be grateful. I can assure you that some day she will be. Right now she can't feel grateful because she's too distressed. She's been through an awful lot more than most kids her age. She may be acting out more with you now because she feels safe to express the anger she feels. When children are distressed, they often express those feelings in anger and temper tantrums."

"I don't see her as distressed."

"Well, that's the thing—kids don't express how stressed out they are feeling the way adults do. They don't mope around; they throw temper tantrums. There are different kinds of stress that can cause a child to feel depressed. There are two kinds of depression. A child can have one or the other or a little of both kinds. There is the depression caused by a chemical imbalance and another type that comes from a single major or a string of minor to major traumatic events. The latter can actually cause the former to occur."

"I've never heard of that," Gretchen said.

"Children who are chemically imbalanced as a result of major traumatic events become hypersensitive to criticism, delayed gratification, and redirection. They've learned that the instant they think things are okay, everything gets turned around and upside down. They learn to expect chaos and confusion.

"This chaos begins to feel normal to them. They are at home when things are out of whack. At least they know what to expect. They begin to feel uneasy, scared—even homesick—when things are calm and quiet. For them it is the calm before the storm. They strongly object to being caught off guard by the storm. A lot of their behavior is a defense against the storm hitting them by surprise. They feel if there is to be a storm, let it come from them. In that way they are in control of the coming and going velocity and ferocity of the terrible winds, thunder, and lightning. They know no other way to be. For them, this is reality. They feel more secure when they can feel that they control their own reality."

I turned to Katy and asked, "Are you angry, too?"

She stuck out her lower lip. "When she's mean to me."

I needed to shift the focus off the aunt and the child's current circumstances and reflect back to the age Katy was at the time she lost her parents, and the years and circumstances leading up to that event. I sensed that her emotional age was stuck at that earlier developmental stage when all the trouble started.

"Are you angry at your mom and dad for not taking good care of you?"

Gretchen interrupted and reminded me that Katy was only four years old when she was taken from them. I nodded and repeated my question. Katy nodded.

"Did you ever tell your aunt that they made you angry?"

She shook her head.

Her aunt said, "I really don't think she remembers. She was too young and it was over two years ago. She's been kicked out of fifteen foster homes in those first two years for her behavior! This didn't just start in August when she came to my house. She's used to people giving up on her. She knows how to get their sympathy and to make them feel sorry for her, and then she starts to show her butt. She knows what she's doing. She'd love for you to think, 'Poor Katy.'"

I took a mental health break drawing in a long, slow breath. Gretchen was absolutely formidable. Instead of reacting, I practiced what I preach, reminding myself that she was speaking and acting out of concern for the younger children, herself, and her husband—and quite possibly even for Katy. I wanted to grant her the benefit of the doubt. Still, it was getting harder for me to tell if she did in fact, love the child.

I could imagine how Katy felt by now. I had only listened to Gretchen snapping at her for a little over an hour. Katy had been on the receiving end of this type of tone and insinuation for over five months.

At the same time, I knew that Gretchen wasn't expressing hatred as it might have appeared. She was clearly frustrated and didn't know where to turn. She may have thought that, if I didn't focus on her complaints, nothing would change. She seemed to fear that she would be returning home having accomplished nothing. She was growing impatient with my excursions into the child's feelings and thoughts about remote, recent, and immediate events. She wanted me to align with her in demanding that the child think and feel whatever she needed to think and feel in order to behave the way she was expected to behave. The aunt didn't want me to approach this from any other direction.

I wondered to myself if she hadn't taken too literally the precepts and practices of behavior management. It didn't seem as though she had found any use for compassion, nurturance, or the slightest display of affection. I imagined that she didn't think Katy deserved any of that. In Gretchen's mind, those would have to be earned.

Each time I attempted to approach the child's pain, Gretchen tried to take control and redirect me back to her issues with Katy's behavior. It was interesting to note, though, that when I wouldn't allow the aunt to redirect me, the child opened up and was more and more receptive and attentive to what I had to say. It may have appeared to the aunt that I was ignoring her needs, but, by engaging the child, I was getting closer to the core issues that were at the heart of their problems.

These perceptions ran through my mind as I ignored the aunt and continued my questioning of the child.

"Katy, you don't seem to feel as if she loves you. You need to feel loved. You need to be able to crawl up into her lap, feel her arms around you, and hear her say that she loves you and that everything will be all right, don't you?"

"Oh, you can say that again!" Gretchen interjected. "Every time I hold one of the babies she has to start teasing them, chanting, and trying to get them upset. She hates to see me hold them."

"You want to be held too, don't you, Katy?" I asked sympathetically.

Katy nodded with big, sad eyes looking at me as if I had hit on something that she had wanted to tell me. She then smiled at me before pointing to her aunt and saying, "See, she is mean!"

The aunt responded defensively. "Well, if she wants to be held she's going about it in the wrong way. I'm not about to pull her into my lap when she disrupts the entire family day in and day out."

I disagreed. "Nurturance goes a long way in situations like this, Gretchen. I personally believe it goes a lot further than scolding. The more you hold her off and refuse to nurture her, the worse she gets. I tell parents and guardians of traumatized children, "Whenever you feel the urge to push, pull instead."

"Traumatized? She wouldn't be traumatized if she learned how to behave. She brings it all on herself. If she behaved I wouldn't have to scold and correct her. I might even want to hold her."

"She was traumatized by her home life and the behavior of her parents. If she wasn't, they wouldn't have taken her from the home. Most of the anger you see her display comes from that situation. She's angry with her mom and dad for not being good parents and for not doing the right thing so they could keep her and her siblings. She probably went through the past two years thinking they were going to get them all back, but they never did what they were supposed to do to get them back. She's not only angry for the hurt they caused her when she was in the home, she's also angry at them for not getting it together to take them all back again. This hurts. When kids get hurt, they get angry, just like everyone else."

Before Gretchen could challenge what I had said to her, I turned to Katy and asked, "Did you get mad when your mommy and daddy would drink and start fighting, Katy?"

She nodded.

"Did you ever get to tell your mommy and daddy you were mad at them?"

"No!"

The aunt interrupted sarcastically, "Yeah, right! She has no problem speaking her mind. That's probably why they hit her often enough to finally lose her to the Department of Children and Families."

Uh-oh! Now I had to turn to the aunt. I could not allow her to blame Katy for that. "I understood that they abused alcohol and drugs and that they were abusive to each other as well as to all of the kids?"

"Yeah. Well, that is right."

I addressed Katy again. "Honey, have you seen your mom and dad since you were taken from them?"

"No."

"If you saw them, would you be able to tell them they made you mad because of the way they treated you?"

Katy's eyes got big and she nodded. I decided to borrow from Fritz Perls' empty chair strategy. I pushed the chair closest to me around so that it was facing her. "Pretend they are sitting in this chair and tell them how you feel."

She started to move to get up and then thought twice about it. She laughed nervously and refused to do it. I encouraged her. "Go ahead. Tell them just how you feel. You can talk softly or shout at them. It's okay. They won't hear you." I nudged the chair with my foot so that it was a little closer to her.

She backed up a bit and then, pointing her finger at her parents, she started to scold them for beating her and her siblings, for leaving them in the house without any food or heat, for yelling and fighting, and for disappearing at night. The more she remembered, the louder she yelled, and then she started hitting the chair with her fists as she spoke, accentuating each word with a punch—until finally she wore herself out. At that point, she threw herself on the couch, with her back to us again, and whimpered, "I'm done!" She lay there crying, holding her knees up to her chest.

The aunt didn't budge. That little girl lay there hurting and completely alone. Had I been the guardian or the mother, I would have scooped her up in my arms and rocked her until she felt better, but her aunt just sat there and watched her cry.

"You can hold her if you want."

"She'll be all right. She's gotten a lot of attention tonight. That's all she wants. Anytime she can be the center of attention, she's fine."

I looked straight at the aunt, put my hand to my chest, and said, "When you can change the way she feels in here, you'll see her change her thinking and her behavior. You can't get her to change her thinking or her behavior while there is still so much hurt and anger in here."

"We all have hurt and anger."

"We're not all six years old, and we haven't all gone through what she's been through."

"Her siblings went through it, and they don't behave that way. They're a lot younger than she is and according to their fathers, they're no trouble at all."

"Well, there could be a number of reasons for why they're not as disturbed. I'd say the biggest reason is that they weren't in the home as long as she was before DCF took them away. Part of the problem you are having with her is that she sees how you coddle, protect, and care for your younger children. From what I hear, no one took care of her like that, when she was their age. She sees you coddle them and compares it to what she remembers about how she was treated, and it fills her full of anger and resentment. She feels they are more loved than she ever was. That anger and resentment is played out in her relationships with them and in her interactions with you and your husband. In order for her to get past this, she will have to be coddled as she should have been, when she was their age."

Gretchen crossed her arms against her chest and stared at me.

"The more she sees you nurture them, the greater her pain. The greater her pain is, the greater her rage will be. She needs to be nurtured and coddled as if she were between two and four years old. Until this happens, she will not heal. For some people this never happens. She's still young enough to benefit from coddling now, and you are in a position to give it to her."

I then introduced a subject that always pops up when I find out children who have traumas in their background have been treated for ADHD with Ritalin. She may have had ADHD, but that might not be her only Axis I diagnosis. She may also have had Post-Traumatic Stress Disorder (PTSD). I encouraged Gretchen to ask a psychiatrist to rule out PTSD.

I explained that although the symptoms and behavior are very similar, the causes and treatment are very different. Ritalin won't help a child suffering from PTSD. If she did, in fact, have ADHD too, Ritalin would help to alleviate those symptoms, but Gretchen had already said it wasn't helping at all. Psychotropic medications and behavior management techniques alone don't work well with kids who have PTSD, especially when orders and expectations are given harshly.

I put my hand on my chest again and said, "The source of behavior is the way she feels in here. You can't change her behavior by making her feel worse in here. Often when a child has PTSD they also develop clinical depression. This is especially true if the child hasn't been properly diagnosed and treated for that disorder. Children use aggression and rage to act out their depression."

I then asked that Gretchen keep an open mind and at least ask a psychiatrist to assess the child for PTSD. I also advised her to seek weekly counseling so that she could get some help and learn how to manage a PTSD child, if the psychiatrist agreed with my diagnosis.

The aunt was very skeptical. She may have felt as if she were being manipulated. She may have even felt some guilt for not having nurtured the child up to now. She surely wasn't going to start in full view of me. At least that is what I thought and felt.

By now the child had turned back around so that she could see me. She made eye contact with me. We smiled at each other, and I winked at her. I understood and expressed something that she felt and could not say. Even if the aunt never gave her the affection she needed, she now knew that she was entitled to it. I was fortunate to have been able to validate her needs.

Gretchen would need more support in learning how to respond to a traumatized child. I asked her to sign a release of information form that would allow me to explain the work we were doing to the child's guardian ad litem. I felt that was the only avenue open to me to ensure that follow-up services relevant to the child's needs were made available to her once they left the CSU.

I praised Katy for the work she had done with the chair and for her honesty. I told her she did a great job in expressing her anger. I then suggested that they go home, since it was getting late. I told them I would walk them to their car.

Katy got up and came over to me. I took her hand and we walked out together. Just as we got her seated in her car seat in the back of the van, Gretchen said, "Well, I learned something tonight."

"What did you learn?" I asked skeptically.

"I never knew she was so angry at her mom and dad. That's new to me." And then she bowed her head and in a contrite tone, she added, "I'm so sorry Katy. I thought you hated me."

Finally, Gretchen was able to see that she wasn't the sole target of Katy's rage. It wouldn't have struck her so undeniably had she not seen and heard Katy's anger toward her parents as she just had, directly from the child, in that exercise with the chair.

Katy began to cry, but her aunt was already in the drivers' seat. I was still standing by the side door of the van where I had helped Katy climb up to her seat. I reached my hand up and pulled the lamb's wool protector down that was there to keep the seat belt from rubbing up against her neck and ear. As I positioned it, I asked, "What's the matter, honey? What are you thinking?"

She then cried out to her aunt, "I'm sorry I've been bad. I won't be bad anymore." It appeared as though Katy had been able to contrast the relationship she had with her aunt and the one she had endured with her own parents. By her last comment, it seemed that she realized she had been angry with the wrong person and that it made her feel bad enough to want to say she was sorry.

I let them both know the nights I would be there, and I invited them to come back. Katy was calmer now and said that she was hungry. When her aunt told her she could have a snack when they got home before she went to bed, Katy gasped and said, "But you don't like me to have bedtime snacks."

Gretchen turned over her shoulder so Katy could see her face, and in a soft and affectionate tone she replied, "Katy,

I have been too harsh with you. It makes me sad to think you were so angry at your parents. I thought it was me you were so mad at the whole time. I should have known that. I don't know why I didn't see it until now. Of course you would be angry about the way you were treated. Well, things will be different now. I'm going to make sure of that, and we're going to start by changing that silly old rule about bedtime snacks, okay?"

Katy put both her hands over her mouth and then started giggling and kicking her feet as she said, "Okay!" They were both smiling ear to ear as Gretchen put the car in gear and drove away.

I know Gretchen felt angry at first and let down that she wasn't able to carry out her threat of having Katy locked up. Her husband's threat of having Katy live at the CSU for good wasn't played out either. I'm sure that, in that respect, I had been regarded as the idiot who couldn't see the forest for the trees, but she now had information that would help her to not take Katy's anger so personally.

The day after they were there, my supervisor got a call from the Department of Children and Families. They were about to have a hearing on the status of the adoption in process and wanted permission to talk to me about the observations and recommendations of the night before. I spoke to the case worker for almost an hour. We talked about the difference between ADHD, for which the child had been treated unsuccessfully for two years, and PTSD.

The case worker told me she liked the advice that Gretchen apparently had relayed to her from our session: "Whenever you feel the urge to push, pull instead." We talked about Gretchen's tendency to withdraw and punish when nurturing could have solved a lot of the problems she was having with the child. We agreed that home- and school-based counseling services would help alleviate a lot of the stress that was mounting in their home. I wished that I could have pursued that situation further. The CSU seems to fill up in spurts, and there is rarely time to do intensive crisis interventions. Most of the time, parents bring their child in out of sheer frustration because they can't manage her. In sheer exasperation, such parents use rejections as a disciplinary device and threaten to have their child locked up if she continues to thwart their authority. But we can't lock them up for misbehaving. They have to be a danger to themselves or others to meet the criteria for placement in the CSU.

We don't want the CSU to be thought of as a place you go when you're bad, either. Children and adults need to know that the CSU is a safe place where children can come when experiencing suicidal or homicidal thoughts, as a result of acute stress, depression, or an onset of psychotic symptoms. They shouldn't fear it or think of it as a place for punishment. Once admitted to the unit, they are stabilized within twenty-four to seventy-two hours and then returned to the home with a discharge plan that often includes referrals for family counseling and case management services, to be accessed through their local community mental health facilities.

The community-based programs are often allotted a limited amount of tax dollars, by the state, to service children whose families can't afford to pay for services. They can also receive case management services that might help the family access money to cover costs. When that isn't possible, they operate on a sliding scale, in accordance with the family's size and income.

I once heard that it costs something like $30,000 to house an inmate per year. I began in-home therapy making ten thousand less than that. I serviced up to six to ten different families every two to four months on that salary and worked sixty to seventy hours per week. And yet every day, when I went to work, I didn't know if my program would be shut down for lack of funds and I would be out of a job.

The services are so minimally budgeted by the state that more experienced and seasoned professionals who have their own families to support are compelled to move on. There's no job security and barely enough of a salary to run a household. The result is that we have young adults who are just out of school and still resolving issues with their own parents, while they are out there trying to tell parents how to raise their children.

These "therapists" are often too young to have examined themselves for attitudes, postures, beliefs, and prejudices that compromise their ability to provide an effective intervention. They need case-specific training to compensate for that lack of life experience. And, they need seasoned, experienced supervisors out in the field with them until they can demonstrate the insight and skills it takes to provide evidence-based interventions. By providing intensive counseling services to troubled individuals, young and old, we are improving the quality of life for all. When we empower troubled children and their families to begin to heal and grow, we heal a part of ourselves and our society as a whole.

Chapter Nine

Tomika — The Runaway

Tomika was a sixteen-year-old girl referred, by the Department of Children and Families (DCF) to our mental health agency, for being ungovernable and running away from home. The case report indicated that she skipped school and refused to do any classroom or homework assignments, causing her grades to drop in the past year from A's and B's to D's and F's. She defied her parents' rules and curfews, made friends with the wrong type of people (many of whom were much older than her), and she acted out with verbal and physical aggression toward her parents and siblings when she didn't get her way.

I was assigned to assess her and her home environment to determine if she would be a candidate for either a therapeutic foster home or a residential treatment program.

Tomika had three sisters aged ten, seven, and four. Her father, Justin, was a law enforcement officer who worked the night shift so that he could be home when the four children got home from school. The mother, a registered nurse, worked the day shift at a local hospital so she could be home to get them off to school in the mornings.

I had hoped both parents would be home for our first session, but I was told the mother would be getting home a little late due to staffing problems they were having at the hospital.

When I arrived at her house, Tomika was still grounded and confined to her room for running away. The father answered the door and let me introduce myself as the one who had called and arranged for the counseling for his daughter, but he didn't invite me in at first. Instead he just stood there, a huge Paul Bunyan bulk of a man, looking down on my slight, 5'4", 115-pound frame as if he wasn't sure he would let me enter.

Finally, in a gesture of resignation, he shook his head, stepped aside, and said, "Well, come on in." He turned his back to me and lumbered over to an overstuffed chair that faced the TV, picked up the controls, and raised the volume slightly on the program he had apparently been watching prior to my arrival. He didn't offer me a chair, so I chose one for myself that allowed me to have a panoramic view of the living room and the hall that separated the living room from the kitchen and led, I assumed, down to the bedrooms.

His other three daughters climbed up on the couch and sat posed like mannequins. No one smiled. No one except the father spoke without permission, throughout the introductions, and then only in monosyllables once he gave them permission to speak. The father made it quite clear that he didn't appreciate having to submit to receiving counseling as a result of his child's antics.

"She's down there," he said in an irritated tone, while waving the remote in the direction of the hall. "It's the third door on the left, if she hasn't escaped out the window again. Go ahead and do what you came to do." He obviously thought that since she was the focus of treatment, he would be able to resume watching his program as soon as I went about my business.

I had to ask him to turn the TV off so that I could gather some collateral information from him about her behavior. When he realized that he would have to participate, he was not a happy camper. I tried breaking the ice with casual conversation, even a little humor, to no avail. He made it quite clear that I was to get it over with as soon as possible and get out, so the children could resume their after-school activities and he could get back to watching TV.

I soon learned that he ran the home with an iron fist. The children received their orders and were expected to carry them out with military discipline and precision. What happened when they didn't shape up? It took me several minutes to get the answer to that question. It came finally from the youngest one: they were "whooped." The others' eyes widened in fear of what the father would do, now that she had spoken out of turn as well as divulged what might have been a very private matter.

"Whooped with what?" I asked.

No one said a word. After scanning all of their faces, I turned to the father with the same question on my face. He squirmed slightly in his chair as he moved his big hand to the buckle on his belt. The tension in the room was incredible. You could hear a pin drop.

"Is it working?" I asked the father.

He raised his eyebrows and glared at me. Yes, I had challenged him. I don't believe he was used to being challenged. I softened my tone and asked, "Is it working with your kids?"

"They know I mean business," he said, nodding his head in the direction of the younger ones. "Now the other one—that's a different story. She used to listen, but she's gotten so you can't even speak to her. She's got a bad attitude.

She mouths off to her mother and me. She's setting a bad example for her sisters."

"Oh, she's getting to be more and more defiant?"

"Defiant? That's a good word for it."

"And mouthing off? She is responding with sarcasm, belligerence, or what?"

"That too."

"I see."

"She's got a garbage mouth. She gets into more trouble with her mouth than anything else," he said.

We were making some headway. Once I had made it clear that he would need to talk with me, he wanted to conduct the direction of our discussion. He had filled me in on how he ran the home and what his expectations were. He let me know that their mother had tried to get him to ease up on them, but he wasn't about to give in to her either.

"This is how it has been, is now, and will be, and if you think you're going to come in here and take over or change anything, you can just pick yourself up and go back where you came from," he said defiantly.

He was resistant and defensive in his speech, tone, and posture. He seemed to want to show the little ones that no department or agency was going to enter his home and tell him what to do or how to raise his children. He said he wasn't going to take any more from us than he would take from his own wife or daughter. It was his way or the highway. It was how he was raised and how his father was raised before him. It had worked for them, and it sure as hell was going to work for his children, or they would regret the day they were born.

The more pompous his articulation, the more obvious it was that he felt he was losing control over his oldest daughter. His tried and true, die-hard methods weren't working. The more defiant she became, the greater the frequency and intensity of the punishment. Conversely, the greater the frequency and intensity of the punishment, the more defiant she became. I sensed that he felt he was losing her and that it scared him.

That isn't how it looked on the surface, though. On the surface, it appeared as though he was refusing to accept the loss of power and control over her. Whenever anything that obvious strikes me, I always think something else is in play. It would have been easy to make that snap judgment. I could have written him off as just another manly man who had to have the power and control over his own domain and everyone in it. I could have called him on it. I could have spent my time challenging that apparent need.

In the process, I could have applauded Tomika for taking a stand against him and for holding her own in the face of his unabashed wielding of that power. In doing so, I could have given each of the younger three the message that their father was a bad parent. They would have understood that all their protests were warranted and that he was in the wrong.

This is what he probably expected me to do. He expected me to undermine his authority by attacking his methods and his power trip. He was prepared to defend himself in that regard.

In order to connect with him and to engage him in the treatment process, I had to reinforce his authority while helping him to recognize and examine the futility of his methods. I needed to disarm him without attacking him. In order to disarm him, I had to look beneath the obvious. I needed to see that it wasn't the loss of power and control, but his love for her that was disturbing him. It was the fear of losing her that fueled the fiery emotions he felt when addressing and correcting her behavior. Now that I had that figured out, I knew where to focus my intervention.

I shared with him my observation that it was the fact that he was losing her that disturbed him most. It disturbed him in the deepest stratum of his being. It was that loss, manifested in her defiance and belligerence that triggered the adrenaline and toxic emotions with which he wielded his open hand against her cheek and that belt on her rear. It was that loss that was fueling and deepening a greater and more profound sense of responsibility for her well-being. And yet, he hadn't been inclined or able to communicate that to her.

I also explained that with that sense of responsibility there was an element of impending doom. The sensation of doom from deep within him now filled the atmosphere of his home. It was the result of the unbearable grief, fear, and panic he felt as he watched his own flesh and blood rise up against him and then run further and further away from him at a stage in her life when she needed him the most.

By explaining this perception to him, I was able to plant the seeds of trust. I felt he was now comfortable enough to continue with Tomika in the room. "Let's ask her to come out here and join us, okay?" I said.

He turned his head toward the hall and then, in a deep bear growl, he ordered her to come out. No response. He growled again. I counted to five before I heard her door open. She walked passively into the room and sank onto a hardback chair that sat next to the wall between the living room and kitchen. It was the farthest seat from her father she could find.

Her attitude was written all over her face and expressed more emphatically in her stiff and deliberate body language, as she eased herself down on the seat. She didn't look up at him or me, but sat staring at her shoe. It was as if she were trying to say, *Whatever this is about, I've heard it all before. If I have to hear it all again, fine! Just get it over with, so I can go back to my room.*

Recalling the father's attitude when I first arrived, I could see where she got her attitude. There were other similarities too. Her features were a lot more like his than those of the other girls. I shifted the focus of our session for a few minutes, taking the opportunity to point out their likenesses.

"You two look a lot alike," I observed.

The father looked over at her. She didn't look up. "She used to be daddy's girl."

"You aren't daddy's girl anymore, Tomika?" I put a little baby talk tone in my voice when I asked the question. It was enough to make her smile slightly as she shook her head.

"Nooooo, I don't think so!"

"How come?"

She shrugged. "I'm grown now, I guess."

"Oh? So, it hasn't always been this way, huh?" I threw the question out for anyone to answer. No one did, so I shifted my eyes to the girls on the couch. "What do you think—is this a new thing?"

They looked at each other and then at the father. He answered for them. "It's been the past couple of years. It's gotten worse since she got interested in boys. She thinks she should be allowed to date. I told her if dating was going to cause all that, she wouldn't have to worry about dating for a long time. She's too young to date, anyway. That's why she's been grounded—she thinks she can show herself around here and then go and hang out with her friends. I ground her and then she sneaks out. We don't know where she goes. We've waited up for her night after night. She doesn't come home."

"Oh, so she has gotten more defiant since age thirteen or so?"

He nodded.

I looked over at the oldest one on the couch and asked, "How old are you, again?"

She said, "I'm almost eleven."

I winced and looked back at the father. "Uh-oh, another one is coming up close behind her."

"Yeah, well, she's already got that one covering for her, or she tries to. They stick up for each other."

This family was a perfect example of how everything that is supposed to be right goes wrong. There was parental presence and involvement, structure, and discipline in a highly functional family system. Both parents were educated. Both were working. They provided plenty of shelter, food, and clothing—and yet, this family was splitting at the seams. The atmosphere of impending doom was shattering their dreams. This is not how it was supposed to be.

Going all the way back to the day they took their vows, these parents planned everything to work out the way it was supposed to work out. They built their home together and raised their family. They had four beautiful daughters that used to bounce happily on Mommy's and Daddy's knee.

One has to look beyond the layers of stress and strife to the goodness and light that has existed within this family home, to find the source of the father's grief, fear, and panic. That source was his love for each of his children.

Most of us have heard of the parent who says, "This will hurt me more than it hurts you." The fact is, corporal punishment does hurt the parent as much as it hurts the child, because it frequently brings about a result that is contrary to the aim of the parent, as well as the needs of the child. The child withdraws from or rebels against the punishing parent just when the parent is attempting to draw the child in to listen and to act on what the parent knows is right.

While this father was acting on his love for the child, his love wasn't apparent in his actions or tone. The one thing that was neither felt nor demonstrated by either of them was the very thing tearing them apart. His love could have strengthened the bond between them, had it been expressed and felt.

By now, I had let him growl to her without raising an eyebrow. He had watched for me to react, but I had deliberately kept a relaxed facial expression as he growled to her to get her to come into the room. I brought out that he and she were alike in many ways. I got him to recall better times when she and the others use to bounce on his knee. I then shifted some of the weight of the discussion to the fact that he was also losing his second-born daughter.

Now I had to show them that it wasn't his need for power and control, but his love for her that was at the heart of the trouble.

"You love them all very deeply, don't you?" I asked in an understanding and empathetic tone. When I turn the spotlight to the strengths and goodness at the heart of the trouble in a family system, I shift the mood of the discussion from one of resistance and defensiveness to that of mutual recognition, acceptance, and regard. He feared all the things that he knew could happen to her if she continued to thwart his authority. It was his love that filled him with the tumultuous waves of panic in confronting her.

It was his love, cloaked in the guise of a need to wield power and control, that was behind the force of his hand and belt. That love, and his intention to parent and protect her, was buried behind harsh, incriminating words, epithets, decrees, and demands for obedience and respect. "You will do as I say, when I say it! When I say jump, you'll ask, 'How high?'"

The love was buried but it was there, plain as day—at least to me. Had I perceived the problem as being his need to wield that power, I would have missed the solution. It was that love that would heal the relationship between him and his daughter. I didn't need a bag of tricks and potions to help this family; I had to first expose and then lift the cloak of fear, anger, and frustration that was keeping their love for each other from being felt and expressed.

When he met me at the door with defiance, he was defending his right to love, parent, and protect his daughter in the only way he knew how. He knew what was at stake, and he doubted anyone else could possibly know how deep his commitment was. He truly believed that if he didn't wield the rod, he wouldn't be a good and responsible parent. He would have let them all down. He would have let himself down.

As much as he may have hated to be the disciplinarian, he stood up to the task and accepted it without hesitation. He would continue to do so and wouldn't hear any recriminations. He wasn't willing to risk compromising the quality of her character development and life experience for some new-wave sensationalism against corporal punishment.

At the same time, his daughter felt the absence of her feelings for him and his for her. The love and bond between them both was buried, over time, beneath layers of defensive and counter-defensive behaviors and arguments. These behaviors and arguments played out in a series of negative events in which they both participated in defense of their own idea of the way things were supposed to be.

It would have been counter-productive and self-defeating on my part to focus on his methods without giving credence to the love he felt for his children. He may have ultimately acquiesced, verbally and for appearance' sake, so he wouldn't get in trouble with the Department of Children and Families. He didn't want to be accused of resorting to excessive disciplinary measures. He would have had to demand that his children keep family affairs to themselves. They would have been hushed and warned to keep secret the fact that he would continue to use his belt and raise his children as he saw fit, whether his way was working or not. He might threaten to leave rather than stay and look the other way. The children could have feared his wrath even more and lost all hope that those things would change and return to the way they were before he had become so fearful for his daughter's welfare.

Were I to focus on admonishing him for his methods, I could have turned him and the whole family against the idea of participating in counseling. Our time together would have been spent going through the motions of an intervention without making any progress.

I could have spent six weeks or six months in there without being the least bit effective in bringing about a positive outcome that would continue to develop once I was out of the home. He wouldn't have changed his ways. I would have alienated him when I needed to connect with him. If I had let that happen, I would have had myself to blame.

I allowed a long pause and then repeated the question. "You do love them, don't you? This time my accent was on the word *do.*

That enormous 6'4" bulk of a man stared back at me in abject silence. And then, before me and everyone else in the room, a tear fell from the corner of his eye and rolled down his cheek. I paused to let everyone take in what had just happened. Then I turned to Tomika.

"He treasures you, Tomika. He doesn't approve of your behavior, but he treasures you with all his heart. He's afraid he's losing his first-born daughter."

She tsked and turned her eyes away.

I continued, "The way you talk to him and disappear at night scares him. If he didn't care about you, he wouldn't be scared. He'd say, 'Good riddance.' A lot of parents do. Instead, he is in here trying to parent and protect you. He isn't trying to be mean."

She responded with a sarcastic laugh. "You don't know him like I do. You think whatever you want to think." Her response confirmed what I already knew: she saw him as hateful and mean. Her actions were defensive reactions. She wasn't ready to accept that he cared about her—in fact, she had stopped asking whether or not he cared for her a long time ago. She was convinced that his intention was to make her miserable and to ruin her life.

Had he not softened and allowed that tear to escape his eye, she wouldn't have had the nerve to speak out the way she was now. I had hoped his sentiment would expose her love for him, but instead it empowered her to attack him.

"Okay," I said, pensively, "do you want to know what I think?" She ignored my question, but since she didn't object, I looked over at him for a brief pause and then turned back to her. "In your father's mind, he is doing everything he can to keep you safe and sound. Are you making that hard for him?"

"Safe from what?" she asked defensively. "The only thing I need to be kept safe from is him. He doesn't know my friends. Their parents don't yell and smack their kids. They don't have to be in by dusk every night. He needs to just leave me alone. Then he wouldn't have a problem."

The father sat up and appeared to be about to interject something, but he remained silent when I held up my hand. "Let's let her vent. She has some confusion and anger too. I always try to get families to agree that they can speak their minds in our sessions without fear of recrimination once I leave. Can we all agree to this?"

I waited for the father's response. So did everyone else. I wouldn't go on without that agreement. I explained further, "Open, solution-focused, assertive communication is always the first thing that needs to be re-established in family systems. This is true especially where its members have learned only to express their objections once things have gotten out of control. We need to learn to communicate without using criticism, demeaning or threatening tones, and name calling. Beyond that, we don't want to censor anyone. We want everyone to feel safe in expressing themselves. This is true even when they are expressing their disappointments and anger. Venting in a calm and controlled manner can clear the mind and open the way for a better understanding of what each one thinks and feels. Before we go any further, I need to know that they each have your permission to speak their minds."

"She vents enough around here," he said sourly.

"Yes, but not with your permission and not in a controlled setting with a detached observer. Usually, when family members vent anger, they do it as they are storming out of the room or the house, or they stand still but turn their ears off to the response of others. Somebody says something mean, and then doors start to slam. Glassware and furniture flies across the room. In this setting, each one would be given a turn to speak, as well as to listen, and then rebuke what the other is saying."

Everyone laughed a little at this, as if they realized I knew more of what it was like to live there than they had previously supposed.

"Come on. There will be no flying furniture, I promise." I laughed, and he laughed a little too this time. Then he waved his hand in a gesture that said to go ahead. "Great! There, Tomika, now you have his permission to speak your mind, but no yelling and no name calling, okay?"

She folded her arms and rolled her eyes before answering me. "I'm not saying nothin'. This is stupid."

I waited and watched her. She could see that I wouldn't be easily dismissed, so she continued.

"He thinks he can yell and smack me in the mouth. Whatever! I'm not saying nothin'."

"So why does he yell and smack you in the mouth? What's that about? It sounds awful. When does he do that?" I was baiting her just enough to get her to make the connection between her behavior and his reactive behavior, but I used a tone that expressed shock that he would smack her in the mouth for what must be, in her mind, no good reason.

She wanted me to think he was the cause of her negativity and misbehavior. She kept trying to focus on the reactive behaviors that would put him in a bad light while she made herself appear to be the victim. She wasn't accepting any accountability for the escalation of intensity in their confrontations.

I surreptitiously winked at the father while I continued to appear to be accepting her perceptions. He relaxed his facial expressions but shook his head slightly, as if to say that this wasn't going to get me anywhere with her.

"He's got to be all up in my business," she said.

"Well, he's supposed to parent and protect you, Tomika, right? He has to parent and protect you until you show him that you're responsible enough to parent and protect yourself. Have you been showing him, in the choices you've made and the way you behave, that you're responsible enough to parent and protect yourself?"

"He's just mad because I'd rather hang out with my friends than come home and take care of everybody and make dinner every day. All he wants to do is sit in that chair and tell me what to do."

While I made a mental note to remember to address the fair distribution of chores, I couldn't allow her to shift the focus of my inquiry. "We'll talk about that in a bit. Right now I'm trying to understand why he feels he has to parent and protect you so much. Do you have a good relationship with your parents and siblings?"

"I would if they didn't get all up in my business and mess up all of my stuff. I don't go messing with their stuff."

Now I was hearing that she had some valid boundary issues that would need to be addressed, but not right now. Instead, I re-directed her back to my question. "We can talk about that later, too. Right now I'm looking at why he feels he needs to parent and protect you so much, now that you are all grown, as you say. Do your friends get along with their parents?"

"Her friends don't have parents," the father interjected.

"Yes, they do! Why do you always—never mind. See? He's always got to start with that stuff."

"She hangs out at her friends' houses until the parents get home. They all hang out together down at Barbara's or Raj's. The parents are down at the bar and come home drunk half the time." He addressed his daughter directly. "How many times have you come home upset because Raj's dad comes home cursing and yelling at Raj?"

"So? That's him—that's not my fault. I'm not supposed to be Raj's friend just because his dad gets drunk?" After asking him that, she turned to me. "He watches his little sister and baby brother until his dad gets home. Their mom walked out a couple years ago. Me and Shirese help him sometimes after school. What's wrong with that?"

"Oh!" her father exclaimed, "So you'd rather take care of his sister and brother than come home and help out with your sisters?"

"You're home, they're your kids—why should I leave him by himself? That's stupid! Why should I come home and do your job while you sit there and boss me around? I already have to take care of them every weekend while you're asleep and mom is at work. You just want me to stay here and do everything and not have any friends. It's not fair! They're your kids, not mine. I have my own life, and I should be allowed to have friends. I'm only sixteen." Tomika started to get tearful and frustrated as she listened to her own arguments. It did sound justified to me, and I had to admit that to both of them. But I couldn't help but smile when I heard her shift from *I'm grown* to *I'm only sixteen*. .

"Tomika, let me interrupt a minute, okay?"

"Sure. Go ahead." She shook her head and smirked as if to say that she wasn't getting anywhere with either of us, anyway.

"This is the second time you've brought up the issue of what you're expected to do here, after school, with the house and with the kids. We'll talk about that later, I promise. But right now, I want to focus back on the question of why your dad feels he needs to parent and protect you. What do you think he's trying to protect you from? Do you really think he just wants you home so you can do stuff around here? Is that really the only reason he gets upset when you don't come home and he doesn't know where you are or when you'll be home?"

"I don't think—I know! He just wants me home so he doesn't have to get up and take care of stuff."

"I see." I replied pensively. And then, turning to her father, I said, sympathetically, "You must be exhausted after policing all through the night." I then turned to Tomika before he had a chance to respond and said, "I think you're right. I think you might be only half-right, but half is good. We can't overlook that."

She was surprised and disappointed at the same time. She wasn't used to having her view heard and considered, never mind validated. At the same time, she was being told that I wasn't agreeing with her whole point of view. I saw that there was more to it than she saw or wanted me to see. I had validated him, too. It wasn't easy to work and run a household, especially with young children to raise. It stood to reason that he would lean on her for help.

I advocated for the delegation of chores in the family home. I addressed the father and said, "I see nothing wrong with children taking a part in the upkeep of a home and the care of younger siblings. I say this for two reasons: It has become more and more necessary in homes where both parents are working. And I have found that it actually gives the children a stronger sense of belonging and importance within the family system. We just have to be sure that they don't feel as if that is the only reason we want them around. It sounds as if Tomika thinks you only want her home so she can be here to take care of things. She doesn't seem to think that you really care about what happens to her. You do care, though, don't you? You care very much about her."

I felt as if I were holding several frayed threads in each of my hands that had just become unraveled during the unfolding of this conversation. Now I had to weave them into a pattern that would meet the needs and expectations of both of them.

"I care about her," he said. "She knows that, but it's not worth it to have her help. I'd rather do it all myself than to put up with her mouth and attitude."

"You are saying you care about her and you could use the help, but you don't want to have to deal with her mouth and her nasty attitude."

"That's right."

"Hmm. What do you think, Tomika? Are you hearing what he's saying? He's telling you that he cares about you and he needs the help. You've been saying that he doesn't care about you and that he only wants you here so you can help. The part about how much he cares about you is the half you were leaving out earlier. What do you think now—do you think he cares about you?"

She snickered and said, "Nooooo."

"Her response is sincere," I said to her father. "She isn't trying to be difficult. She genuinely believes that you no longer care for her. I believe that's what is at the core of the problem you've been having with her mouth and her attitude. It's not so much an objection to doing chores and helping out as it is an objection to being forced to hang around someone who doesn't care about her."

He looked shocked, and I continued. "When children stop feeling that their parents care about them, they stop caring about how their parents feel. I'm not saying they're right. What I'm saying is that this is what happens in a lot of families, for many of the same reasons. Notice that I'm saying it's when children stop *feeling* that their parents care for them, they stop caring how their parents *feel about them*. I'm not saying that the parent and child have actually stopped caring for each other."

"She should already know I care about her and how she feels about me," he said.

"I hear the same substance of arguments in most of my family homes where teenagers have grown and begun to speak their minds. She doesn't know that you care about her. She might even think that you care more about the others than you ever cared for her. Those feelings can contaminate her relationships with them and make her resent them. She might even wish, deep down, that they were never born. They'd be safer and better off if she didn't have much to do with them. She doesn't have the same grounds for resentment with her friend's siblings. That would explain why she is more inclined to help Raj with his siblings than she is to help you out with her sisters."

The father looked up at me and then over at his daughter, and said, "Of course I care about you. How can you think I don't care about you?

"Yeah, right! If you did, you wouldn't yell at me, smack me in the mouth, and whoop me with your belt."

I nearly collapsed when she said that. I'd had everything going so well. I had hoped she would realize he cared and that once that was understood, they would want to make up for all the years of spit and spatter between them and all would be well from this point on. But that wasn't going to happen. Not yet, anyway.

She continued to try to get me to focus on the inflammatory "no-no" of his striking her. Children have been taught to call DCF if they are being abused or if they know of someone being abused. This is a good thing; I'm not going to sanction abuse. But neither am I going to address it without pointing out the share and distribution of accountability that leads up to it. It would have been easy to do that, but it wouldn't have addressed the problem on the level that it needed to be addressed if there were to be any significant changes in the way they related to each other. I wasn't going to single him out and be used as her weapon against him.

"Tomika, that's not what this is about right now. I can't just focus on how he reacts to your behavior. I feel as if you want me to say that he's out of line without looking at what might be behind the behaviors that upset him. This isn't all about him. There are problems on both sides. I'm trying to focus some of the discussion on what your part might be in the problem here. I believe I have identified two areas. He cares and you don't know it. We have to do something about that. He needs your help. This is true. But he cares about you as much or more than he needs you. I think if you realized how much he cares about you, then you'd feel better about being home. I think you'd be more willing to take on some of the tasks that need to get done. What do you think?"

"If he cared about me, he would let me have my friends. He would let me have some fun after school. He wouldn't make me come straight home and give me stuff to do until dinner. By then, I have homework, and then it's time for bed. When am I supposed to see my friends?"

"Why don't you pick friends that I would want you to be with?" her father asked. "All of your friends are in trouble with their parents or doing poorly at school. Two of them have dropped out. One just got suspended for sassing one of his teachers. One got busted a few weeks ago for having pot on the school grounds! Maybe, if you chose to hang out with better friends, I'd feel better about letting you hang out with them."

"I should never have told you anything!" she stammered. "You always turn everything around. I like them. That doesn't mean I am *like* them. Why do you have to act like I'm going to get in trouble just because they get in trouble? I'm not like that. I don't smoke pot and I never got suspended. I was getting A's and B's in all my classes. You just like to blow everything up and think the worst, and then you make me feel like I'm no good, just because they have problems. I'm not going to turn my back on my friends, just because they have problems. You don't know what it's like at their houses. You don't even know their parents. John doesn't even have parents. They're gone all the time. Some work all the time. Eric's dad has two jobs and his mom works nights. They aren't all bums just because they can't handle all the junk at school right now. You don't need to put people down that you know nothing about—it's not fair! That's why I don't even talk to you anymore. You think the worst about everybody. I'd have no friends if you had your way. So..." She shrugged at the end of that tirade and turned her eyes back down to her shoes, assuming the same resigned posture she'd had when she first entered the room.

Her father threw up his hands and shrugged as if to say the situation was hopeless. I could see how he would think that way. It did seem as if we were right back where we started. On the other hand, we had covered a lot of ground and identified several areas that complicated their relationship. Now all we had to do was agree on what we were going to do about them. I had to figure out how to shift the focus back around to why he felt he had to parent and to protect her as much as he did.

I said, "Tomika, it sounds as if you feel that he's putting you down when he puts your friends down. Is that right?"

"He is! He treats me like I'm out there doing all this *terrible* stuff."

"Are you saying that you don't feel that he trusts you?"

"He doesn't trust me. Listen to how he talks about my friends."

"I listened and frankly, it sounded to me as if he didn't trust them."

"Well, if he doesn't trust them, then he can't very well trust me either."

"Exactly!" her father exclaimed.

She realized how this came out and started to smile. Then she explained, "I am my own person. I'm not them."

"Yes, but he has a right to be concerned. You're hanging out with people who are in a lot of trouble or acting out in ways that lead to trouble. I think that if you chose better friends, he would feel better about giving you more freedom. I really think it's them that he doesn't trust. Why don't you ask him if he would let you out more if you had better friends?"

The father didn't wait for her to ask. Instead, he said, "If I thought you had friends that were doing well in school and not getting in trouble with the principal or the law, I'd be a lot more lenient with you. Especially if you changed your attitude about helping out here and you kept up with your schoolwork. I'd have no problem letting you out with your friends."

She looked up at him and asked if he thought Marisha and her brother were okay.

"Marisha is the one who plays the clarinet, right?"

"Yeah, I like her."

"She's in the band?" I interjected. "That's great! Have you thought about joining the band, Tomika?"

"I used to play the clarinet but I quit the band last year and we sold my old clarinet to Marisha."

"Well, the band room has instruments kids can rent or borrow. I really like the idea of kids getting into something like sports or band. It gives you a group to belong to that has a common interest. Kids your age like to feel they are part of a group, and the band is as good a group as any. Do you want me to look into getting you back into the school band?"

"I doubt I could get in," she said with a dramatic sigh.

"Want me to try?"

"Sure, I guess."

Her dad smiled at this and said, "Honey, if you can get in and want to stay in it after a few weeks, I'd be happy to take you to buy your own instrument. I'd do anything to help you get back into something like that."

"You would?"

"I sure will. That's a promise."

Tomika unfolded her arms and brightened up for the first time. "Really?" she asked him, looking surprised and happy.

He brightened up too, and repeated his promise. I said to her, "See, he must like you a little bit, huh?"

"Maybe," she teased.

Ah! Now we were getting somewhere, I thought. "Okay, now can we get back to the question I've been trying to get answered here?"

"What question?" Tomika asked.

"The one about why he feels he has to parent and protect you. I'm trying to help you understand that he really cares about you. If he didn't care, he wouldn't try so hard to parent and protect you."

Although I was addressing her, I was speaking to the father as well. Rather than reinforce his earlier demands for obedience and respect, I was able to reinforce the true sentiments behind them. I was saying to both of them and to the other children that I understood that he had a right to parent and protect her. I was standing up for that right and encouraging that responsibility, despite her objections to it.

However, it was equally important for me to help him understand that, while children do need to be parented and protected, they also need to *feel* parented and protected. When children feel parented and protected, it gives them the security they need to grow into healthy and productive adults. And, when they feel parented and protected they are more obedient and respectful, in turn.

Sometimes the demands for obedience and respect create the opposite impression and bring about an entirely different result.

She needed to be reminded of his actual intent and that I supported him in that intent. Had I agreed at the onset, that he was wrong to raise his hand to her, I might have led her to think that he was wrong in parenting and protecting her. I needed to make sure she was able to see and to agree that he had that right and responsibility before I shifted the focus to his methods. I had to do it in this order to keep from alienating him in the process. Losing his faith and attention would not have served her purposes at all, in the long run.

"Are you starting to see that he cares about you and that he needs to parent and to protect you?"

Much to my surprise, she nodded and said with a smile, "I guess."

Finally! At the risk of at least momentarily appearing to sanction his abusive responses, the words "parent" and "protect" had penetrated her walls of defensiveness and resistance. Now the tears fell from her eyes. "He treasures you, Tomika."

She looked up at him, and I prompted her, "You love him too, don't you?"

She nodded.

"Don't misunderstand me, Tomika. I'm not saying he should continue to use his hand and belt on you."

Her eyes widened. Now that I had exposed the love they felt for each other, I could turn the focus back to the question of the effectiveness of corporal punishment.

"Before you came out here," I said, "he and I had already established that physical slaps and spankings are not working." I then turned to her father and said, "It rarely works for the smart kids."

I now had the attention of both parties. I had empowered them both personally, while demonstrating that I wasn't going to take sides with one against the other. I continued to focus on the love between them without sanctioning their behaviors.

In most arguments about behavior, the individual is attacked first. These personal attacks spur counterattacks. "I," "you," and "me" statements take the focus off the specific behaviors that put the child at risk. The parent comes off as objecting to the child. The child feels rejected and knows it's wrong for a parent to reject her. She arms herself against the rejection with indignation. The more forceful the parent is in their objections, the more indignant the child becomes. The parent then takes up the arms of indignation against the child, and a standoff occurs.

Anger flares the nostrils of the parent and the child. There follows name calling, personal vendettas, and an exchange of threats—if not made audibly by the child, they are uttered under the child's breath. At a time when the specific high-risk behaviors need to be discussed, there is a total communication breakdown. The child begins to feel rejected and in turn rejects the caring and concerned parent. The specific behaviors are no longer the subject of discussion.

The caring and concern for the child must be verbalized by the parent and then recognized and felt by the child. Those sentiments need to be stated and restated, particularly in the discussion of the high-risk behavior that is to be modified or extinguished. We need to find a way to parent and protect that disarms our children. We need to disarm them with loving arms and spoken sentiments. We need to express and demonstrate our love and concern with tender words of endearment and encouragement. We need to be able to discuss their behavior without alienating them.

I wanted to make this clear to Tomika's father. "You might try beginning discussions about her behavior with, 'C'mere.' Let her know that you care. Convince her that she is too precious and too special to be ungoverned and unsupervised in today's world. Let her know that you are scared for what might happen to her out there. And then, turn her attention to the behavior that puts her at risk. Once a child has been pulled in and the force of your objection is placed on the behavior, rather than on the child, there is far more cooperation in making the necessary changes."

I paused. Once I had brought the parent's real sentiments out, Tomika seemed to be a lot more attentive than she had been earlier in the discussion. She brightened and relaxed her features. She no longer looked hard and defensive. She lost her arrogant airs and softened, looking very much her sixteen years.

"I'd like to go into this a little further with you, but, first, you might want to let the little ones go out and play. They have been sitting here for quite a while already."

"Go on out, but stay in the yard," the father said.

Tomika got up, playfully pretending that she had been excused as well. "Tomika!" I scolded, in the same playfulness she was exhibiting. She quickly sat back down while pretending to be sorry for the feigned misunderstanding.

Chapter Ten

Tomika—Amazing Grace

Tomika's father expressed his pride in the twinkle of his eye and broad smile as each of the girls wasted no time in jumping down from the couch. They ran to the door chattering about what they were going to do. Suddenly, the oldest of the three stopped, put her arms out to stop the other two, and then turned around to face her father.

"Daddy!" she exclaimed. "Look." And then she held her skirt out in each hand, while looking over at what the others were wearing.

"Oh! You're right—go change out of your school clothes."

The youngest of the three groaned as they all ran down the hall to change their clothes before they went out to play. Tomika asked if she could help them. Her father looking surprised, waved his hand in the direction of the hall, and said, with a broad smile, "By all means! Thank you."

It occurred to me that with the younger girls and Tomika out of the room, I could speak more directly to the father, so I called out after her, "Hey! Tomika. If you have homework to do, you could do that while I talk to your dad.

We will call you back out here in a little bit when your mom gets home, OK?"

Tomika came back into the room and started to protest but her father gave her a look that let her know she should go and do her homework until we called her back in, so she whined an involuntary, "OK" and went back down the hall.

I asked Justin if he had any questions or comments about anything we had discussed so far. He responded enthusiastically, "Tomika is listening to you!"

"Yes, it seems that she is listening to me. But that's because I'm talking about the way I believe you really feel about her. And I am taking the time to explain why you're so concerned. I'm saying that you want to parent and protect her, that you treasure her, and that you believe she's too precious and too special to be ungoverned and unsupervised. The message isn't that she's too stupid, too irresponsible, too young, or too anything negative—that caring and concern is what she needs to hear. The more she hears it, the more cooperative and compliant she will be."

He nodded as if he understood that. There was a long pause before the silence was broken and then I explained further, "By taking her behavior to a personal level, using harsh admonitions and corporal punishment, things are only getting worse between the two of you. You run the risk of losing her to the receptive arms and negative influences of her peers."

Just as I ended that sentence, we heard the children shut the back door behind them as her mother, Helena, walked in through the front door. I could see at once that she was perfectly poised, about 5'9, and graceful in her movements as she entered the room. Aside from appearing to be a bit worn for wear from a long day's work, not a hair was out of place, I could also see that she had taken the time to freshen her makeup and lipstick before she got home. She pouted slightly as she learned the girls were changed out of their school clothes and playing out in the back yard, as she had been looking forward to seeing them. But then, she smiled warmly as she introduced herself and apologized for being later than she thought she would be.

We shared with her the gist of what we had already discussed. She was glad that we had talked about getting Tomika back into the school band. She thought that was the main reason Tomika didn't have any good friends—they were all involved in after-school activities. The only ones left to hang out with were the ones who had nothing worthwhile to do.

She agreed that it would give Tomika a greater sense of belonging if she were to take a more active part in the upkeep and care of the house, too. But what she liked most was that I had, inadvertently, taken her side on the subject of corporal punishment. That was something she and her husband had disagreed about since the birth of their first child.

She knew that Tomika and her father had lost the relationship they used to enjoy. It pained her to watch as they turned on each other over the past couple of years. She worried that the same thing might occur between him and his other daughters.

"You both want what is best for her!" I said thoughtfully. "Neither of you want to lose her to the negative influences of peers that are unsupervised and undisciplined.

"From what I've heard from both of you today, she has already begun to turn to them for acceptance, approval, and affection. The greatest danger is that in her quest for those things outside of her family home, she might open the door to the experience of intimate relations. She may already be sexually active."

Justin broke in with a scolding tone directed at Helena, "I have been telling you for months that she has been fooling around out there!" And then, to me, he said, "Her mother thinks she can do no wrong! I tried to tell her that Tomika has been throwing herself at boys and her mother just shakes her head and says I am being too harsh!" He was clearly flustered and angry.

Helena protested, "She isn't throwing herself at boys, Justin! She's not like that!"

"Helena," I countered, "how can you be so sure? Have you asked her?"

"Well, no, but I think I would know if she were sexually active!"

"How would you know?" questioned the father. "She doesn't even talk to us, anymore! She cuts us off when we ask her where she's going! You are in denial! She is not the little angel you want to believe she is, when she walks out that door! You never listen to me! It doesn't help for her to think that you see her as this perfect angel that could do no wrong, while I have to get after her for acting out! You're crazy if you think this is all about me and what I do wrong! She is no angel, Helena! You need to see her for what she is and help me get her turned around. Take off your rose colored glasses and help me keep her out of trouble!"

"I am not crazy and I am not wearing rose colored glasses!" Helena interjected, defensively. "It's not all about what you do wrong, but I do think you tend to blow things way out of proportion and see her as having no sense at all! I just don't agree with the way you see her or the way you get on to her all the time. You are constantly picking on her as if she were this horrible child that needs to be punished and put in her place! It's no wonder she doesn't want to be home when you are here!"

Both of them were exasperated with each other as evidenced in their volume, tone, animated body language, and facial expressions. They were opposing each other at a time when they needed to present themselves as a cohesive team to Tomika and their other children. The mother seemed to be blind to her daughter's antics while the father imagined the worst. Moreover, neither one had any patience for the other's points of view. Both were equally convinced that their perceptions were facts while neither one would give any credence to what the other thought. It was clear that they were so exasperated with the bucking of their teenage daughter that they had turned on each other.

They had just displayed a total communication breakdown, where one was name calling and both were pointing fingers at the other, while neither one listened or reflected on what the other one was saying. Furthermore, from my perspective, neither one was right in their approach to the teenager's attitude and behavior. The father was too authoritarian and the mother was too permissive. Neither approach was working.

"Hold on, you are both getting upset with each other. I don't want her to think she has the power to split you apart. It all seems to be turning the atmosphere of your home from what could have been an Island Oasis into a shipwreck. Let's talk about this for a minute, before she comes back in here."

"We are split apart! Our home is a shipwreck!" Helena cried. "It has gotten so we don't want to be in the same room with each other. I get so mad I can't see straight! He won't let up on her and it just makes everyone upset! I just wish he would not be so hard on her!"

"She thinks Tomika can do no wrong!" he answered, emphatically. "Every time I try to discipline her, her mother jumps to her defense! She accuses me in front of her of being too quick to judge and then Tomika gets away with whatever she wants to do! She tries to be her best friend instead of being her mother! How am I supposed to parent her by myself with her mother interfering in everything I try to do?"

"You are both right!" I said with a smile. To Justin, I said, "She is too permissive, and then to the mother I said, "And he is too authoritarian! Neither approach is very effective as you both can see. When one is too authoritarian, the child becomes more defiant and when one is too permissive, the child bucks against boundaries, limits, and rules wherever she encounters them. She rebels against her father's unrelenting decrees and in response to her mother's permissiveness, she feels entitled to having her way and refuses to obey anyone. Why don't we strive to achieve some middle ground so she can see you are both on the same page when it comes to guiding and disciplining her. Right now you are neutralizing each other's authority with her. Neither one of you has the power to keep her on track with her responsibilities at home and at school, her peer choices or her use of free time."

"What middle ground?" asked Justin, impatiently, and then nodding toward Helena, he said, accusingly, "She isn't going to accept any kind of middle ground! She thinks she has to cater to her every whim and that I am a monster for not agreeing with her!"

Helena began to object, defensively, but I interrupted her saying to him, "She may feel that she has to overcompensate for your authoritarian approach. And, you might feel she is so permissive that you have to be more and more of a disciplinarian in order to compensate for her mother's permissiveness. I suggest that you both try to be more authoritative."

"What's the difference between being authoritarian and being authoritative?" Helena asked skeptically.

"There is a huge difference between the three types of parenting. Authoritative means to teach in a kind and motivating way. Instead of being too harsh or too permissive, you would both agree to teach her what you want her to know and how you want her to behave. When authoritarian you boss and order, command and make demands of her. No one likes to be ordered about! She learns to fear your wrath and learns to hide and to deceive you. When permissive you turn a blind eye to all her wrongs and encourage her to believe she already knows all she needs to know about herself and life. She loses respect for you, believing she can pull the wool over your eyes and have her way whenever she wants to do whatever she wants to do. The more she exercises that perceived right the more challenging she becomes to the authoritarian parent."

"Oh!" exclaimed Helena. To Justin she added, "She's right! We have been creating a monster! In trying to outdo each other we have totally done ourselves in!"

Justin shook his head and smirked slightly before asking, "So how do we do this authoritative thing? How do we handle her authoritatively when she sneaks out at night, or doesn't do her homework, or yells and intimidates one of her sisters?"

"We can address that in her treatment plan. We will introduce parenting practices that have proven to be highly effective."

"What kind of parenting practices?" he challenged.

"There are tools and strategies parents can use that actually motivate their children to make good decisions. Rather than using threats to get them to do what you decree we can agree on incentives that reward her for compliance with your expectations."

"Can you give us an example?" asked Helena.

Justin raised his eyebrows.

"Yes, of course!" I answered, enthusiastically.

"You have both alluded to the fact that her grades have dropped. She hasn't been applying herself. She has probably been skimming through reading materials, careless in completing math assignments and missing some assignments altogether, in her haste to be done with it. Right?"

They nodded in unison.

"Well, I have designed and implemented a strategy I call, 'Equal Minutes' that parents have told me works like magic. Here's how it works. Instead of trying to punish them by taking away their electronics and favorite things for indefinite periods of time as many parents do, I suggest that they use them as leverage. While some parents complain about how kids today are so driven by their electronics, I use it to my advantage."

Justin sat up ready to defend taking everything away, but I quickly spoke to keep him from interrupting.

"For every minute that your child spends doing homework or some other assigned task, she would get a minute to do what she wants to do, such as play on her computer, use her phone or spend time with her friends. Most of the children on my caseload are up to doing 90 minutes of homework just so they can have ninety minutes to use their phones and IPADS. If they don't have much homework they can earn minutes reading, practicing writing, or working on math problems off the Internet. The minutes do not roll over into the next day, unless their time was used up at a sports or band practice or some other school related activity. When that happens minutes can be saved for the weekend. Some minutes can be earned during the school week, for cleaning their room, getting up and out the door on time, etc., to be used on Saturday and Sunday, as well."

Both parents brightened up when hearing that idea. Justin was the first to speak. "I'd be willing to try anything to get her back on track with her school work! But, she isn't as into her electronics as she used to be. Now she just wants to bust out of the house to spend time with her friends."

"We will be putting reasonable limits on that too, which will give her more free time at home to use her electronics."

"I'd be willing to try it if you think it would help!" Justin said somewhat skeptically.

Helena nodded enthusiastically and added, "Me too!"

"Good! I think you will be pleased with the result. By using equal minutes you are offering an incentive that causes her to develop the internal controls it will take to earn a privilege. You won't have to struggle with her while using all the externally imposed controls you have tried up to now. I have had kids earn A's and B's that had been earning D's and F's! We can get her back on track, earning higher grades again if we can agree to use this strategy."

Justin sat back and then sitting up again with impatience he protested, "Wait! So, I have to bribe her to do what she knows she is supposed to do?"

"It isn't bribing!" I explained. "It is a way of enticing, inspiring, and motivating her to do what she has to do. Kids ask, 'What's in it for me?" If you can answer that question, you'll get their cooperation. Besides, that is exactly how we all operate. You get up every day and go to work to provide for your family. That is your responsibility. That is what you are supposed to do! But, you wouldn't be working the hours you work if you didn't get that pay check at the end of the week, would you?"

"That's a good point," he said, "But, I still don't know how to keep her from sneaking away at night!"

"We need to encourage her to be more compliant and cooperative with your rules, limits, and expectations. To do that, we have to reestablish your authority and her mother's credibility in a way that encourages less defiance and more cooperation and compliance.

"We have to work together to encourage her to enjoy being a teenager without allowing her free reign to come and go as she pleases." I was about to explain myself further but Helena interrupted me.

"I don't want her going out of the house in the middle of the night. She could be taken advantage of or get herself in trouble!"

"Yes! She is at a very vulnerable stage. She is half woman and half child. One minute she thinks she is all grown and the next minute she is curling up in the fetal position whimpering like an infant. Puberty is an exciting time, but a scary time as well. All children begin to experience the same sensations at varying degrees during puberty. They all develop the same curiosities about intimate relations. But what is it that causes some of them to satisfy those curiosities in desperate ways? I don't believe that desperation defines their drive for sexual satisfaction. I believe they actually feel that it's the only way they can get the acceptance, approval, and affection they so desperately need and no longer feel from their parents. Once they seek acceptance from their peers instead of their parents, they then turn to their peers for guidance, too."

Justin took in a deep breath, shook his head, and then said, regretfully, "So you are saying that I am the reason she is leaving the house at all hours of the night? I've been setting her up to being taken advantage of?" Before I could answer, he rolled his eyes, as if he had just had a revelation, and then under his breath he swore, "Oh my God," And then, turning to Helena, he said, "I am sorry! That is not what I was trying to do! I should have been listening to you!"

Helena intercepted his self-admonishment and countered it, saying, "It isn't all you! I have been just at fault. By undermining you and being such a pushover, she hasn't any respect for either of us! This is awful!" And then turning to me, she said, "Is it too late? Can we fix this? Will she ever listen to us?"

I agreed things had gotten way out of control and let them know that it would take all of us working together to turn her back around.

"We can't waste any time. We need to come up with a parenting plan that shows her you are both on the same page and have the same set of rules, limits, and expectations for her. We need to let her see that you both have her best interests at heart and a unified plan to see that she is on the right track. This is a critical stage for her. You want her behavior to reflect a good, strong moral character. You want her to develop self efficacy and independence while honoring your family values and boundaries. We can't do that if she continues to feel alienated by her father and entitled to do as she pleases by her mother. There are too many boys out there ready to intercept her, not out of any real malice, but out of sheer desperation to feel that they too are important enough to be valued by someone. Kids today are sexually active at eleven years of age or younger. They're out there, and they are ready and willing to receive her."

Justin's chin dropped down to his chest as he looked up at me with a look that said, he'd knock any kid into the next millennium, if he caught him taking advantage of his daughter!

Helena tried to reassure him saying she felt Tomika had better sense than to let someone do that to her, but again, he saw her protests as another example of how she allows herself to believe her daughter can do no wrong. He took her attempt at reassuring him as a direct hit.

"There you go again! It's hopeless! She's hopeless!" he stammered. And then, he added, "For all we know Tomika is taking advantage of them so she has some place to run off to whenever she feels like avoiding her responsibilities at home!"

"She's not hopeless, Justin!" Helena countered. "I just won't believe that Tomika is out there doing that with anybody! She is a good girl!"

Justin did have an entirely different picture of his daughter. He argued, "The way she runs her mouth in here, using the "F" word and the "B" word under her breath and the way she tries to dress, when she goes out tells me that she is capable of that and a lot more! I've caught her sneaking out of here with short shorts and heels in her back pack!"

"Oh, Justin!" Helena protested. "Most girls her age are doing the same thing. They like dressing up. It makes them feel grown up. She is probably feeling excited about how she is blossoming into such a beautiful young woman and wants to show herself off a little, to her female friends."

"That is a good point, Helena," I said. "Girls her age are very self-conscious and worried that others are developing faster and better than they are."

Helena appreciated the validation of her point but then shifted back to asserting that Tomika couldn't possibly be trying to get attention from boys. She said, to Justin, "We have taught her to have good morals and to honor family values. I think she would tell us if anyone tried to get too fresh with her and I can't see her running after boys for attention. That's ridiculous!"

Oh brother! I thought to myself. *She can't be that naive!*

The father, unfortunately, read the expression on my face and rolled his eyes. By allowing my reaction to Helena's apparent naivety to show, I had just initiated a triangulation between the three of us that I had to dissolve. I didn't want him to think that I thought Tomika was a bad girl, or that I was taking his side against her mother. So before he could comment, I interjected,

"Kids that act out sexually aren't motivated so much by sexual cravings as they are by a perceived need to be accepted and to feel wanted. They meet each other eye to eye. When they first reach out and agree to be exclusive, neither one is hurting the other, physically, emotionally, or mentally. On the contrary, their touch is ever so sweet. Their embrace lends absolution. They're okay in one another's eyes and arms. It feels good. They begin to feel better than they've felt at home in a long time.

Kids aren't out there having sex to upset or even to disrespect their parents. When they act out sexually they are doing it because it makes them feel better. When a parent tries to stop them, the teen thinks the parent doesn't care about whether they feel better or not. They aren't defending their right to act out sexually—they're defending their right to feel good, to feel approved of, and to receive acceptance, love, and affection."

"I won't believe she would do that!" said Helena, but her tone carried more doubt than before.

"Well? Let me ask her. Let's call her back out here and I'll try to ask her in a way that doesn't shut her down."

Before Helena could agree, Justin called out to her but in a more cautionary tone than he had used when he first called her to join us earlier in the session.

Tomika didn't require a second or third call as she had when I first arrived. She walked right out and over to her mother, gave her a kiss, and then, took a seat on the couch a little closer to her father than the one she had sat down in, so defiantly, during our introductions.

"Hi, Tomika! I said. "Were you able to get some homework done?"

"I got most of it done. I still have to do some math."

"Well, I will try not to keep you too long. I know it has been a long day for you, too. We have been talking about dating. It seems your parents haven't agreed on what age is appropriate for young girls to start dating." I embellished a bit here by addressing the first argument she and her father had addressed with me in the beginning of our session. "A lot of girls have boyfriends long before they are actually allowed to date, don't they?" I inquired.

"Yeah! I guess," she answered cautiously.

"How many boyfriends have you had already?" I asked her.

She nervously blushed and answered, "I don't know. A few, I guess."

"What was the longest relationship you've had, so far?" I asked in the friendliest tone I could muster, as I smiled at her.

She gave me a sheepish smile back and said, "I don't know. Do you mean, how long have I been hooked up with someone?" She shrugged and squirmed a bit.

What I knew, is that there are three phases in current relationships among this pre-teen and young teen population. They either say they are friends, they are talking, or they are hooked up. Hooked up usually means they are sexually involved.

"Either talking or hooked up. What's the longest relationship you've had?"

I let her off the hook in front of her father. She wouldn't have wanted to admit, in front of him, that she had ever actually been hooked up with anyone. I'm sure she feared she'd be grounded for the rest of her life if she confessed to that. But now that I had said "talking or hooked up," she relaxed considerably.

"About two months, I guess."

I smiled and deliberately caught her eye. She lowered her eyes, clearly hoping I would take the spotlight off of her. I couldn't. "Are you in a relationship now?"

"No," she answered sadly. "Not anymore."

I could tell I had hit on a soft spot. "Uh-oh—have you broken up with someone recently?"

"No. It's more like he broke up with me." Her voice carried the disappointment and deep sadness she felt about the breakup.

I could tell from the way they reacted that her parents were disturbed by this information. They had been alerted to the fact that she might have been having intimate relations—and then that she had been dumped. I could tell that her father was riding an emotional rollercoaster and didn't quite know how to react.

I turned to him and asked, "You didn't know she was going through a breakup?"

He shook his head and rolled his eyes, letting out a deep sigh.

"I didn't think so," I said. "She wouldn't be able to come to you about it without telling you about the relationship. This happens to so many girls her age. When the communication between the parents and child has broken down, the children have no one to turn to when something goes terribly wrong. They begin to feel lost in the throes of despair with no one to comfort them."

"Tomika," her mother cried. "You can always come to me. You know that don't you?"

Tomika shook her head slowly and then looking up at her father, she said, "He doesn't want me to have a boyfriend. He thinks I am too young for boyfriends! He treats me like I'm still a little kid."

"That's not it! Tomika, I don't want to see you get hurt or into some kind of trouble."

I interrupted him. "I wouldn't try to prevent her from experimenting with relationships. She needs to know that you trust her to honor your values and to test the waters in relationships with boys, while she is still under your wing. She needs to learn how to choose the right boyfriends and how to build healthy relationships but she will make mistakes. It would be so much better for her to know that when things go wrong or she has made a mistake that you and her mother are there for her, to comfort her and to help her figure out how to cope with the disappointments."

"That is what I have been trying to tell you, Justin. We need to trust her and to be there for her. We can't keep her locked up until she's eighteen and then expect her to know how to get along in the world!"

"I'm not trying to keep you locked up, Tomika, but I get what your mother is saying. I guess I have thought of you as my little girl and I probably always will!"

Tomika sighed and shook her head at him, but in a non-offending way. She seemed to understand and even appreciate that her father would see her that way, forever, but on the other hand, she wanted him to see her as grown too. That latter part was implied in her response to him.

"Daddy, I will always be your little girl but I want to have a boyfriend too. All my friends have boyfriends and they're allowed to date. They have been going on dates for two years, now. You won't let me have a boyfriend or go on dates. That's not fair."

"Tomika!" her father said, impatiently. I am not interested in hearing about what your friends get to do. I make the rules here and you will follow my rules while you are under my roof!"

The force of his speech and tone chilled the air once again. Tomika protested. "That's not fair! You and mom dated when you were my age. Why can't I date?"

Her father would not back down. "How can I consider it when your grades are falling, you are sneaking out of the house at all hours of the night, and refusing to help out with the chores?"

"Maybe I would be able to do better if you let me have a boyfriend."

"Tomika," I said, "you have had a boyfriend despite your father's expressed objections, and you haven't been able to keep your grades up, obey your father's rules, or help out, right?"

"Yeah, I guess. But that's only because he broke up with me and it hurt so bad that I couldn't concentrate. Even when I do study, I don't remember what I read and I can't do good on my tests when I can't remember anything!"

"Oh boy!" I mused. And then, to her parents, I said, "Teenagers' hearts are so sweet and sensitive and break so easily. With each breakup, they get more and more sensitive. Their sensitivity fuels their intolerance of any criticism and disapproval they might get from their parents. Their quest for comfort begins to overshadow their ability to interact and function appropriately at home and at school, too. Their family and peer relations decompose. Their grades begin to suffer. For some, their failures slap them in the face wherever they go. They have nowhere to turn where they can feel good about themselves. They become angry and act out their anger on others and on themselves. Some may even begin to loathe and hate themselves."

Both parents shifted their body language and turned their deeply sympathetic eyes toward Tomika. They had begun to understand that her attitude and behaviors were not solely a result of their interactions with her. This was new to them and it seemed to spark an understanding that had escaped them up to now. He father was the first to speak.

"I had no idea you were hurting from a break up, Tomika. Where is the scoundrel?" And then, in a half-teasing tone, he added, "I'll take him out if it would make you feel better!"

"Me too!" her mother chided. "We'll pulverize him!" And then, she made like she was boxing with her fists in the air. Both of them seemed to tickle her with their exaggerated intent to even the score. She couldn't help but let an involuntary smile erupt into a nervous giggle.

Then her father conceded, in a gentle loving tone, "Honey, if I had known you were hurting I wouldn't have been so abrupt with you. I had no idea! I wish you felt you could tell me. I thought you were just angry about having to do as you were told. I thought you were angry with me!" He had missed the fact that he was no longer the center of her universe. He realized now that he was not going to be able to kiss away her every bump or bruise as he was able to do when she was his little baby girl.

To both parents, I explained that theirs was a common reaction to such acting out behaviors and then I explained further as follows:

"Children get angry when they are hurt, just as adults do. It can be quite disturbing to them to experience these new felt emotions at such a tender age. The parent receives their child's anger as a personal attack and reacts on a personal level, often adding salt to the wound without realizing it. The child then counterattacks with greater force, because they take it as insensitivity and meanness coming from the parent, at a time when they need and would be most receptive to their parents' sensitivity and kindness. They feel they have a right to protest."

"I would protest too!" her mother said, emphatically.

"I never intended to come across as insensitive and mean," said her father."

I answered, "As children mature, their ups and downs are triggered by personal struggles or conflicts with their peer relationships. When that happens, the child's anger isn't about the parent at all. But, by taking the child's attitude personally and by reacting in a negative way, the parent isn't available to receive and comfort the child. When this occurs the parent disappoints and alienates the child. Each time it happens, the parent is given and yet misses the opportunity to strengthen the bond between them. After a time, the child stops turning to the parent for acceptance and guidance."

"I get that," Justin said, but then in a more aggravated tone he added, "but I can't have her throwing her weight around in here, upsetting her sisters, slamming doors, and stomping around here the way she does."

"No! you can't. I agree. But you might be able to get her to calm down if, instead of focusing on her outward behavior, you could call her to you and show an interest in finding out what or who is upsetting her."

"I can't let her take her anger out on me and everybody else in the family! If she wants to put herself out there to be with boys, then she needs to learn how to handle herself!" Justin decreed.

Tomika started to get upset and pled with her mother to intercede, "Mom!"

I held my hand up for Tomika and Helena to let me continue and then to Justin, I said, "Her being upset and stomping around as you say might not always be about a boy. Teenagers experience a tsunami of emotions for all kinds of reasons. It could be something a girl said to her or about her. It could be that she is struggling with meeting a deadline. She could have a new pimple in the worst possible place, or be totally dissatisfied with her reflection in the mirror. She could be miserable without a clue as to what is upsetting her. The point is that once kids reach puberty, their ups and downs are not always going to be about something you have done or didn't do, as it may have been in the past.

"She won't talk to me!" he exclaimed.

Tomika asked again and whined, "You never ask me why I am upset. You always tell me to go to my room or to get my work done and stop upsetting everyone but you never ask me what is wrong!" Tears started welling up in her eyes as she confronted him.

"I guess I am guilty of that too, Tomika," her mother said. "I worry about how you are affecting the children and I don't want you father to get on to you so I admonish you for acting out without first asking why you are upset!"

"I wouldn't get on to her if she had come to me and told me someone or something was troubling her but she won't. She won't talk to me!" her father said with mounting exasperation.

"Maybe not right then," I said, "but you will have let her know that you are there for her when she is ready to talk. You can acknowledge that she is upset and let her know that she can come to you or go to her mother, if she needs or wants to talk about what or who is upsetting her."

"Well, it is hard to ask her anything when she bucks up against me and starts uttering epitaphs and curses at me under her breath," he said to me. And then to Tomika, he asked, "How do you think it makes me feel when you call me stupid or start telling me to get away from you and leave you alone?"

"I only do that when you start yelling at me! I'm already upset and when you get upset I just want to get away from you! I just want you to stay away from me. You only make everything worse!" Tomika said angrily.

This was not the first time that Tomika complained of his yelling at her so I took the opportunity to introduce another strategy that I have found to be effective in addressing the explosive yelling that goes on behind closed doors.

"Justin?" I interceded, "Tomika yells too from what you tell me. From what you are both saying, it seems there is too much yelling going on in here. I have a way of nipping that in the bud if you two would like to hear it."

Tomika tsked but her father said, "If she'd listen I wouldn't have to yell. I don't start out yelling. I ask her the same thing over and over again and it's like I'm talking to a wall. She blurts out her two cents before I can finish a sentence! You can't tell her anything she doesn't want to hear!"

"That's not true, Dad! You get mad if I don't move fast enough and start yelling at me to "get out here," or "get in there," and to do this or do that! You don't even talk anymore. You yell when I'm not doing anything wrong! You have yelled my name so many times that I don't even like my name anymore. It scares me! Now when I hear my name I get all tense and nervous and want to run away from you so I don't have to hear what you have to say!"

"We would all like to run out the door when you start up with your nasty mouth!" Justin countered. "I'm not going to sit here and let you terrorize everybody because you left the peanut butter out on the counter and don't feel like putting it away when you are told!"

I turned to Helena and said, "When kids or parents report that yelling is going on, I give them what I call Pillow Power!"

Helena looked very interested in hearing how Pillow Power works. Justin asked skeptically, "What is Pillow

Power?" Tomika, asked, "So what? Are we supposed to start hitting each other with pillows? That is stupid!"

I waited until they were all ready to have their questions answered, and then I said, "It works like this. When someone yells, the one who is getting yelled at gets to put the yeller's pillow in Time Out for the entire night!"

The idea eased some of the tension in the room as they all reflected on how it would be to have to sleep through an entire night without that one treasured, often taken for granted, gift from the gods.

"Wait!" Justin said, with an interested grin, "so you are saying if I yell she can put my pillow in Time Out?"

"Right—and you could do the same when she yells."

"Right!" countered Tomika. "He would just take Mom's pillow or get his out of time out when he was ready to go to sleep."

"Oh no!" I said, shaking my head. "Neither one of you can replace the pillow if you are caught yelling. You would both have to agree to give the other Pillow Power and you would both have to agree to concede your use of your pillow if caught yelling. Can you both agree to that?"

"I don't know," Justin said, half-serious and half-amused. "I don't want to give up my pillow!"

Helena laughed as Tomika agreed with him.

"It is crazy how much we revere that seemingly innocuous item when it comes to having it taken away from us," I said with a chuckle. "But, it works for that very reason! No one wants to give up their pillow for an entire night. I've been surprised to learn how effective this one little strategy has been for countless families. No one wants to give up their pillow!" I laughed again, as they both grimaced and groaned.

"So, what do you say? Do we have a deal?"

Tomika looked over at her dad and then back at me.

Justin looked pleadingly at Helena's anticipatory face and then threw up his hands in a dramatic concession as he said, "Pillow Power, it is! I will agree to give up my pillow if she will!"

Before Tomika could answer, I asked him, "Are you sure? You will let her take your pillow for the entire night, if you yell at her?"

"If that would keep her from yelling her head off in here, I'd gladly agree to that! It's worth a try!"

Helena asked, "So what if they both yell? Is it the one who yells first or the loudest or do they both lose their pillows?"

"Oh, they would both lose their pillows for the entire night!" I accentuated the 'entire night' part.

"Tomika, how 'bout it?"

She rolled her eyes, but had a big smile on her face as she imagined her dad having to sleep a whole night without his pillow. She answered, "Ok, Dad, you can take my pillow if I can take yours!"

"It's a deal then!" I decreed. "Pillow Power it is!"

At that, Tomika and Justin regarded the other as the feared enemy and target of the worst possible threat they could imagine. I looked up, as if to heaven, and smiled, saying, "A-ha! The magic of Pillow Power!"

"Now, it might take a night or two of sleeping without a pillow for either of you to actually stop yelling when you are upset. But it shouldn't take more than that."

Tomika, asked, "Can it go for name calling too? Can I take his pillow if he gets mean and starts accusing me of stuff and calling me names?"

"You both need to learn how to communicate with each other when you are upset. If you feel angry, say you are angry without acting angry. If you are feeling bad, say so. Own your feelings, though. Don't blame the other for the way you are feeling. Don't say, "You are making me mad," or "You are mean!" Say, "Tomika, I feel angry when you do this or that," or "Dad, I get scared or feel unloved, unappreciated, unwanted, or irreparably flawed when you criticize me like that."

"I don't get mad! I get frustrated! I wouldn't criticize her if she did what she is told!" Justin argued.

"Well, I understand. But when we are too critical, they stop listening to what we say. They are too busy defending against criticism and how we are saying it to pay any attention to your words."

"So, I'm not supposed to react to the way she is acting, but she can blow up at me for the way I talk?" Justin asked.

Helena collapsed against the back rest of her chair and said with mounting exasperation, "No, Justin! That is not what she is saying. She is just saying we need to be less critical and more inquisitive. We need to ask her why she is upset."

"Yes, Helena. That is it exactly!" And then to Justin, I added, "You can react to the way she is acting, but when you do, you will shut her down. She won't tell you what she is upset about."

"Well, I call it as I see it. When she blows us off and struts around here like she's grown, she deserves to be punished for her attitude." He ignored Tomika's protest and continued, "I don't want her teaching her sisters how to act like that. It's enough with one of them. I have to put a stop to it or we'll have all four of them stomping and strutting around here!"

"I agree, we don't want that! But by improving the communication between you she will learn there is a better way to handle stressful situations. Tomika was hurting from the breakup with her boyfriend. But, she couldn't talk to you because she felt you would come down on her for having a boyfriend. She couldn't possibly tell you, for fear of being punished. And then, to make matters worse, you took her behavior personally and began to admonish her for how she was acting. When parents start admonishing kids for the way they act when they are upset they think the parent doesn't care about what is upsetting them. From their perspective the parent should not have been so insensitive and mean."

Justin dropped his head down and sat quiet for a moment and then, to Tomika he said, "You're right! If I had known you were hurting I wouldn't have scolded you! I don't want to hurt you or make you feel worse!"

"I am sure that Tomika didn't want to make you feel bad either. I understand that she has no right to call you names or to be disrespectful. But, she sees you trying to get her to shift her focus from the pain and anger she is already feeling to your issues of disrespect and insubordination. That makes her feel even worse because she is already feeling more vulnerable than she has ever felt before in her life.

When a child perceives their parent as being insensitive and mean they just might tell their parents to shove off, —and then, they really are in trouble. Whether they face the parents with this shove off attitude or not they have no choice but to escape the wrath of the parent one way or another. Does this sound at all familiar to either of you?"

"You've about hit the nail on the head," said Tomika's father.

Her mother just shook her head.

"I never told you to shove off," Tomika protested.

"Maybe not in so many words, Tomika," I said. "But every time you sneak out of here and run off, you're telling both of your parents to shove off, aren't you?"

She shrugged but smiled. "Uh huh!"

I said with a laugh, "See? You do."

She smiled nervously back at me.

I then turned my attention back to her parents.

"They often act out the same level of loathing and hatred on themselves that they've demonstrated to you and others. This self-loathing begins to show in self-defeating and self-destructive behaviors. We say that adolescents believe they are indestructible; the truth is some seem to reach a point where they don't care if they self-destruct or not. They begin to feel anything would be better than the way they feel now.

When their attempts to escape fail to comfort them, they can, and too often do withdraw and give up on you and themselves, or they attack everyone who slights them—with mounting, uncontrollable rage. When they internalize that rage they can become dangerous to themselves and when they externalize they can be disruptive and even dangerous to others." I nodded to Tomika's dad. "Justin, I'm sure you've met more than such children in the course of your career as a police officer."

"Oh yeah. We haul the suicidal ones off to the crisis stabilization unit and the assaultive ones off to the detention centers. I'd say once or twice a week on my shift alone."

"That many?" the mother asked.

"Oh yeah! At least that many. They come from good homes, too—a lot of them."

"I guess that would depend on your definition of a good home. Are you saying they come from affluent neighborhoods?"

"Yeah, I guess you could say that."

"Teenagers from all walks of life are vulnerable and acting out. Cohesive families that enjoy an open and loving communication fair better than those that don't. The financial status of their parents has little to do with it.

"When teenagers feel alienated from their parents, they often cop the attitude, 'What you don't know won't hurt me!' There are several others in the neighborhood who have the same philosophy. Many of them are what we call latchkey kids. They congregate after school, at the homes where both parents are working until after 5:30. Some know just how to time it so that they can leave before the parents get home. Those parents haven't a clue as to how many have been hanging around at their house or what goes on when they aren't there."

"I've told her not to go into homes when the parents aren't there," the father said.

"Tomika," the mother said, "tell her what happened a few weeks ago when you gave me Jenny's number."

Tomika dropped her head and winced. "You tell her."

"Okay," the mother said with a sigh. She turned to me. "She gave us the phone number of where she was staying overnight. It was supposed to be at Jenny's house. I called from work a couple of times, and either she or her friend's brother would answer the phone. Both would say that the parents were outside, in the bathroom, or asleep. As it turned out, the number she gave me wasn't Jenny's. It belonged to a friend whose parents were out of town."

"How did you find that out?" I asked.

"One of her old friends called and told us that she was worried about her and wondered if we knew she was over there."

"What did you do?"

"Her dad took the belt to her and grounded her from leaving the house and using the phone."

"So, did that teach her not to deceive you in that way again?"

"No. It didn't faze her in the least. She just started sneaking out after her dad left for work. That's how she got herself into this mess with the Department of Children and Families."

"Well, it isn't such a mess after all, because we're going to work on things so she'll be more compliant at home, aren't we Tomika?"

Tomika looked relieved as she answered, "Uh huh."

"Well, I hope so," her mother said. "Things have gotten out of hand. It's not just her, either. A couple months ago, I got a call from someone's mother. She called to say she would be a few minutes later than she had planned to pick up her daughter. I hadn't heard anything about her daughter being at our house, and so I asked if she was sure her daughter was here. The mother said, 'Well, yes, don't you recall? I talked to you last night to make sure you were going to be home before I dropped her off?' I didn't recall because I wasn't the one she spoke to. My daughter covered for her and a few of her other friends who were going to a party at the same house we spoke of earlier."

"Tomika!" I scolded. She dropped her head again. "So," I asked the mother, "what happened then?"

"I waited for all of the girls to show up, sat them all down, and then made them explain to all their mothers what they had been up to when the mothers came to pick them up. I made Tomika apologize to all of them. She got a beating, and she got herself grounded again."

"There's that 'What you don't know won't hurt me' posture that I was speaking of before," I said.

"Well, it did hurt her," said the father, crossing his arms over his chest. "She got a beating and she got grounded."

"Those consequences were effective?" I asked.

"No," the father interjected. "She just runs off more and tells us more lies. She isn't stopping. She's just getting better at lying and sneaking out."

"Well, that's what I was talking about before. When parents use punitive consequences, troubled kids become more and more defensive, resistant to your authority, and deceptive. The more punitive your response, the more she'll react with high-risk behavior. I'm not saying it's right; I'm just saying that it's what happens. You can see for yourself that it's a losing battle—not just for you, but for her as well. Punitive consequences can drive a wedge between you that is irreversible. You have to struggle with the fear of what can happen to her. At the same time, you are struggling with being lied to and betrayed over and over again, by your own child."

"I can't ignore it," said her father. "She has to learn that if she gets caught lying to us, she will get her butt beat."

"But, she has gotten her butt beat, as you say, and it doesn't seem to be changing the way she behaves. Her behavior has been getting worse. Hasn't it?"

The father's face turned red, his cheeks filled with air, and then as he let the air out, he answered, sounding exasperated, "No, nothing works. She's getting the best of me and there's nothing I can do to stop her. She's completely out of control and she doesn't care what I have to say about it—she's just going to do what she wants to do, no matter what I do."

"That's not true, Dad," Tomika said. "I care about what you have to say." She paused then, looked over at me and then back at her father, and said, "Most of the time."

"Yes, you care most of the time, when you're doing what you want and not getting caught."

"See, you always say things like that. You always say I don't care about you and that I'm trying to hurt you and Mom. You act like I'm this horrible person and like I'm—" She stopped herself and then turned to me, as if she wanted me to finish her sentence for her.

I understood immediately.

"I think what she's trying to say is that she wasn't acting out because she wants to hurt either of you. She is being openly defiant and brazenly willful and noncompliant because you seem to be oblivious to her perceived needs. The truth is, she would have been happier if you never found out what she was up to."

"Of course!" her father exclaimed. "Then she could do whatever she wants and not get her butt beat."

"No, Dad! I don't want to hurt you. Never mind, you just don't get it. Think what you want to think—I don't care."

"You do care, Tomika, and so does he," I argued, "but neither of you is responding in a way that makes that clear. I think you all care very much about each other."

Her father snorted and said, "If she cared about me and her mother, she wouldn't put us through this."

"So you think she's acting out because she doesn't care about the two of you?"

The mother nodded, appearing to sympathize with her husband. "She's acting out because she's mad at him for using the belt and for forcing her to listen to his rules. She thinks his rules are stupid and that she shouldn't have to do anything he says."

"Hmm…is that true, Tomika?" I sked.

"No."

"No, what? What part of that isn't true?"

"None of it." She threw her hands in the air.

"Talk to them. Tell them what part isn't true. You need to be more specific. I'm not sure they understand what you mean," I prodded gently.

"Why? They won't believe me anyway, so they're just going to think what they want to think. They don't care what I think. All they care about is their stupid rules. They don't even care about me," she blustered sarcastically.

I held up my hand just enough to keep the parents from interrupting her. With that gesture, I was telling them that what she had to say, whether right or wrong, was important. I wanted them to listen without judging and without censoring her comments. With my eyes and facial expression I communicated that I wasn't sitting in judgment of them either. I let them see that I was taking an objective view of all that was being said. My objectivity eased the tension in the room, and Tomika felt safe enough in my presence to voice her thoughts and feelings.

Up to this point, the parents had been telling me what her motives were, and she had explained what she felt their motives were. Both perspectives were extremely hurtful, yet neither was factual. Everybody was hurting for reasons that were based purely on speculation, and false assumptions.

"Justin, she isn't acting out to hurt you or her mother, any more than you are whipping her to make her miserable and to ruin her life."

"I'm not so sure about that!" he countered. "She lets me know what she thinks of me! She'd rather make her own rules and not have any parents!"

Tomika was about to object again but I was able to interrupt her saying, "That negative thinking is forming a wedge between all of you. Her acting out is wrong, yes, but your punitive responses are ineffective and her mother's lenience is making her feel too willful and insecure.

Tomika is not trying to hurt you any more than you are trying to hurt her. That is what Tomika wants me to help her explain."

Justin became defensive again and said, "Still sounds like I am supposed to show her I care how she feels when she is showing her butt around here! Isn't that going to make her think all she has to do is show her butt and she will get my sympathy? She'll play me the way she plays her mother!"

On the surface, it didn't appear that we were getting anywhere. I mean, this wasn't a casual conversation or argument. We had slipped into an area that was saturated with mutual frustration and confusion. They were exposing the ineffectiveness of his using the belt which as it turns out has been an issue that had caused considerable defensive and offensive reactions on the part of the whole family.

I tried to dissolve his defeatist attitude by helping him to see there was a better way to respond to her behavior. I answered him, saying, "In order to get her to feel safe telling you what is wrong, you need to first give her some space to deal with whatever is troubling her on her own. Timing is the second most important part of a good communication!"

Tomika asked, "What is the first most important part?"

Helena answered her with a question to me, "Listening?"

"Yes, listening!" I said. "But, be careful of what you are 'listening' to. Instead of listening to her words and tone, listen and try to identify what she is feeling. Is she feeling hurt, frustrated, ugly, too fat, too short, too tall, or is she feeling unloved, hopeless, defeated, or all of the above? Once you have identified her feelings you will know how to respond to her."

"If what you are saying is true, then I have taken a belt to her when I should have comforted her." He turned to Tomika again, and said he was sorry if he ever did that.

"I realize, Justin, that you felt you had no choice." I consoled and then continued, "Corporal punishment is used when parents feel that they are powerless and have no control over a situation. They use it to regain that control. Having no control over a situation isn't a powerful position to be in, and that doesn't change for the better, no matter how severe the thrashing. While corporal punishment may cause fear of being physically hurt, it doesn't instill reverence or respect for the punishing parent. Often, the less powerful the parent feels over the situation, the more abusive the thrashing becomes."

"I don't lose control when I use my belt!" Justin exclaimed. "She knows she has been beat but I don't cause her any real harm! She's got to learn to respect me. I can't let her walk all over me and her mother!"

"I agree that you can't let her walk all over either of you, but you do need to use more effective corrective measures. We need to exemplify our capacity to communicate, in a solution-based manner. We need to resolve to solve issues that compromise relationships, without resorting to verbal and physical violence. We have to learn how to live together without hurting each other.

The first thing we have to do to accomplish that is to stop acting on false assumptions in our interactions with each other and our children. And then, we need to practice more effective communication skills."

I deliberately allowed for a long pause.

I had to make them understand that they were all working against their own goals. They were each their own worst enemy. It was, primarily, their own thinking that was at the root of a good part of their pain, frustration, and anguish.

I reflected back on what Tomika had said. In her defense, I broke the silence. "She isn't acting out in order to hurt you or to get back at you for hurting her. She's trying to get her needs met!

"Children need to feel that they belong. They need to know they can come to their parents for the approval, comfort, and affection they need, in order to heal and grow throughout adolescence. If you push when you could pull her in, you are only complicating and severely compromising your relationship with her."

Justin bolstered up almost as if he were about to get up and demanded, "Again, how do I pull her in when she bucks up against everything and everyone? She talks back, runs out the door or down to her room, and makes a scene if I go after her!"

"If you reach out to her when she is most vulnerable, such as Tomika has been since the breakup with her boyfriend, there is a good chance that she would be receptive to what you have to say."

Helena nodded and looked up at Justin with a look of hope that he would hear and understand what I was telling him.

He looked perplexed and then asked, "What do you mean by reaching out? If I tried to put my hand on her when she is upset she would push me off and claim I was trying to abuse her! I can't go near her when she acts up!"

"By reaching out, I'm talking about sensing her pain and confusion, and then being a comfort to her. Refrain from pushing her away with harsh admonishments. Give her time to work things out on her own without jumping in to question her or to fix her problems. Just step back and give her space without reacting until she calms herself down. And then, when she is calm, ask her if there is anything wrong? Tell her you noticed she is upset and ask if there is anything you can do to help. If she feels safe enough to confide in you that she has had a break up, for example, pull her in with gentle words of encouragement. Speak to her tenderly, and say, 'This is one of the things we wanted to protect you from, honey,' showing genuine empathy and then invite her to cry in your arms."

I turned to Tomika and said, "Your parents aren't trying to ruin your life. They aren't out to keep you from experiencing love and pleasure. They are here to protect you from confusion and pain. They want you to wait until you and whomever you choose to relate to on that level are mature enough to handle the emotional ups and downs that can come with the intensity of intimate relations. You're going through these ups and downs now, aren't you, sweetheart?"

Tomika turned her eyes away from us. Her affirmation got stuck in her throat, but we heard it. I continued, "Your parents want you to wait until you have met someone mature and morally responsible enough to care for your well-being. They don't want you to be any boy's good time girl. They don't want you to be the object of some boy's desire who has no interest in taking responsibility for you and your welfare."

Her father interjected, "If she didn't hang out with sluts and tramps, she wouldn't have to worry about it!"

Whoa! I thought to myself! *What just happened? He didn't just say that! I was just about to wrap this up when Bam! He had to go and throw that out there! Did he miss the whole discussion about name calling?*

Before I could object he blurted, "Tell her about your friend—what's her name?"

"Who?"

"The one that just got herself knocked up."

Tomika tsked and turned to face the back of the couch, but not without expressing considerable disgust toward her father for bringing that up.

I had to come to her defense. I leaned forward, facing him squarely in the face and said, "I have to say something about using such labels. When children and their friends are put down with harsh words and demeaning labels, they become more and more deaf, distant, and ungovernable."

"Well, I call it as I see it."

"And you can do that, but when you do you are actually strengthening the bond between Tomika and her friends. They already have a common bond by the mere fact that they are of one generation and you and her mother are from a different generation. This is what is referred to as the generation gap. That common bond causes her to see her friends as a reflection of herself to some extent, so when you call them such names, she internalizes the same complaints to be about her.

"She takes it in as if you were saying that she too is a slut merely by association. You don't want her to think of herself like that. You want her to value herself. You want her to know her daddy values her!"

"I do value her!" he insisted. "But I don't have to value her friends if they can't exhibit socially acceptable behavior! How is she to know not to be like them if I don't give her my opinions about the way they act?"

"You could start by focusing on what you value about her. Tell her that you know she is a good girl and that you are relieved that you don't have to worry about her the way her friend's parents have to worry about them."

"I don't think her friends parents worry about much of anything, and even less about their kids," Justin retorted.

Tomika chimed in with a direct question. "Do you even know that, Daddy?"

"Know what?" he asked.

"That I am not like them! I don't drink or use drugs! I don't bounce from one boy to the next, flirt, and curse and run the streets. I'm not like them!"

"How can I know that? When you walk out that door I don't know what you are up to. You say you are helping your friend babysit and that is a nice thing to do but are you really there to help him or are you there to do what you want because there are no parents around to supervise you?"

"I am really helping him!"

I then said, to Justin, "It is easy to shut them out thinking of them as sluts and tramps but are they sluts and tramps? Or, are they, as she sees them; immature, hurting, and stressed out kids that don't know how to cope with the way things are for them? I think you and your daughter would have a much better relationship if you considered her point of view. She seems to regard them as the latter and resents your negative view of them."

Tomika sat up a little straighter and leaning forward facing her father, she said, "That's true, Dad! They aren't bad kids! They are having a hard time with everything! I wish you could see that and not be so mean!"

Helena came to his rescue. "Your dad just wants you to choose friends that are not so stressed out. Honey."

I acknowledged the tender way that Helena had addressed the issue, saying, "You put that very nicely, Helena. That is exactly what I am talking about when I speak of authoritative parenting versus authoritarian or permissive parenting. You are using a kind and sympathetic tone while telling her exactly what you both expect and want for her. You both want her to make good decisions and good choices when you are not there to guide her.

"If you want her to pay any attention to what you are saying, you need to refrain from using such harsh labels and instead explain things to her in loving ways."

To Justin, I said, "You can object without being crude and offensive. You can't call the girls sluts and the boys tramps and then expect her to listen to you or to care about what you have to say."

"So I'm just supposed to keep my thoughts to myself? How will I teach her right from wrong if I'm not supposed to tell her how I see things?" her father asked.

Helena jumped in, saying, "You don't have to use such harsh words!"

"You need to hold her and reassure her that you are here for her because you love her," I said. "You aren't here to punish and admonish her. You are here to protect and to shield her until she is mature enough to make choices that will be good for her. As much as you might see her friends as being sluts and tramps, you are defeating yourself by calling them that. You can hold her with loving kindness in your facial expressions, tone and word choices, as close to you, as if you were holding her in your arms."

"It's hard to be reassuring when she tries to dress like she has no morals and stays out all night doing God only knows what!" he argued. "She could be shacking up with them and I have no way of proving it or stopping it. I don't want my daughter shacking up period, never mind with the likes of any of her so called friends!"

"She's not shacking up with anybody, Justin!" Helena insisted.

"How can you be so sure?" he asked accusingly.

"I'm not, Daddy. I don't shack up with anyone!" There! We finally got the answer to the question we had raised before calling her out here. But, he wasn't convinced.

He rolled his eyes and shook his head at her.

"I would like to believe that!" he spluttered. "But you want to hang out with the worst of the lot. They have no morals or boundaries. Those girls are disgusting the way they dress and parade around boys that are just trying to get into their pants. That's all they ever think about," he added, with the most disgusted tone he could conjure.

He had totally dismissed her expressed sympathy, concern and regard for her friends. She had tried to show him that it was their circumstances that had contributed to her friend's behavior. She wanted him to understand that they were struggling with circumstances beyond their control and that they were not bad kids, at all. He wouldn't listen. By not listening, he failed to recognize and acknowledge his daughters remarkable ability to look beyond appearances. She understood that there were underlying forces that caused her friends to be so troubled that some failed to do well in school while others rebelled against laws and rules. His daughter demonstrated compassion while he shielded himself, behind an opaque wall of moralistic brick and mortar. He failed to consider the truth of what those kids were about, and worse, he cast shame on her for not joining him behind that wall. In fact, he was implicitly accusing her of having no morals. How was such a degrading verbal abrasion going to open her mind to what he had to say?

Helena seemed to shrink back into herself and her chair as he roared and rambled on but Tomika rose up in hers and came back at him with a startling force.

"What are you talking about?" she demanded, angrily. "You don't know them! You can't call them names! You don't understand what they have to deal with every day! Why do you always have to be so hateful and mean?"

"Mean? There you go again, trying to get your mother's sympathy by saying I am being mean! I am not mean, Tomika! Stop saying that just because you don't like me telling it like it is!

"I said it before and I will say it again! I call it as I see it! I don't care what their circumstances are! They can make excuses for their behavior, but I won't! They have choices and if they choose the wrong way then they deserve to suffer the consequences! If you continue to hang out with them you will suffer the consequences too! I'm not going to allow it! You can forget going anywhere until you can pick friends who make good choices and that is the end of it!"

Oh Brother! I thought to myself. *Here he goes spouting off a rigid, cold morality barren of that one thread that runs through all the religions of the world just as plain as it is expressed in the Golden Rule! 'Do onto others as you would have them do unto you!" His is an 'us and them' mentality that belies the very heart of any true morality. It is perfect examples for why I say leave the preaching to the Ministers. It is the very reason I tell parents to model, guide and teach rather than to moralize and preach.* I made a note to go into this much deeper with him in private. For now I wanted to get back to addressing the futility of his whole parenting style. I had to at least confront his approach.

"Justin?" I called out his name abruptly, to get his attention and then paused before I spoke. I took in a long breath and slowly let it out to ease some of the chill and tension in the air.

"Justin," I said more patiently, this time, "when parents use admonitions, alienation, and shame to instill morals in their children, the kids tend to close their ears and tune their parents out. They run for cover and don't hear the wisdom behind their words. It becomes impossible for you to parent and to protect them at a time when they need your guidance the most.

"We must find a way to teach with love and approval in our eyes and facial expressions. Approval needs to be expressed in affectionate ways by the parents. Parents need to practice demonstrating love to their older kids every day in heartfelt words and nurturing ways, just as they did during the infant and toddler phase. The only difference is that, rather than giving them a kiss or a lullaby to calm them down or to soothe their bumps and bruises, we must lift their spirits with daily expressions of kindness. Only then will they open themselves to our direction and guidance. Harsh reprimands and threats of corporal punishment do not do the trick! It only makes them more defiant!"

"She gets affection! She gets if from her mother and she gets it from me when she does what she is told," Justin said.

"There is a risk of creating an even greater problem when affection and corporal punishment coexist in the home. Another message presents itself in destructive ways to these children. It tells them that pain and affection go hand and hand. That message sets them up for an acceptance of aggression and violence in future relationships. They could either become the aggressor or the victim of aggression in their adult relationships. I know you have had your share of domestic violence calls since you have been on the force."

"Yes, I have but I have never thought there was a connection between domestic violence and corporal punishment," he murmured.

The session had gone on for an hour longer than I had intended. I felt that we had come a long way from where we were at the beginning of the session, but I wasn't about to leave without the assurance that he wouldn't use his belt on any of his children in between sessions.

"The problem here is that children who are spoken to harshly or not at all, and then on top of that, disciplined with verbal, emotional and/or physical violence, often turn away from the shepherding of their parents and guardians and run further astray. They become masters in the art of escape. You are trying to parent your children in a way that will keep them safe."

Helena said to Tomika, "She is right! Your father and I both want you to be safe!"

"I know, Mom," said Tomika.

Nodding to the three of them I continued, "It's important to remember why being too permissive or using harsh epithets, verbal slaps such as 'slut' and 'tramp,' and corporal punishment aren't working. The undesired behavior and the punishment escalate and alienate the parent from the child even further. There develops a total breakdown in communication. Neither hears the other. Words between them become sparse and cold, while affection and kindness are rarely expressed.

I turned to Tomika and explained, "Remember when I said he isn't trying to be mean? He may think that if he isn't as consistent with the threat of corporal punishment, as his own parents were, then he isn't being a good parent."

I then turned to the father. "It appears to some kids that their parents are all about control and power. Teens tend to respond to control and power by engaging in a power struggle neither side wins."

Facing Tomika again, I continued. "He is about protecting and rearing all of you in the best way he knows how. He wants to be a good parent. He wants and intends to stay involved, whether you like it or not, because he knows if he doesn't, you'll be at risk of being hurt, physically or emotionally, in ways that could ruin your chances of having a good and productive life. Considering how many teens are out there who don't have responsible parents, this is a huge responsibility that he takes very much to heart. Can you understand what I'm saying, Tomika?"

She looked up at him, smiled, sighed, and said, "Yeah, I guess."

The fact that Tomika was smiling and agreeing with me wasn't as much to my credit as it might have appeared. I simply capitalized on her need for love, acceptance, approval, and affection from her father. I was telling her that, although his behaviors made it look as if he didn't care, it was, in fact, testimony to how much he did care. This information made her feel more secure with him than she had felt in a long time—and it was clear that this wasn't something I had just brought in to their relationship. It was something that had been there all along. I didn't create it; I exposed it.

Now that I had built him up, I aimed to hit the bull's-eye. I looked him squarely in the eye and said, "I won't sanction spanking and 'whooping' kids. I have raised three daughters and have never had to spank them. In fact, the only time I ever really have a problem with any of them is when I am hurting, tired, or upset about something. Then, it's more about the way I am feeling than anything they've done. I find that when I'm less tolerant, I speak sharply to them or become overly demanding or insensitive, simply because I'm too tired to be more gentle and kind.

"I can give you a recent example. Just the other night, I got home late and noticed that my daughter had made dinner and washed all of the dishes from the night before. But I had had a miserable day. I ran into difficulties at work and got stuck in traffic. I was anxious to get home to my girls, but I had to drive through a thunderstorm on the turnpike for over an hour at 30 mph. I missed my kids and hated not being there when they got home from school, or at least in time to make dinner.

"By the time I finally got home, I was feeling anxious, frustrated, angry, and sorry for myself. However, I thought I could squelch those feelings. I entered the house, gave my hello hugs and kisses to each of my girls, and set to work to help put the dinner on the table.

"But then, as I took glasses down from the shelf, I noticed that the counter was covered in water. With all the anxiety, frustration, anger, and self-pity I had brought home with me, I spat out her name and asked her how many times I'd told her, 'Wipe off the counter after you've washed the dishes!' My tone failed to reflect the heart, energy, and time she had spent doing the dishes. And I knew asking how many times I said anything was rhetorical and ludicrous.

"But worse, by not expressing my recognition and appreciation for all that she had done, I got an attitude back that could easily have escalated to a mutually assaulting verbal exchange. But I stopped myself before it got to that and remembered I started it. We could argue the one who didn't wipe off the counter for the hundredth time started it. We could say that if she had wiped the counter as she was supposed to, the argument never would have occurred. The message we would end up with was, if she wiped the counter next time she wouldn't get yelled at. But in her mind, if she hadn't done the dishes, the counter wouldn't have been wet.

"More importantly, if I had continued with my venting, I would have missed an opportunity to reinforce the personal pride in herself she may have felt for all that she had accomplished before I came in and spoiled everything. So, instead, I caught myself and apologized for my tone and words and profusely expressed my appreciation for her and for everything she had done for me."

"I am guilty of that too, I think," said Tomika's mother. "I get so tired and caught up in the details of my job and the bills and everything that I can be very short with my girls at times, too." She then turned to Tomika and said she was going to watch herself from now on and try not to be so insensitive.

"I'm proud of you for seeing that," I said. "That's good insight and just the kind of self-awareness that can help to turn things around." I went on to discuss how children are negatively impacted by the put-downs and corrective tones parents use when a kinder approach could have been used instead.

"Let me recap what we have been talking about," I said to all three of them. "Children are frequently cited for what they do wrong before they are acknowledged for everything they've done right. The little things they forget to do or that they've done wrong get blown way out of proportion, while the big thing they did accomplish goes without notice or merit. Over time, these kids become frustrated and angry at the parent and at themselves. As they are more and more troubled by that parenting style, they turn off their ears and shift their eyes so as not to hear or see the punishing parent. They not only act out in disrespectful ways, but eventually lose all respect for the punishing parent. They fail to feel their love for the parent or the parent's love for them. They begin to dread, rather than look forward to seeing their parents at the end of a school day."

"So is that why you head out the door the minute you get home?" Justin asked Tomika. "You don't want to hear me grumble and growl?"

Tomika looked up at him and laughed a little as she said, "You do growl, a lot!"

Helena looked over at him and sympathized, saying, "If I had been more help you wouldn't have gotten so exasperated. You wouldn't have had to grumble and growl quite so much."

He sat back with a look of satisfaction on his face, as if to say, *"Finally! Helena can finally see that I have had to be the heavy because she was too easy on the child."*

I let out another deep sigh and said, "I am so glad you can both see where things have gone awry in here. It isn't just that Tomika is getting worse. It's that the methods you have both been using have only complicated and compromised your parenting of her. When parents use ineffective practices, to discipline their children, the children become more unmanageable.

"Eventually, they become more alienated from the parent and the family system. That alienation comes to a head during adolescence. Children that are disapproved of and always in trouble give up on their guardians, teachers, and therapists—and worst of all, they give up on themselves. They begin to lose hope."

Helena turned to Tomika and asked her, "Have you lost hope, Tomika?"

"Not now," Tomika said, looking over at me. Both of her parents then turned to me as they all smiled.

"Good," I said. "I think we are getting somewhere. Tomika is a sweetheart. I don't want her to feel she is a bad girl. I don't want her to continue giving up on herself."

"Have you given up on yourself, Tomika?" her mother asked as she softly cried.

Before Tomika could answer, I wanted to drive the point home that their parenting styles could cause a lot more damage and distance between them and their daughter if they didn't change the way they both responded to her.

"A troubled child who is always in trouble and who has pushed guardians and teachers to the edge is often getting negative feedback all day, every day. Such a bombardment of negative feedback destroys the child's chances for success as it destroys her self-concept. Over time, the child simply begins to live up to the expectation that she is bad. She begins to seek out 'partners in crime' and to associate only with those who get the same 'rap.' Once that occurs, they begin to compete in the 'bad' group by trying to be the baddest."

"Are you trying to be the baddest, Tomika?" asked her father in a teasing tone.

"No," she answered, smiling, "but I can see how that could be true for some of my friends. They like to brag about how many times they get away with skipping school and even about who has the most suspensions. John and Gerard were high-fiving each other today about that."

Her father shook his head and said, "I want you to know that I appreciate your not falling in with that type of behavior. It's only going to hurt their chances for getting a good education and for making something of themselves in life later on."

"I know, Daddy, and I won't do what they do. I want to go to college and be a registered nurse someday like Mom."

This was the first time I had heard that—and from the look on her parents' faces, it was the first they had heard of it too.

"Wow, Tomika!" I exclaimed. "That would be wonderful."

"Really, Tomika?" said her mom. "When did you decide you wanted to be a nurse? I think that's magnificent! I'm very pleased to hear it."

"I was talking to my guidance counselor about career goals, and she and I looked up the education requirements and pay schedules on the computer. It got me to thinking that I could really do it if I wanted to, and I think it would be a good career choice for me. I didn't want to tell you until I was more confident that I could get my math and science grades up and actually qualify for a nursing program. My guidance counselor said she would help me stay focused on raising my GPA and then submitting applications when the time comes."

Both of her parents made surprised and encouraging comments about her plans to improve her GPA and her showing an interest in going to college. They were amazed and excited that she had decided to do that for herself, and they asked her to thank the guidance counselor for encouraging her and helping her prepare for college.

That guidance counselor had given Tomika hope! That was such a contrast with the messages she was getting from her parents at home. They had been focused on her non-compliance with the house rules, her defiance and willfulness and peer choices, without any idea of what her personal hopes, dreams, and goals were, up to now. Had they shown more of an interest in her goals, perhaps they would have opened the door to a side of her they hadn't seen before. Instead, by focusing on what she was doing wrong, they had shut down any communication about everything else that was going on in her mind and heart.

Thankfully, the guidance counselor was able to pull her in when her parents seemed to be pushing her away.

To both parents I said, "To get our children to begin to think of what is in their own best interests, the way her guidance counselor did, we need to rise above our indignation, unfold our arms, and reach out to them. We need to pull them in and turn them on to the idea of joining us in a solution-based team approach to resolving the trouble they are experiencing and expressing in their behavior. And then, we need to help them gain the confidence they need to even imagine earning the quality of life they all deserve.

"We need to learn and use techniques and practices that promote healing, learning, and growth. Adolescence requires the same degree of shepherding required during the terrible twos. Unfortunately, in many homes, just when they need the shepherding of their parents the most, they are turned off and tuned out from their parents' lack of expressed approval. We need to approach our children with an inquiring mind, if we want to be taken into their confidence. We can't be so focused on what they are doing wrong that we miss all the good they have going on."

I sat back a little and gave them a moment to reflect on all that I had said.

"You're right!" her father said, as her mother nodded in agreement. I continued to drive the point home.

"When teens are torn between needing and fearing their parents, they become more and more troubled by their parents' tendency to push them away with excessive admonishments and criticism and then pulling them in with orders to get in and stay put. Corporal punishment, admonishments, and criticism are the least effective corrective measures with them. People say, 'Spare the rod and spoil the child.' I find the reference grossly misinterpreted. At the time the Bible was written, the rod was a stick used to nudge and guide the sheep to greener pastures. I can't fathom it being used to beat the sheep up and over the hill. But I can easily imagine how it would have been used as a guiding rod to nudge and guide the lambs to nourishing soils and greener grass."

I had deliberately made this last point directly to the father. His face reddened. He let out a bit of a half cough half chuckle as he nodded and said, "That's a good point! I never thought of it like that!"

"Right?" I said, raising my eyebrows at him. "Some parents spare the rod in a physical sense but believe they're entitled to use it in an emotional, verbal, and psychological sense. Children who are taught to fear God, their parents or guardians, and other authority figures often rebel. That's what her friends are doing—they're rebelling covertly by relinquishing their own power and becoming extremely dependent on others, or they're rebelling overtly by becoming the behavior problem from hell.

"A child's behavior tells. The question is, 'Who will listen to what is being told? More important, who will empower such a child to heal and grow?' When we focus on changing the behavior, without acknowledging their strengths and changing what the child must endure, we are running up a very slippery hill. We will continue to alienate them when they need us the most. We can then blame the child, or we can work on cultivating a greater understanding of how life is for them and then draw on that understanding when we respond to them."

I let a few moments pass in silence. Then, looking up at him again, I said, "I'd like to contract an agreement with you that you will not use physical punishment during the duration of our intervention."

Tomika let out a little laugh and said, "Yeah, right! That'll be the day."

But he surprised her. "I'll contract for longer than that. I never liked using my belt in the first place. I just thought it was the only way, but now I see I'm just making things harder on myself. It isn't working with my kids. I've just about lost my little girl here!" His eyes started to fill with tears again.

"How about you, Tomika?" I said. "Are you willing to accept the rules, limits, and expectations—that your mother and father set up in order to keep you safe while you're still so young?"

Tomika lowered her eyes and said, "I can try."

"Helena?" I added, "Are you ready to join him in setting and endorsing clear and reasonable rules limits and expectations for Tomika and your other daughters?"

"Absolutely!" Helena said to Justin.

The father laughed and rolled his eyes. He could see the game was afoot. The transition wouldn't be easy, but it appeared they each felt there was enough at stake to give it their best shot.

"We could make a statement to her and the rest of the children," I said, in a half-tongue in cheek manner. "Is that the only belt you've used on them recently?"

"I've had this old thing for years," he replied.

"How about let's bury it out there somewhere in the back yard. We could have a little ceremony before I leave."

He chuckled.

The mother laughed.

"I'm serious. Let's do it."

"Sure, why not?" he said, smiling as he rose up out of his chair. When he got up, my mouth dropped to the floor! We all quickly followed him out to the back yard, as if to keep the momentum going before he changed his mind. When Tomika told her sisters to come, they each stood in disbelief as we explained what he was about to do and why.

And then, as Tomika gestured for everyone to form a circle, holding hands around her father, she began to hum, "Amazing Grace!" We each looked one to the other and then back at her and before long, we all joined in singing "Amazing Grace," in rounds, as that huge, once-thought-to-be-ferocious man buried his belt in the sand.

Chapter Eleven

Tommy—Part One

Approaching the open door of my supervisor's office, I overheard him discussing a new client with two of my associates, Ben and Brian. Ben, a retired New York City police detective, towered over me. He was over 6'5." Brian, a retired high-ranking officer in the Marine Corps, was a tall drink of water too, at 6'4", the irony of which will become apparent as you listen in on the conversation we had.

"There's no way this fifteen year old kid is going to be appropriate for our program," my supervisor said adamantly. "He pulled a knife on his father, and when he was told he was going to have home-based counseling, he threatened to shoot anyone that came anywhere near his property."

I listened as the others laughed out loud at the thought of Tom being allowed to receive outpatient therapy instead of residential treatment in a juvenile correctional facility. They all agreed that he should have been placed in Juvenile Detention until he could be sent to a more secure correctional environment. They were speaking of Tom as if he were Jack the Ripper.

I felt they had come to their conclusion rather abruptly. I stepped just inside my supervisor's office and, after responding to their morning greetings, asked the first question that popped into my mind.

"Does Tom have guns?"

"Apparently, he does," my supervisor said. "According to the report we received from DCF, he had more than one gun—and no one knows where they were hidden."

"Cool! Let me have that one," I said.

All three of them bellowed out laughing. They thought I was kidding. I wasn't.

"Come on," I said. "Let me check him out."

My supervisor saw that I was serious and said, "No! This one is too risky for any of us."

I argued that I would be alert and aware of the risk going in, that I wasn't scared, and that he just might be asking for help. My supervisor made eye contact with the others, raised his eyebrows, shook his head, and said I was a real sucker for losers.

They all roared with laughter.

I did see the irony in the whole thing and was amused by it myself, but not so much that I wanted to let this kid slip through the cracks before I even had a chance to assess him. I sensed there was more to the story than what had been put in the report, so I prodded my supervisor for more details.

"What does the referral say was going on between the son and the father when he pulled the knife?"

"The kid had called 911 to report that his father had punched him in the face and stomach. But he already has a reputation in that town. He's been in and out of trouble, and known on a first-name basis by the local law enforcement, since he was eleven. He's been in a school for emotionally disturbed kids since he was in fourth grade. He's just another fifteen year old with a reputation for being in trouble, and he's out of control at home, school, and in the community."

At that point one of my associates said, "He needs a walk to the shed out back—that's what he needs."

I thought to myself, *He's probably already had more time behind the shed than he needed.*

The three men in that office were enjoying the idea of how Tom could and would be corrected if they were his father. It was obvious that I wasn't going to get anywhere by sympathizing with the boy. I had to use a different approach, or I was going to lose the battle. So, with my hand on my hip, I bragged, "Yeah, well, somebody needs to go out there and knock him down a notch or two—and I'm just the gal that can do it."

There were more asides and laughter, but my persistence actually won in the end. I had to promise that I would be very cautious. I was to let the local police of the little rural town escort me to the home, until I was confident that Tom wasn't going to pull a gun on me.

Tom had a court hearing pending on the assault charge and only a short time to clean up his act before appearing before the judge. My supervisor reiterated that our intervention was futile and that the court should recommend that he be sent to a residential treatment program, such as the Sheriff's Boys Ranch or some kind of therapeutic corrections program. He advised me to work with the juvenile justice system to set those recommendations in motion.

As I turned to leave his office, I looked back over my shoulder at all of them and asked, "Is there a program for his parents?" I then left without paying any mind to their jocular responses.

My first meeting with the rebel was a piece of cake, as I knew it would be. The police officer pulled in right behind me. I motioned for him to stay in his car, and then I went up the few steps that led to the front door of the single-wide trailer where Tom lived. The door was open; through the screen I could see his mother, Trish, sitting at the table. Once she knew who I was and what I was there for, she called to her son.

He called out from his bedroom that he was busy and that he wasn't coming out. I asked the mother if I could come inside. She said, "Sure, but it won't do you any good."

I smiled, dismissing the implication that I was there for my own good, and walked right in, indicating to her that I was going to pester him a bit. I continued walking straight past her and down the little hall to his room.

"Hey, let's blow this dive!" I said to Tom through the door. "Let's ditch the cop and go out for a burger."

Tom was silent. I had thrown him off guard. My language wasn't typical of someone in an authoritative position. I was putting the control in his hands by making such a seemingly bizarre suggestion. He may have felt it was a trap. He might have thought I was there to lure him out, so that the officer could arrest him. Even if that wasn't the case, why would he want to go anywhere with some middle-aged woman?

Mustering up just the right amount of arrogance, he said, "What?"

Ah! I had him talking to me already. Two points for me.

"I'm supposed to come out here and make you think I'm trying to help you get out of the mess you're in, while I secretly connive to set you up to be sentenced to a correctional program." I looked back at his mother and smiled. She smiled back at me.

He was silent again, for several long seconds. I again imagined what must have been going through his mind. I wasn't pulling any punches. I let him know that I represented those who believed he belonged in the juvenile detention center or a residential correctional program. That was no surprise. He knew it was only a matter of time before that ax would fall.

When he saw me pull up in front of that trailer, with the police in tow, he must have thought his worst nightmares were about to come true. Maybe he was thinking, *But wait! Didn't she sound as if she wasn't agreeing with them? Wasn't she letting me know that I might be able to swindle her into protecting me from the consequences everyone was saying I would get for what I did?*

I believe I had confused him with that little twist—but not for long.

"Yeah, right, you're not one of them," he exclaimed sarcastically. "Nice try lady. F**k off! I'm not going anywhere. You better just leave me the f**k alone."

I answered, "Okay, fine!" and went outside, letting the screen door shut itself behind me with a bang. I walked slowly and deliberately to the police cruiser to tell the officer that the coast was clear and that I wouldn't need him.

As I turned my back on the exiting cop and headed up the path to the door again, I saw the curtain to Tom's window drop back into place. I let myself back in and sat down with his mother at the table, knowing I had hooked him. He would wiggle and fight to get off that hook, but I knew that I had caught him and would be reeling him in. All in good time.

I made a point of talking loudly enough for Tom to hear what I was saying. I asked his mother to tell me what was going on the day that he pulled the knife on his father. She said that the two of them didn't get along and that she didn't know why. I asked if she and her husband ever fought. She said that her husband got irritable sometimes. Recalling the beer cans that were strewn about the yard, I asked her if he drank.

She answered, "Rick will have a beer or two after work." She added emphatically, "He's a logger." I took that to mean that she believed he deserved a cold one after being out in the hot sun all day.

I then asked her if they fought more when he drank.

She shrugged. "He doesn't drink that much."

I felt she was covering up just how much he drank. I also knew that Tom was listening through the door. He would be filtering everything I said through a wall of skepticism, but perhaps he had just enough curiosity to benefit from our discussion in spite of himself. I couldn't let such an opportunity go to waste. I wanted him to hear that I believed there were two sides to the story.

I asked, "He's not more irritable after he's had a few?"

She said she didn't know.

I then asked, "Had he been drinking the day Tom got arrested?"

She answered, "No, I don't think so."

Hearing her say that, Tom threw his door open so that it banged against the wall. "You're lying, Mom! He's always drunk. What are you lying for?" He then turned on me and said, "Why don't you just get out of here?" as he stormed out of the trailer.

Her minimization of Rick's drinking had made him angry. It did go through my mind that he could be digging up one of those guns that were supposed to be hidden out there somewhere, but then, he had heard me question his mother about his father as if he might have contributed to the fight they had. I had deliberately let him know that I wasn't taking sides against him. Furthermore, I couldn't leave the discussion hanging on the faults of the father, without putting the mother, the son, and the outcome of the whole treatment process at risk. Nor could I leave with him calling his mother a liar. I was stuck.

I scooted myself down in the kitchen chair, looked around, and let myself imagine how it would have been for a kid to feel stuck in there. The place was small, dreary, and dirty. The floor hadn't been swept in a while. There were dishes half full of dried food on the counters. Huge patches of sheet rock were missing or hanging by threads of wallpaper. Water spots the size and shape of Missouri and Arkansas decorated the ceiling. No roaches though. That surprised me. Perhaps they were sleeping somewhere after a night of fun and folly.

By now Trish had started to squirm. I knew she was worried about what I thought of her housekeeping. "So," I mused, "you care a great deal about both of them, don't you?"

She looked a little surprised, as if she wondered how I gathered that from my survey of the room. It was close to 4:30, but it looked like she hadn't combed her hair since getting out of bed. Her blouse was a dingy white, old and tattered at the collar and pocket, and missing a button. She had it fastened at the waist with a safety pin. Her shorts were just as old and tattered as the shirt and flip-flops she had on.

I asked her another question before she could answer that one. "What do you do for fun?"

Her face darkened, and she just looked at me.

"You're not having much fun lately, huh?"

She shook her head.

"Now that's not good. We're going to have to do something about that."

She smiled and rolled her eyes at me as if to say I was crazy.

"I'm serious! You can't just sit in here all day. Is there anything you do for yourself that's just for you? Do you take walks? This is a beautiful country road. How about bubble baths by candlelight?"

She laughed and said, "Yeah, right!"

"Why not? You deserve a little pampering, don't you?"

She then said that she did go to her brother-in-law's place with her son and husband once in a while. They had two little girls, and she enjoyed spending time with them on the occasional weekend.

"Where do they live?"

"Just up the road from here. He barbecues one of the pigs. The men drink beer and we play gin rummy. That's about it. Sometimes the men go fishing and me and Aunt Carla sit around and wait for them to get back." She then lamented in a dreary tone that she rarely went anywhere unless Rick was home. Once a week she took the car into town to do the shopping. That is, when they had the money for gas. Sometimes he picked something up on his way home, or they made do with what they had in the house.

As she was talking, I heard a truck lumbering up the rocky dirt drive. It sat rumbling in the yard for a few seconds. I asked her if that was Rick. She gave me a quick nod and shifted around in her chair so she was facing the door as he came in. I squinched up my face and upper torso and asked her if he was going to be upset to see me there. She said she didn't think he'd care. I told her I would introduce myself and play with him a little.

As I said that, I rubbed my hands together, as if to say that I was going to mess with his mind and stir up a little trouble. She raised an eyebrow; there was a little glint in her eye that told me that was something she'd like to see.

Rick clomped up the steps, flung open the screen door, and walked straight into the kitchen to the sink, barely glancing at her. He washed his hands, totally ignoring the fact that I was sitting there.

She said, "This is the counselor that came to work with Tom."

He turned around, introduced himself to me, and then asked, "What'd he do, take off?"

I shook his hand and gave him my name, and then answered him in a way that wouldn't put Tom in a bad light. I could have said that Tom stormed out when his mom minimized the amount of drinking Rick did and how drunk he was the night all of this started, but I didn't.

Instead I said, "He was here long enough for us to get acquainted. I couldn't take too much of him at once, you know!"

He laughed, as if to say, *You can say that again.*

I then embellished a little more and said, "I wanted him to scoot so I could get the goods on the two of you from his mother."

By now he had a can of beer open and had come over to the table to sit down. I was surprised; I had expected him to leave the matter of counseling to the mom, but he didn't. He sat right down and started asking me questions about what I thought could be done about his son.

"Nothin' probably," I said. They both laughed. "He's probably beyond help," I added with an exaggerated sigh, while shaking my head remorsefully.

The father agreed with that.

"But, I don't mind giving it a shot," I continued, "if that's all right with you?"

Let me explain that I don't present myself as your typical professional home invader. I had on a T-shirt and a pair of blue jeans and had made myself right at home in that dilapidated little trailer. For as long as I was there, I was just another one of them. I wanted them to feel at ease so I could see what they were like on any given day. This would have been impossible had I presented myself more formally. They would have felt they had to put on airs with me. I wanted to avoid that as much as possible.

I also didn't want either of them to think that I had any answers or that I could do anything for them that they couldn't do for themselves.

"Has there been any more trouble with him since he got arrested? Has he been any more disrespectful or volatile?" I wanted to create the impression that I was accepting the fact that their son was the core of the problem. If I were to suggest that Tom's behavior was symptomatic of a dysfunctional family system, I would have increased the parents' defensiveness and resistance. In doing that, I would not only have severely compromised the development of a therapeutic relationship, but I could also have put the son at greater risk once I left the home.

The father sat up a little straighter, puffed out his chest, and said, “Well, he’s a good kid. He just doesn’t listen. He gets something in his head and starts butting in to things he doesn’t know anything about.” He then nodded toward his wife and said, “She and I get to talking, and he’s got to get in his two cents. He doesn’t know when to butt out.” He nodded in her direction again and added, “She loves it. He starts fighting her battles for her. He ought to learn to leave it alone. What goes on between me and his mother is none of his business.”

I nodded, as if I were in agreement with what he was saying. The mother appeared to be hopeful I would contradict him. Instead, I turned to her and said, “Wait till he’s got his own woman to reckon with. We’re not all that easy, are we?” I smiled at her. She smiled back. She knew I was referring to a woman’s right to speak her mind and to set things straight when things go wrong.

Her husband shook his head at both of us, and we all chuckled about it. But what they didn’t realize is that I had artfully played a little “blame ping-pong” with both of them. The ping-pong ball of blame went first from the father to the identified client, then it was my serve and the father played right into it, hitting the ball with a twist so that it landed in the mother’s court. I intercepted it from her court and bounced it right back into the father’s court without his realizing what had happened. In doing that, I had empowered the mother at a point in the game where I was appearing to join the father in blaming her as well as the son for what had happened.

It was great fun, but enough for one session.

"Well," I said as I stood up, "I guess I ought to be going. It's getting close to dinner time. A logger must get pretty hungry by this time of day. I'll mosey on in to his school on Wednesday. Perhaps I'll take him out to lunch or something."

The father protested, "That's all he needs! Another excuse to miss school."

The father had a point. Tom either skipped school or was suspended more days than he was in attendance. He was in special education and still failing all of his classes. The teacher had already decided to administratively promote him to the next grade in the coming school year.

I stood there with my eyes to the floor in consideration of what the father was saying, and then I agreed. "I can't argue with that." It was important to give credence to the father's expressed concern for his son before interjecting any argument of my own. I sat back down and said, "His attendance will be one of the first goals of his treatment plan. I've found, though, that in working with teenagers, particularly, it helps to begin by appearing to be rescuing them from something they want to get away from."

The father's face told me that he couldn't argue with that. I had said it in a way that implied that my way could be wrong. I shrugged and paused to let the father know his point was well taken, but, still, I had one-upped him. Now I was coming off as the smart one—and he had to concede. That wasn't how I wanted to end the discussion. Before I could say anything though, the father dismissed the whole issue.

"Just do what you want to do." His tone implied that he was through with trying to figure it out himself.

I couldn't accept his resignation. We were playing ping-pong again, only this time the ball was not one of blame but of responsibility for the son. He had just put that ball in my court, and I needed to give it back to him.

I asked how he would feel about my meeting with his son during school, until I was able to build a rapport with him.

The father waved his hand as if to say, *"Whatever!"* I could see the imaginary ball of responsibility for Tom drop short of his father's court and roll off into nowhere land. The only way to get him to pick it up was to convince him that I wouldn't proceed in any fashion, without his informed consent.

I turned and made eye contact with the mother, who had withdrawn from the whole discussion, and then I turned back to him and said, "May I share my thoughts?" Without waiting for an answer I went on. "Teenagers are the least receptive to treatment. They are at a stage when they are developing autonomy. They are breaking away from bonds with adults and authority figures. An attempt to create a therapeutic relationship goes against the grain of that stage of their development." In saying this I had taken the focus of the discussion off their son and put it on his developmental stage of life.

"It's hard to engage them," I continued. "You're lucky if you can catch up with them, never mind have an intelligent verbal exchange." We all chuckled in agreement, and I said, "Hey, that's why I dress in running shoes and blue jeans—I never know where the chase is going to take me." Here I was asking for a little leeway. In doing that, I openly displayed my fallibility and limitations. I showed the parents that we had that in common. I reduced my role down to a level they could relate to and to the level they had been on with him for some time.

They now knew that I shared in their frustration and that, although I wasn't easily diverted, I was aware of the obstacles before me. I had no illusions about the effort it would take to achieve our treatment goals.

I shrugged again and said, "I've found I have the most influence with teenagers when I appear to be playing into their hands. Besides, he isn't getting anything out of sitting in class. He keeps getting into trouble, but if his attendance and performance should improve in the next six weeks, his next three years could be far more beneficial.

"To be successful, I have to be ready to answer his question, 'What's in it for me?' An hour out of class is more readily accepted than a promise of increased attendance and improved academic performance. That all sounds well and good to us, but doesn't amount to a hill of beans to a troubled kid."

Without questioning that he was a troubled kid, both parents nodded in agreement. Whenever I take the time to explain things to parents, I'm not only keeping them abreast of what I'm up to, I'm also saying that I believe in them and in their intelligence, and that I believe in their capacity to see the logic in my methods. The result is, more often than not, a mutual recognition of intelligence and goodwill.

I'm also modeling a way to take control without ominously appearing to be the one who is in control. Parents who find themselves in endless power struggles with their children are often very receptive to such examples. Control and power struggle issues run rampant through family systems when there are one or more teens involved. At the same time, I had run head-on into the issue that brought me to their home in the first place. The night that Tom pulled a knife on his father, there had to have been a power struggle between him and his father that they both fought to win. The result was that they both lost.

I wasn't ready to confront the father directly with his part in that event. I hadn't built enough rapport or trust to start hitting him where he was the most vulnerable. So, rather than addressing him personally, I began by speaking in general terms again.

"I have to be careful not to come on too strong with adolescents. While I'm not here to live up to their every expectation, the last thing I want to do is to get into a power struggle with them. I've learned that the more we try to authoritatively assume and enforce our control, the more resistant and rebellious they become."

Rick snorted and then said, heatedly, "He won't listen to you anymore than he listens to me or his mother! He's got all the answers and knows better than anyone else! You can't tell him anything! He is too bull headed!"

"I understand!" I said. "He will buck up against me and the whole idea of getting counseling. I'd be surprised if he didn't. But I have a way to approach kids that seems to make them think they could benefit from at least making it look like they are playing along I teach, by example, how to achieve and maintain control with the least amount of resistance and rebellion.

"When I'm trying to build a rapport with teens, I explain things in terms of what their best interests are, rather than as a way of satisfying my expectations. I say, '*You* want this,' not '*I* want this' or '*Your* parents want it this way.' Nor do I ever say, '*You* should want it.' I avoid *shoulds* as much as possible."

I focused my attention on Tom's mother. "When we scold them, saying, 'You'll do as I say or else,' we end up alienating and infuriating the child. We also exhaust ourselves in the process. This is especially true when the 'or else' escalates into physical corrective methods. Such methods rarely work with the smart kids."

Trish looked up at Rick saying, "The smart kids?"

Rick answered, "Smart A-- would be more accurate!"

"He is smart!" Trish said, "He just doesn't like to be told what to do."

"No he doesn't but you are right, he is smart. I think he gets that from me," he said half joking, and then he added, in agreement with Trish, "He could be doing a lot better if he wasn't so lazy!

When I tell parents that those tactics rarely work with the smart kids, I nip the proverbial argument, 'But my dad beat the hell out of me, and I turned out all right,' in the bud. If the father said that, he would be saying that he wasn't one of the smart kids. I've never met a dad who wanted to say that. Cats get their tongue every time, but in a positive and empowering way. I'm complimenting and validating the child and the parent at the same time.

The parent might think to himself, *Hmm, so that's why I didn't get along with my old man. It's not that I was a loser after all. It's that I was too smart. Why, yeah, I knew that all along!*

Whenever I say that to parents they seem to begin to see themselves and their children from a different and more positive perspective. Perhaps they see that their teenagers aren't so hopeless after all.

I felt the father's eyes on me and could hear him snorting behind my back. I turned to him and asked, "You were one of the smart kids, weren't you?" He turned a shade of red as he peered at me over the top of his beer can, taking a good, long swig. "Well, am I right? I bet your dad had you behind the shed a couple of times, huh?" I used a very intentional sympathetic tone. "I bet Tom is just a chip off the old block."

I turned again to the mom. "It's true. The smart kids don't buckle down under corporal punishment—they pull back and counterattack in a way that causes misery for them and everyone in the family. The worse it gets, the more powerless you feel. The harder you try to reel him in, the further away he gets from you. It's been a losing battle! I wouldn't want to be in your shoes right now."

I had moved from general to personal, and I was getting away with it. I had their attention. I knew they were feeling very mixed emotions. I was criticizing them in a constructive and empowering way, and I was showing them that I understood what they were going through. While holding them partly responsible for their son's rebellion, I was also empathizing with the effect it had on them.

I wanted to leave with some assurance that Tom would be safe being left in that home, so I felt I couldn't leave them without clarifying further how the whole corporal punishment thing compromises a parent's position with their child. I wanted to get the focus back on how corporal punishment affects the smart kids. To do this, I had to move out of the personal and back into the general realm. In so doing, I was able to take the pressure and the spotlight off both of them and still keep their attention.

So, with an expression of shared defeat, I said, "I've found that, the smarter the kid, the more effective their counterattack. When they counterattack, the parent experiences an increase of adrenaline that then contributes to an escalation of physical reactions. This is true whether the attack is covert and in your face or overt and behind your back."

I turned and made eye contact with both parents as I said, again in a very sympathetic tone, "Whether the counterattack is overt or covert, it can be extremely frustrating and painful to the responsible, concerned, and caring parent."

I paused, looking down at my lap for a few seconds. The frustration and pain that both of them were feeling had just been exposed. I took in and let out a deep breath, to give their raw and inescapable emotions their due. I was at a critical point, holding the trust and ego of the parents in the balance. I had opened and exposed them. I wasn't saying anything they hadn't already known and felt. Perhaps they had never verbalized that knowledge, but it had been there all along. I didn't want to cause them to feel guilty of abusing their son; rather, I wanted them to be clear about the negative impact of corporal punishment.

Guilt could shut them down. It could cause them to become extremely defensive and resistant to treatment. That would serve no purpose. The wrong facial expression, body language, tone, or word from me could turn them both against the whole treatment process and against me. Moreover, I could easily become the target of their frustration—and that would be even more counterproductive.

Without lifting my eyes, I said, "It's like being caught between a rock and a hard place. This is how many parents end up getting reported to DCF for physical altercations with their children. The physical correctives increase in intensity and frequency. Before you know it, some of the most concerned and caring parents are being accused of being uncaring, unloving, and even abusive."

Now that I had sympathized with the father, I felt it was time to hit him point blank with the crux of the problem he had been having with his son.

"Hey, I know you love your son," I said, looking him in the eye. "I know you want the best for him. You feel you've lost control of him and of yourself, and you don't know how to keep from losing control again. You resolve not to lose control, and then he turns around and figuratively slams you right into a corner. You feel that you're stuck with the choice to either correct him, or watch his life go down the drain."

I have learned to end a confrontational exchange with a positive statement. I turned to the mother and added, "If Rick didn't care or love Tom, he wouldn't get so upset. A lot of parents just throw up their hands and walk away. Rick is in here trying to keep your son on track, and Tom is fighting his dad every inch of the way."

The mother said, "You can say that again!" She looked up at her husband. He squirmed slightly in his chair, took a long swig of his beer, and then wiped his mouth aggressively with his arm. He appeared to be energized and empowered by that point of view.

Without justifying his behavior, I had validated his intention, which was to love and care for his son. He needed to know that I was aware of his intentions. They would have been the crux of his defense of using corporal punishment, if I hadn't separated the two and been able to draw distinctions between them. But, more than that, he needed to get in touch with and learn how to express his underlying care and concern *without violence.*

Tom had learned to expect to be the brunt of his father's fatigue and frustration. He had also learned that, after six or seven beers, his father's fatigue and frustration turned into an intoxicated rage that came into play, with very little provocation. That rage was expressed as disappointment, disgust, and even hatred. Tom felt toward himself what his father expressed toward him. He then felt and expressed the same toward his father.

If I had focused my intervention on the negative feelings they each expressed toward the other in their thoughts, words, and behavior, I would have fallen into the same pool of fatigue and frustration. I wouldn't have been able to show them how to accomplish anything. There wouldn't have been a significant change in the atmosphere of that home.

"You've about hit the nail on the head," his father said as he set his beer down on the table. "Tom called DCF. He'll call them again, too, and he'll keep calling them until he gets me busted. He'd rather see me in jail than straighten himself out."

"Well, he did call DCF. Instead of busting anybody, they sent in a counselor to work with him and his parents. That's why I'm here. The department isn't about to bust you or remove him while the family is trying to learn and practice more effective ways of dealing with the problems you're addressing now.

"As long as I can document that both of you, and Tom, are participating in counseling, the department isn't going to interfere. As hard as it is for you to open your door to an outsider, you are both sitting here with me, exploring alternative ways of parenting. You've both been upfront with me. You're both being honest and open in your disclosures.

"Everybody in this house has become expert at expressing fatigue, frustration, and rage. Rick, you and your son express those feelings overtly with dramatic gestures of violence against each other and against yourselves with the drinking and drug abuse. His mother expresses the same negativity, in more passive ways, toward herself and each of you by resigning to a hopelessness and deflated will to improve herself or her environment, never mind correct the two of you.

"The one who doesn't adjust to that environment gets the outside attention. Tom is young enough to question the permanence and righteousness of that lifestyle. In Tom's mind, all he has to do is walk out that door to be removed from it. But the sad thing is, when he walks out that door, he takes his fatigue, frustration, and rage with him. Therefore, there's an internal storm of mixed emotions that seems to follow him wherever he goes. It appears to him that his internal storm is a fact of life. He doesn't realize that it originates inside himself and within the walls of his family system. He begins to think that he needs to fight against the winds of that storm in order to survive."

"He wouldn't have such a so called internal storm if he would just do what he is supposed to do!" his father said emphatically. "He's lazy and arrogant! He walks all over his mother and stands up to me, talking back, and tearing down the road, fit to be tied! She knows if I tore after him that there would be a fight so she starts up with her yelling and pulling on me to back away from the door and to let him go."

"Well," I said, "I'm glad you listen to her and let her keep you from going after him. But, I understand how you would want to. No one likes to be blown off the way he blows you off when you are trying to correct him. And I know you worry about whether he'll run into trouble or meet up with peers you wouldn't want him to know, but in the heat of an argument, as volatile as you two can get, it is best to allow for some space and time for the two of you to settle down."

"That's what I try to tell him!" Trish whimpered.

"I understand," I said empathetically.

"He doesn't run out of here to settle down! He goes out to find someone to buy him beer or to smoke that pot! He has his little girlfriend up the road too! She and her brothers have been suspended for having pot and pipes twice in middle school," Rick retorted.

"I know! It sounds as if he gets so tired of fighting that he looks for an escape. He begins to seek refuge in his peers and in other high-risk behaviors. He may easily slip into smoking marijuana, drinking alcohol, and taking other drugs in order to feel better. He could easily become dependent on sexual relations and the effects of drugs and alcohol, because, while he is having sex and high, he is removed from the noise and banter of the storm of emotions he feels inside. He begins to see these forms of escape as absolutely necessary and essential to his peace of mind and even to his very survival."

"Yeah," Rick said, "he's a storm alright!"

"She's saying the storm is inside him, Rick! Not that he is the storm!"

"He is a storm, the way he tears out of here, slamming doors and cursing us out back over his shoulder! If I had talked to my dad the way he talks to me, I'd have been knocked from here to the moon!"

"The tendency to escape becomes more important than anything else he does. He's struggling so hard to squelch the storm he feels inside that he can't look toward tomorrow. Inevitably, the result is that he goes into his tomorrows, unprepared.

"Those who criticize and interfere with the ways that he escapes, are felt as a threat to his existence and peace of mind. We have nothing to say that he wants or needs to hear."

"You've got that right!" his father said, adamantly. "He'd prefer to go and hang out with his bum friends!"

"He only wants to be with and speak to those who understand how important that escape is to him. If he follows that path, he'll begin to believe that his health and well-being depend on his ability to keep sexually active and intoxicated or high. He'll be determined to exercise that need no matter what it takes. He may even begin to commit crimes to obtain alcohol and drugs. He won't steal from his own kind to support that perceived need, but he'll have no problem stealing from those who would, in a snap of their fingers, attempt to deny him the freedom and means to get his needs met.

"He'd better never let me catch him stealing from anybody! I'll have him locked up! Rick said, raising his voice. "I don't care whether he has a storm inside of him or not!" he added sarcastically.

"By denying him what he is convinced it takes to survive, he truly feels you're threatening the quality of his very existence. If he steals someone's car stereo for his survival, he thinks his gain is far more significant than their loss. Those are the thoughts of a thief of this type. Any attempt to interfere in or thwart his escape causes even greater fatigue, frustration, and rage. Nothing positive can come out of it. You've already realized that, I'm sure."

I paused and faced Rick directly. Since he first walked in the door, he had blatantly and inappropriately chugged down one can of beer after another. I had fully intended to address that behavior from the start, when I could do it appropriately. It was time.

I said, "Tom isn't drinking and using drugs because you drink; he's drinking and using drugs because he's just as fatigued, frustrated, and enraged as you are. The only difference is that he's younger than you are. He stands to develop a serious addiction at a younger age than you did. He may get sick and die from it, end up in prison, or get clean and sober quicker than the other kids. Tom knows no other way, from your example or from his own knowledge and experience, to keep himself calm without it. And yet, as we all know, the way he's trying to cope with his life could kill or seriously impair him for life."

Rick bristled up and objected, "He's a kid! He doesn't have to work or pay the bills! He doesn't have anyone he has to worry about except himself." He then took in and let out a deep breath before he continued." You can't sit here and tell me that he has the same amount of stress that I do! He has no idea how hard I work and no appreciation for what I do for him and his mother! All he knows is that I walk out that door in the morning and return sometime in the late afternoon or early evening. He doesn't lift a finger around here to help his mother, either. What stress has he got? He doesn't do his homework and goes to school when he feels like it. He doesn't shower, change his clothes, or bother to comb his hair half the time!"

I let Rick vent through his entire objection to the idea his son was stressed out. He needed to say his piece and I needed to give him a chance to express himself without interruption. Before contradicting him, I needed to identify and address the parts of his speech that were true.

"I understand that you work very hard, Rick. You work hard to keep a roof over their heads and food on the table. You worry about making ends meet and feel frustrated when your efforts fall short of the needs and expectations of your family."

"Well, I don't know about all that!" Rick ejaculated. "I was raised to work and pay the bills! That's what I do! If I acted like him, I'd be laying around here, doing nothing, and then where would they be?"

"That's just it!" I agreed. "Without you here to take on the responsibility of providing for them things would be a lot worse! I can't argue with that. It must also be extremely hard to see that neither one of them is able to meet your needs and expectations. Trish feels isolated and so depressed that she doesn't function and Tom is so defiant and stressed out that he doesn't accept any responsibility for himself or anything else around here! You must feel like you are the only one around here with any sense or ability."

Trish's face flushed with embarrassment in response to my reference to her not being able to function but she didn't deny it. Instead, she fixed her eyes on Rick, as if expecting him to go off on me for being sympathetic to his situation. He didn't! Instead, he seemed to absorb it in gulps, as a thirsty man would down a glass of water in a dessert. His shoulders that had been crunched up so tight I couldn't see his neck, relaxed as the red drained from his face. He sat back in his chair and stared down at the table. His eyes were moving back and forth as he sat there thinking about how to respond to what I had said.

He then asked, uneasily, with a nod in Trish's direction, "You think she is depressed?"

I turned to Trish and asked matter of factly, "You are depressed, aren't you Trish?"

"No!" she declared. "I'm just tired."

Rick puffed out a puff and demanded, "From what? All you do is sit around here doing nothing all day. You don't clean up the kitchen, wash the clothes, or bother to put dinner on the table! No wonder Tom doesn't do anything! He sees you doing nothing so why should he?"

"I'm tired of all the fighting!" she countered with a piercing whine, that I didn't know she had in her. "I'm tired of you coming home to the fridge and your beers after I have been in here waiting for you to come home to me, every day of the week! I'm tired of the yelling, cursing, and doors slamming around here! I'm sick of it! I'm sick of you, and Tom and this run down old trailer! I just don't care anymore!"

It may have been my expressed sympathy toward Rick as well as his deflective attack on her that had inspired her outburst of anger and resentment. She exposed layers of dissatisfaction with both of them and her living conditions, in that spiel. Aside from his opening one beer after another, it was becoming clear that there were more reasons for Tom's acting out than had first met the eye. Trish felt Rick had disengaged from her, the marriage, and their family home. The more disengaged she felt he was, the less she was willing to fight or function. She had given up on them and herself. Rick took solace in his beer at night and his job during the day. As long as he could find that solace he was fine. If one of them challenged him or distracted him they would have hell to pay. This wasn't a family home. It was a cold war site, where each one was his own regimen prepared to defend against the other two enemies! Tom was not the sole source of conflict in their home.

"If it is as bad as all that, go!" Rick commanded in response to her.

I held up my hand and got both of them to look at me and away from each other as I spoke.

"In a perfect world, everyone would get along. No one would feel overwhelmed with his or her share of the work to be done. Children would show the same reverence and kindness toward their parents that they consistently demonstrate toward one another, but this is not a perfect world, is it?"

Both of them sat back and shook their heads.

I continued. "You are both feeling tired and stressed out. I suggest you both think about getting counseling to help you alleviate some of the frustration you are both feeling.

Rick? You could get some help to manage your stress without so much beer. And, Trish, you could manage things a lot easier around here if you weren't feeling so hopeless and depressed. Neither of you can help your son if you don't find a way to make yourselves feel and function better. The way you are going at each other just gives him more of an excuse to act out.

"I thought this was counseling!" Rick retorted.

"Unfortunately," I lamented, "our program targets the child. We provide family counseling and home and school based counseling for your son. Couples and Individual counseling for the adults has to be accessed through another branch of our agency. The agency offers evening and weekend appointments. If you would agree to go as a couple, your therapist might be willing to work with your individual needs, too, unless he or she sees it could be a conflict of interest. If it is seen as a conflict of interest a separate counselor could be selected to do the individual counseling for each of you."

"I don't need anyone butting into my personal business! Rick declared. You take care of Tom and leave me to take care of what I've got to do!"

I pushed back my chair, stood up, and kept my eyes fixed on his, as I slowly backed up to the kitchen counter. "I will take care of Tom and work with you and Trish in family sessions to help improve the communication between the three of you, and offer some innovative parenting practices to increase his motivation, cooperation and compliance. But, that won't help Trish with her depression or reduce the amount of overwhelming stress that you are trying to alleviate with all that beer you drink every night!"

"Oh, so now I am an alcoholic!" he stated defensively.

"I didn't say that, Rick! I said you are under an overwhelming amount of stress. Trish and Tom are lucky to have a man who cares as much as you do. You come home every night, sore and tired from logging all day. Logging is very hard work and must cause you to be sore in every muscle in your body, by the end of the day. But they need you to be able to function as a husband and as a father when you do get home. Being a provider isn't enough. Trish needs her husband and Tom needs his dad. A counselor can help you cope better with the stress so that you can be here for them."

"Thank you!" Trish cried. "Maybe we should go to counseling! I do need you," she said to Rick, and then to me, she added, whimpering, "And I think I am depressed. I can't take anymore of the arguing and fighting! I can't leave but I don't want to stay either!"

"It is true, Rick," I said sympathetically. "Trish has shut down. If you can't go for yourself, consider going for her. At least go once to check it out. If you decide it won't help then quit but go at least once to see if it can help. What have you got to lose in checking it out?"

Rick looked away as if to keep himself from blowing up, and then once he had composed himself, he demanded, "Why do I have to go? She can go if she is so depressed she can't function! I function fine! I'm the only one that does anything around here and now you want to stand there and order me to add one more thing to my plate!"

I looked him square in the eye and insisted, "Yeah! I do! I want to inspire you to do whatever it takes to save you from an early grave, to save your marriage and to help your family heal and thrive! If you don't think you are worth all that then I don't know what to tell you!"

He reached for his beer but before it got to his lips he slammed it down on the table and yelled, "Alright! I'll go one time! But, that's it!" and then to Trish he said, "Make the appointment for a Saturday! I'm not going anywhere after work! If you can't get a Saturday appointment the deal is off!"

Trish hastily agreed to make the appointment first thing in the morning for a Saturday.

"I'm proud of you, Rick, and you too, Trish! You just took a giant step toward helping your marriage and your family. You know at the end of the day, all either of you have of any real significance is each other. The work, the bills, the dishes, and the laundry all come second to your own well being and to the well being of your family, right?"

Rick rolled his eyes and turned his head away from me and Trish. He had felt bullied into agreeing and wasn't happy about it. Trish was satisfied that he would at least try it though and told him so.

Shaking her head at him, she conjoled, "I don't mean to say it is your fault, but I don't know what else to do. If we go and it doesn't help, we'll quit! I won't argue! If you say stop we will stop, OK?"

The sympathy in her voice helped him to feel less bullied which helped him to take in a breath and recompose. "Yeah, OK," he said.

I was relieved because it had been quite evident from the beginning that he had been using alcohol to relax and that it was only causing him to lose his temper and increase his stress and the despair of his wife and son, at the same time. A counselor could help him to see that and help both of them to learn new ways of coping with the stressors in their lives. Couples counseling could help them to identify and communicate their marital needs and expectations more effectively and the individual counseling could help them to heal some of their own wounds. Moreover, the fact that his parents were going to a counselor could help Tom to be less resistant to his counselor and that would be a welcome turn, for me.

"So!" I said, with urgency in my voice. "Let's get back to the issue that brought me here. We need to work together to figure out how to respond to Tom's behavior so that he gets back on track. If our response to him is hostile, we only make the situation worse because we increase the level of stress he already feels. We only wear ourselves out and deplete our resources in the process. We can say that if he keeps it up, that he'll end up in jail. One of the greatest problems with that threat is that there simply aren't enough funds or programs to house them all. We don't have the resources or funds to back up our threats. I know—I've stood in court and watched such threats fall to the floor. The kids come to think the whole thing with court and juvenile intervention is a joke. When we do send some to a correctional program, they appear for all practical purposes to turn around, but only because they know if they don't appear to have changed they'll never get out. That's why the recidivism rate is so high."

"Yeah!" blurted Justin. "They fake it to make it and then go back to doing what they were doing before they got incarcerated!"

"That is so true! But it is not because they are all bad and beyond help. It's because they are hurt, afraid, and angry and don't know how to express those negative emotions in a way that would make people aware of them much less want to help them. Just like you and Tom. You get so exasperated by the way he acts toward you and his mom that it wouldn't even occur to you to ask him what is wrong. Right?"

Rick dropped his head and looked up at me as he realized he hadn't thought to ask Tom if anything was troubling him. "I guess I have been quick to react to his nasty attitude without thinking he might have a problem I don't know about," Rick conceded.

"Well, I know that you and his mom are doing the best you can. You feel your responses to his acting out have to be swift and certain and you won't let him think he can get away with it. But, you have to remember, as adults, we're the guardians, not the wardens, of our teenagers. We need to reel them in with patience, understanding, and compassion. We need to acknowledge that they are stressed out and understand what they are feeling. We can no longer say that they don't know what stress is when they are feeling so stressed out they can't even function. We need to begin to show them how to heal from the inside out, by helping them to identify, express and resolve their negative emotions. In order to do that, we need to begin to heal ourselves from the inside out, as well."

Tom's parents were exceptionally attentive to what I had to say. I expected them to become restless and kept watching for a sign that I should wrap it up and leave, but they gave me no such sign. I didn't do the entire session sitting down. I got up and moved about the room. I paced, using dramatic tones and gestures. I got into character when mimicking what the teens think. I moved from one end of the table to the other. I rested against the kitchen counter, leaned up on the doorframe that led to the living room, and then kept them busy following me with their eyes. Sometimes they had to turn around to see me move about the room as I spoke.

Their interest in what I was saying gave me the confidence I needed to stay and speak to them in that way. I was talking about something that concerned them deep in their hearts. I spoke as if they shared most of the same thoughts. They had never heard anyone speak to them in a way that presumed on their love for their child as well as on their ability to understand and accept what was being said. I also spoke of their own internal suffering and sense of entitlement.

When I was talking about their child, I was describing them and what they were feeling and had felt, perhaps since they were his age. They knew their lives were hard, but they hadn't put into words the source of their own discomfort and despair. They didn't realize the extent to which they had each escaped their own pain in the same way and with the same attitudes and postures that Tom was escaping his pain now.

I had given them a glimpse of hope that there might be a better way to escape the storm they were living in, for a very long time. It was time to shift the focus off of them and onto other parents who were struggling with the same levels of frustration.

"You guys should see some of the stuff I've run into in this job," I said. "In an attempt to correct and save their child from high-risk behaviors, parents try spankings with their hands. This often leads to the use of sticks, belts, brooms, and anything within reach, in the heat of the moment. From spankings, it progresses to slaps in the back of the head, one side of the face, and so on. As the teen gets too old to spank, slaps become hits with a closed fist. Add some alcohol, fatigue, or daily stress to the mix, and boom! Somebody calls the police and DCF."

The father got up and got himself another beer. I smiled and asked in a teasing, scolding manner, "Have you been listening to me?" I turned to the mom and said, "See? This is what I mean!"

She giggled nervously. He set his can down a bit harder than necessary, looking right at me. Pretending to get up, I declared, "I'm calling DCF! Where's the phone?"

The mom laughed as he said, "Go ahead! It's right over there, on the wall, by the stove!"

Instead, I sat down, turned on him and asked, using a tone in keeping with my attempts at comic relief, "So are you beastly when you drink or are you one of those happy drunks?"

He answered, "I'm more beastly when I'm sober."

I knew what prompted him to get that last beer—I had just touched a nerve. I hadn't lost sight of why I was there. The father had attempted to "correct" his son by hitting him in the face and stomach with his fist, before Tom pulled the knife off the kitchen counter. Tom was acting in his own defense, against his father. He was taking a stand against being hit again by this man. It wasn't going to happen. Not this time. Not ever again!

And now, for taking that stand, he was looking at possibly going to juvenile hall or a residential correctional program. I thought to myself, *Is that going to save Tom from turning against society as a whole? Will it deliver him from drugs and alcohol as a means of escape or from being the instigator of domestic violence in his own home one day? Will it do anything at all to resolve the source of his rage? No!*

I knew the father was upset about the result of his actions, but I doubted he had the necessary insight to make the changes he needed to make, without my help. He could see the connection now, as we spoke, but that illumination would likely be temporary. As it awakened him intellectually, it also awakened his conscience. The grave result of opening his conscience was that it was too intense. He would drink until the revelation faded, and until numbness took its place once again.

I had to respond to his discomfort now, while it was still felt. I knew it wasn't a lack but rather an excess of sensitivity that brought this man to drink. I struggled with my own tendencies to look down on him and see him as though he were veiled in a shroud of callous ignorance—a man unworthy of my attention. The only way I could reach him was to draw from deep within myself the compassion and patience it would take to extend a strong and helping hand to him. He didn't need or deserve my sympathy. He brought much of what he was going through on himself, causing harm to those he loved in the process.

What kept me from judging him, in a negative way, was that I truly believed the events and disappointments of his own childhood had played just as much a part in who he had become as he was now playing in the development of his son. I began to see the links in the chain of suffering and harm that ran down through his family from one generation to another. If I could have told him that everything was going to be all right, I would. Instead, I slid my hand over the surface of the table to where he sat, leaned forward, and spoke to him in a consoling tone.

"I'll work with Tom and do everything I can to prevent him from ending up in juvenile detention or a program. As long as you are participating in the counseling with Trish at the agency and in family counseling with me and he's willing to participate, there's a good chance we'll be able to get him to turn around. I'm sure, when you held him in your arms as an infant son, you never anticipated what happened between you the other night. Now that it has, let's see if we can't make something good come out of it. I think things can get better if we all work together."

When I spoke of things getting better, I put my other hand to my heart and held it there. I then looked to each of them and then down at my own hand so that they understood what I was saying. They did. We all smiled and nodded.

I then teased the father a little more. "Drinking is bad for you, ya know. It causes hair loss and wrinkles." We all laughed.

I had addressed the issue of his drinking and its relationship to the trouble he was having with Tom—without causing him to retreat behind a wall that would have been so tall, I couldn't hope to get over, around, or through it. Instead, I had opened the door just enough to be able to go in and address the issues of his drinking, temperament, and parenting style more definitively in the next few sessions. I had gotten the point across and was still allowed to feel comfortable at the table with both of them.

I did need to close this session. Two and a half hours had passed, but I wasn't quite finished.

"Where was I? Oh yeah! We were arguing about corporal punishment." I knew they hadn't verbalized their arguments, but I was sure they weren't in complete agreement with me yet. I pushed it a little further. "When parents argue that they have a right to physically discipline their kids and that they have no intention of stopping it, I have to ask them, point blank, 'Is it working with your kid?' And then I repeat with more conviction than before that it rarely works with the smart kids. I need both of you to trust me on this at least for the next six weeks."

I've never worked with a family whose parents didn't agree to refrain from the use of corporal punishment during my six-week intervention.

Rick and his wife looked at each other for the answer to my question. Could they stop for six weeks? Neither spoke. So I let them know that I would only proceed if they agreed to refrain from corporal punishment for at least as long as I was involved with their family. I also offered them an alternative.

"You guys have the right to choose a counselor from our program who is right for you." I paused to give them time to think about what I was saying while thinking back to the comments my associates had made about how Tom needed to be taken to the shed out back. Neither parent said a word, so I continued. "Not all counselors agree with my position on corporal punishment." I added that it was very possible that I wasn't right for them. I always make this perfectly clear from the beginning, and yet I've never been dismissed from a family on the basis of that position. This family was no exception.

In wrapping up the session, I suggested that we all give some thought to what would be the most effective corrective measures for Tom. I added that I would try to see if I could find him a job or something to occupy him after school and on weekends. I told them that I would be tying that in with his attendance at school.

They liked the sound of that. I asked them to make a list of privileges he enjoyed and activities he might enjoy if we were able to provide them—within their means, of course. I also asked the mother to begin a journal of family ups and downs that occurred in between sessions. I invited the father to contribute anything he could to that journal.

Journals can be wonderful therapeutic tools. However, in order for the family to be willing to disclose information useful to treatment, they have to trust that I wasn't there to judge them. I was there to help them sort things out and to look at different ways to deal with the stress, frustration, fatigue, and rage that occurred daily in that family home.

I went further to explain the part mounting stress plays in the destruction of marriages and family relationships.

"Stress is at the bottom of most impaired family relationships. Stress contributes to the neglect, abuse, and exploitation of children and parents of both sexes. Stress serves to blow little things into mountains, to escalate disappointments into outright rage, to immobilize its bearers, and to feed on itself, magnifying and multiplying. Stress is a monster to be tamed. I'll be there to help you identify, reduce, and eliminate some of these stress factors, if you let me."

Both parents looked at each other and smiled. I said, "Yeah, stress? What stress?" We all laughed.

As I stood up to leave, I asked the father, "Is it okay if I meet with Tom at school in a couple of days?"

"Sure! Go ahead! Like you said, he isn't getting anything out of sitting there anyway!"

I reached into my briefcase for the permission slips for him to sign.

After getting everything signed that I needed in order to visit Tom's school and take him off campus, it was time for me to get out of there. Rick went to the fridge for another beer, and his wife walked me out to my car. We smiled at each other as I opened my door.

She asked, "When will you be coming back?"

"Soon! I rarely make appointments after the first session. I like showing up in the heat of things, if that's all right with you."

She winced a bit but said it was okay.

I got into my car, humming a few bars of John Mayo's "I'm not at my best, unless I've got room to move." I learned early on that appointments left me hanging for hours, especially in the initial phases of treatment. Parents would forget about the appointments and be unavailable to reschedule for days on end. I didn't think double booking was the answer either.

Instead of scheduling appointments, I would just show up. If I went to a house and found no one home, I'd just go visit another family on my caseload. My impromptu visits served another function as well. I could see them at varying times of day in different moods and episodes of daily life. This was more grist for the mill during the initial phases of treatment, in terms of targeting areas to be addressed in treatment. Once we were in the process of restructuring, it was an added incentive to stick to the plan, knowing that I could be dropping in at any moment. My drop-in visits therefore encouraged treatment compliance.

Some of my colleagues would argue that this would only encourage the families to put on an act of compliance that would cease once my intervention was over. I had learned, though, that by going through the act of compliance, most families grew to appreciate the result. The act would then become less intentional and more natural over time.

My car somehow dodged the ruts and roots in the drive that led to the dirt road as I replayed fragments of the session, over and over, in my mind. Soon after I hit pavement, I caught an old bike shop out of the corner of my eye. I quickly made a U-turn and pulled into its parking lot. There I was, standing amidst rusty old bicycle parts, practically begging the owner to give my client a job.

"Tom only needs a couple of hours one or two days a week. He could sweep and wash the windows and maybe even learn a thing or two about repairing bikes. He's a good kid and likes to tinker with things. His mother told me that his dad took things apart and Tom would come along and make them work. He was good with clocks and radios. He could be good at fixing bikes, too!"

It was obvious that the man was barely able to keep the shop open with the amount of business he was taking in, but by the time I pulled back out onto the road, Tom had an appointment for an interview with him. All I had to do was convince the guy how much the kid would benefit from working alongside someone who was so well liked by the townsfolk. He'd be an excellent male role model for a kid.

I was glad to be able to leave that town behind me. I couldn't help but wonder what it must have been like to be a teenager in a town that had nothing but a 7-11, a gas station, and a wooden shack with a weather-beaten sign that read Train Depot. You had to drive five miles to get anything but beer and cigarettes. As I left that town I wondered whatever happened to those little soda shops you see in the 50's movies where kids went after school and listened to 45s on the juke box. There was a dance floor, some little tables where they could have a burger and fries, and a counter where the gals would sit and make eyes at the guys. It was a place where gals could meet guys, laugh, dance, and talk, free of alcohol and smoke. And, best of all, from their parents' point of view, they were always well chaperoned by the proprietors and waitresses. Everyone knew where young people were, since that was the only place to go in town. Everyone was there from after school to dusk. Wouldn't it be great if there was something like that for them to do now?

By the time I pulled into my own driveway forty-five minutes later, it was well past our dinner time. I promised myself I wouldn't say anything if I found a pool of water on the kitchen counter, as I briskly walked up to the open door where my own daughters stood smiling and waiting for my hugs and kisses.

Chapter Twelve

TOMMY—PART TWO—TOMMY MAKES A DECISION

By 7:30 a.m. on Wednesday, I was in the office at Tom's school, presenting his parents' written permission to see him on and off school grounds. They accepted the forms and sent for him at my request. Then I waited for several minutes before he appeared at the top of the stairs next to the office. It took him another half a century to make his way down the one flight of stairs.

As he approached me, he swiped the hair out of his face with one hand while pulling his pants up with the other. I had seen the double take in his eyes and his facial expression as soon as he saw it was me standing there. He then slouched even more, as if he was getting ready to tell me that he didn't want to meet with me.

I ignored all that and said, "Hey, I only have a couple of minutes to talk to you," as I beckoned him over to the wall, gesturing that I needed to say something to him in private.

He reluctantly sauntered over to the wall. "What?"

I rolled my eyes and shook my head, and then smiling up at him I said, "Look, I don't have much time either. Listen, that guy down at the bike shop, by your place, wants to talk to you about working for him once or twice a week for a few hours."

"What guy? You mean Mike?"

"Yeah, do you know him?"

"Yeah," he answered skeptically.

"Well?"

"Well what?"

"If you're interested, you need to talk to him about it after school tonight."

He sized me up while trying to appear unaffected by the idea of having a job. After a few seconds he said, "I'll talk to him later." His tone implied he'd talk to him, maybe; he'd have to think about it first.

"It's your decision. I have to get going." In telling him it was his decision, I awakened him to the idea that he was in control of whether or not he would take this job. I had to let him know it made no difference to me.

Even though it was something he might like to do, he hesitated, because it hadn't been his idea. It was an idea coming from an adult, no less. There must be something to it that he wouldn't like. He couldn't just say yes without figuring out what it was going to cost him. Somebody just doesn't come up to you and offer you something for nothing. He had to figure he could take advantage and still see to it that whatever I thought I was going to get out of it wasn't going to happen.

He shifted his weight to his other foot and looked back over his shoulder and then back at me. "How am I supposed to get there?"

"You have a bike, don't you?"

"No. Well, I did, but the gears got all messed up."

"Can't you fix it?"

"Naw. It's missing some parts."

"Hmm. Not good." I dropped my head and left the problem on his shoulders for a few seconds, giving him time to think that the opportunity would have been his but for this one little glitch.

He had come off as though he were doing me a favor by coming down to talk to me. He was a little embarrassed now. He realized that the only way he could get to see about this job was if I was to offer to help him. Why would I want to after the way he had been acting toward me?

I let out a deep sigh, as if I were making an enormous sacrifice. "I can buzz back by here and pick you up if you need a ride."

He looked at me curiously at first and then suspiciously.

"Look, I'm late," I said, glancing at my watch. "Do you want to talk to him or not?"

"I guess!"

"Good! I'll come back by here after school. I'll see you around a quarter after, then?"

I could see him calculating the time in his head. School let out at ten minutes to the hour. The busses and most of the walkers would have cleared the schoolyard by ten after. I gave him one of my wise smirks as I watched him figure out that no one would see him getting into my car. He actually almost smiled.

"Got to go. See you then!" I turned and left before he could say anything.

I had learned long ago that the best way to meet resistance with teens is with resistance. As long as I'm on the go, with no time to spare for idle chatter, I can usually say what I came to say. To build a rapport with them, it helps to narrow down the content to subjects that concern them only—and even then, to use words sparsely.

Without his knowing it, we had just had our second, highly effective therapy session. In those few short sentences I had empowered him to make a decision that would ultimately improve his whole take on life. I had demonstrated that I recognized that he was capable of making an important and responsible decision. What's more, by taking on the responsibility of making that decision, he might actually begin to feel a sense of importance that he hadn't felt in a long time—if ever. Troubled kids rarely get the message that they have a right to make decisions. Usually they are forced to accept decisions that have been made for them. I teach parents to encourage their children to make good decisions very early in their development. This can be accomplished within the structure and standards the parents want for their children.

When children are spoken to as if they can make good decisions, they develop good decision-making skills. A simple example of an everyday decision would be one where the guardian needs to interrupt the child's play to go to the store. In that instance, the guardian might say, "Hey, we need to go to the store. Do you want to go now, or do you want me to wait a couple minutes?"

The fact that they are going to the store is not up for debate. The parent has to go and needs to take the youngster along, or he or she would be left at home alone. Asking if the child wants to go now, or in a couple of minutes, empowers the child to make a decision. It tells the child what he or she is doing is important and it demonstrates respect and patience at the same time. In that single act, the child is learning all of those things. That's good parenting. It serves the parent well to teach these things, as it will cause the child to demonstrate the same level of respect and patience for the parent when the tables are turned.

Unfortunately, troubled children aren't taught respect and patience. While it is frequently demanded from them, it is rarely given. The mother pulls the child up by the arm and says, "We're going to the store. Come on!" Or she might say, "Get in the car. I've got to get to the store."

I've heard parents talk to their little ones as if they were talking to a dog. There is a considerable difference between saying "Get" and saying "Let's get," and the same difference is conveyed in saying "I've" rather than "We've got to go to the store." The bonding and togetherness implied in the latter is totally absent from that expressed to most troubled kids every day.

A mother of a troubled kid will simply pick up a child and walk out the door to the car, without saying a word about the fact that they're going to the store. When a mother does that, she is saying, "You and whatever it is that you're doing aren't as important as I am, or my need to go to the store." We wouldn't say that to an adult in that way. We would say, "Hey, what are you doing?" or "Are you busy?" or, "Will you be free in a bit to go to the store with me?"

With troubled kids, however, parents often swarm in on their scene and scoop them up as if they are objects without a purpose of their own. The message is that they have no power or control over their own bodies, never mind the space they are in, or any of their own things.

I have seen such parents come up from behind a child at play and swoop him up and press him down on their hip or over their shoulder, as if out of the blue, from nowhere. This happens very early, before a child learns to speak, but long after he's learned to understand simple words such as "store." He clutches the toy in his hand for dear life or drops it to the floor. Frequently, the toy that is clutched is grabbed from his hand and dropped to the floor by the parent. If the little one holds on, the parent's grab becomes more aggressive. The child is scolded for impeding the process of getting out the door.

The child might blink, shake his head, and come to in this new state of affairs with varying degrees of disturbance. Some cry and protest, by wiggling and kicking, to get down, while some slap the parent out of sheer frustration and confusion. By the time he gets to the car seat, the child who was playing quietly on his own just a moment ago is now in deep trouble.

By the age of two or three, such children are so used to being disturbed in this way that it doesn't even faze them. They are already acclimated to having no power over themselves, their interests and activities, or their environments. His sensitivity, creativity, sense of security, and any personal pride in what he was doing is diminished down to nothing, in a split second of parental oversight, disrespect, and impatience.

When children are disturbed with more and more aggression, they begin to develop hypervigilance. They learn to remain on alert for some kind of disturbance. They half attend to what they are doing because they've learned to expect to be interrupted without warning. They flit about from one thing to the next so they can try everything before their freedom is snatched away from them again. They don't develop their ability to attend for progressively greater periods of time, as other children do, throughout the toddler phase of their very young lives.

In time, the children learn not to invest themselves in any activity except on the most superficial level. It's not that they wouldn't enjoy or gain anything from greater self-investment; it's that they don't like being caught off guard, so they remain on guard. They wouldn't feel safe taking that much attention away from what's going on behind them or around them. They learn to be guarded against what might happen. The result is that they learn to pay closer attention to everyone and everything other than what they are doing.

From abrupt disruption in the child's activity, for something as benign as being grabbed and taken out to the store, to gross disruption, secondary to hostility, yelling, and/or violence in the home, the child learns early on not to attend to what they are doing half as much as they must attend to what is happening or about to happen around them or to them. That failure to attend and to invest in what they are doing affects the way they learn.

By the time they get to school, they have become alert, vigilant, hyper, and inattentive to the tasks at hand. Many troubled children who have been misdiagnosed with ADHD have learned and mastered the art and act of inattentiveness, hypervigilance, and lack of investment in what they are doing and experiencing. It isn't that they're incapable of attending, as is true for kids actually suffering from ADHD; on the contrary, they are attending. The problem is what they are attending to.

Now that their attention is on what is going on outside their peripheral vision and on what might be coming up from behind them, out of the blue, they begin to feel as if they are sitting ducks for every distraction in the home or in the classroom.

We need to be able to discern the difference between kids who are hyper vigilant and the ones who actually have ADD and ADHD. In the place of the drugs prescribed for actual ADD or ADHD, I provide biofeedback awareness and practices, relaxation techniques, and stress management to help the child regain the comfort he needs to feel in order to attend to the task at hand.

Let's say that you're walking along a busy street when all of a sudden you see a child step off the curb in front of a speeding truck. What happens? You become alert. Your adrenaline increases. You jump into action. What if you weren't allowed to jump? What if you were held back by some invisible force? At that critical moment, you are alerted. Your adrenaline is increasing but you can't move. It's that level of alertness and adrenaline that these children are feeling throughout the day, every day of their lives. If we send the child to a doctor for medication that will slow their mental processes without changing the environment that requires this level of hypervigilance, we'll be setting the child up for becoming even more frustrated and ill-tempered.

As I've stated before, many parents of children who have been misdiagnosed with ADHD complain that the medicine slows them down but hasn't changed their attitude or improved their temperaments in any way. In fact, they often complain that the child's temperament is getting worse. They report that the child is just as oppositional and defiant or even moodier than before.

When I receive such complaints I look further to find the cause of the child's alertness and hypervigilance, oppositional defiance and/or despondency, apathy, and depression. I then initiate environmental controls that encourage an atmosphere of safety, security, nurturance, and belonging.

Such elements are free and should be available to children in every walk of life. With them the child has a chance to develop into a healthy and productive citizen, capable of attending and learning to the best of his abilities. Without them, that same child will be stuck at the mental and emotional age he was in at the time he first began to realize they were absent.

Many troubled children are mislabeled with ADHD and impulsive explosive disorder. Others are misdiagnosed with ADHD and adjustment disorder, depressed type or adjustment D.O. with mixed disturbance of emotions and conduct. The same symptoms often graduate to diagnosis of major depression, or conduct disorder, by the time the child reaches adolescence.

We then assign them to anger management classes and therapy sessions. We give them higher doses of the medication they are on and add more potent medications. Their behavior and productivity levels indicate that they do indeed meet the clinical criteria for one or more of these diagnoses, as they're the same symptoms that emerge in children who are chemically imbalanced. What is different is that the behaviors are learned—and therefore require different treatment.

The focus of treatment cannot be so much on the behavior of the child. For there to be a successful outcome, the focus must be on the behavior of the guardians who are influencing and teaching the child. Such a focus can serve both as a preventative and as an intervention tool. If we could get in and service the families early enough, we might be able to prevent a long-term and even a lifetime of emotional disturbance, learning barriers, and acting out of the troubled child. Were we to prevent that outcome, we would save millions of dollars spent yearly on special education, social security, and social security disability.

The troubled child who has been or is currently being mishandled will either become more and more aggressive with his peers and authority figures, or become more and more withdrawn. He either buckles down under the stress of not being able to defend himself, or he lashes out. Once he has demonstrated an inability to pay attention in class and to complete assignments, he is labeled with any number of not otherwise specified learning disabilities, as well. Teachers then document the evidence of learning disabilities and behavior management problems.

I don't believe these children are as incapable of learning as it may appear. Nor do I believe that they would be better learners if they would only apply themselves. I think they have learned very well. We need to look at what they've learned if we are to understand why they aren't learning what we're trying to teach.

We need to practice what we teach. We can't practice intrusiveness and then demand that they respect another's space. We cannot demonstrate that they have no control over themselves or their activities and then demand that they control themselves and be productive with their time and resources. We can't impose the perception that they are unimportant and then expect them to care about themselves and others. It's more likely that they will conduct themselves in self-defeating or self-destructive ways by the time they reach middle school, having developed an inner disregard for themselves and the rights of others. They will fit in well with everyone else who shares in that opinion.

These children will demonstrate the same lack of recognition of the value of what the parent, another sibling, peer, or teacher is trying to accomplish. They will begin to demonstrate the same intrusive behavior they've learned from the parent and develop an entitlement to be as intrusive as others have been to them. Then, when they get in trouble for their intrusiveness, it strengthens their opinion that others are more important than they are. The sooner they accept that understanding and perception of themselves, the less trouble they will be to others. If they try to protest, they meet with opposition, reprimands, and punishment.

By the time they've grown to adolescence, they have sufficient resentment against these perceptions of themselves—and resulting sanctions—that they inevitably alienate those who have imposed them. The loving bond and communication that would otherwise be in place at this stormy stage are severely compromised.

Their self-concept is damaged further by the negative feedback they get for doing to others what has been done unto them. They've been repeatedly belittled, diminished, and demeaned for acting out what they've learned. Children who've been startled and stupefied several times a day, every day, before they reached the age of five, learn not to attend to anything. By the time they reach adolescence, it's either nearly impossible to startle them, or they make it an occupation to startle others with equal intensity.

Many troubled kids become numb to internal and outside influences beyond their most animalistic drives and inclinations. They've been taught that their opinions mean nothing. They've been taught not to think or to imagine. They've been taught not to dream or to plan because their dreams will be broken and their plans will be sabotaged at the arbitrary discretion of their guardian.

They've been taught that any time they put into beginning a project is time gone to waste, because they won't be given the time or space to complete it—and it probably wasn't important anyway.

These distinctions need to be considered when addressing the learning impediments and behavior problems of troubled kids. Even when we've sited the guardian's behavior as the underlying source of the problem, we still have to focus the treatment on the child. This is even truer when the guardians who have caused the problem are no longer in the child's life (foster children or adopted children).

But what behaviors should we focus on then? Our focus needs to be on changing the negative messages they have received. We need to identify and listen to the negative tapes that run through their minds. We need to use and teach positive, self-affirming speech.

I focus on identifying and eliminating the negative, incriminating self-talk and giving them positive messages to repeat until the negative ones retreat and disappear. My focus is on what they can do, rather than on what they cannot do. I focus on what they are rather than on what they are not. I focus on their strengths rather than harp on their weaknesses.

The tendency to lash out at the acting-out child, disempowering and disarming him, is self-defeating because it's even more destructive to the child. When we retaliate in that way, we foster an escalation of the negative temperaments we're trying to annihilate. This is the primary reason our interventions and IEP plans don't work. This is the primary reason that children who are placed temporarily in ESE classes usually spend the rest of their school years in ESE with little success.

We need to learn and to practice positive affirmations. We have to learn how to reach out to guardians and professionals in an empowering way. We need to understand our own frustration caused by the poor success rates of troubled children. We need to address our own expressed intolerance and impatience—but we cannot sanction or allow them. We have to understand that such reactivity is reinforcing the alienation and persecution already felt by troubled children.

Troubled children are acting out because they already feel that they don't belong and that we don't think they're important. They need us to make them feel that they do belong. We need to convince them that we know they're important. We can't alienate them and demand that they behave. We can't persecute them and then demand that they respect us and listen to what we say.

We need to make eye contact with them with loving and compassionate eyes. We won't engage them with disapproving and angry eyes. We need to open their ears with whispers of encouragement instead of shouting or speaking harshly. They have learned to tune out such battering speech. They will not hear us.

We need to spend a few moments in the mirror and watch our eyes and listen to our speech as we imagine ourselves correcting one of the troubled children in our care. We then need to deliberately soften our eyes, face, and voice. We need to imagine the message we might convey and then how it will be received. We need to call ourselves to the task of softening our approach to solving the problems we are having with each troubled child. We have to soften our eyes, face, and tone and open our hearts to them.

When our faces and hearts are closed and clutched tight as fists, we just might get nothing but their fists back in our faces. When we get their fists in our faces, we can be more and more punitive. We will be seen as the victim of the troubled kids, but in our conscience—and later in our own mirror—we'll know and see the real culprit as we are known and seen by these troubled children. There's no place to hide from them or from the truth in their eyes.

The truth will eat at us and make us more and more ill-tempered and intolerant of their pointing fingers. We'll feel more and more ashamed. Will we then cast that shame upon them instead of on ourselves—where it belongs? When we do, we'll be creating a standoff between ourselves and the troubled child's inherent will to be well and happy. If and when we call them to such a duel, we can't expect them to show up unarmed, time after time.

More and more children are taking up arms. This is a national problem. We can't continue practices that encourage the taking up of arms. We need to disarm them with loving arms. We have the arms that can embrace them, and we must embrace them, especially when we feel the urge to knock them down.

The message Tom received from me during my first school visit was that he had a decision to make—and that he was capable of making it. I knew the short- and long-term effects that demonstration of confidence would have on Tom. I felt lucky that Mike was there to hire him. I felt excited that something I had thought of was going to make a difference in the daily experience of an adolescent. Most of the time, I try to remain humble and not get overly zealous about something I've done. This time, though, knowing Tom would have something to do that could change the way he felt about himself, I sang James Brown's "I Feel Good," the whole way to my next session.

My exuberance was interrupted, though, when I realized I hadn't an hour to bill for that day. That was one of the complications in that type of intervention. How would I bill for the two minutes I had just given him? The twenty-minute drive to the school, the five minutes I had waited in the office, and the twenty-minute drive back to the office—or more, if I was going to someone else's house—didn't count. In fact, certain third-party payment plans wouldn't cover the time he and I were in the car, from his school to the town he lived in, no matter how therapeutic the discussion.

I ended up stretching my forty-hour work week to as much as sixty or seventy hours for this very reason. Ah, but it was worth it. It took me two minutes to get him right where I wanted him. Had I approached him from a more conventional angle and insisted that he sit with me in a conference room for an hour, it could be several weeks before I got him to where I had him already.

With that thought, I slipped back in to bellowing out my James Brown song. "I Feel Good!"

Chapter Thirteen

Tommy — Part Three — Hotshots!

Tommy was waiting for me, right on time, when I pulled up in front of his school. He approached the car with the least amount of enthusiasm he could muster and still lift one foot after the other. In fact, his feet slid along the pavement as he dragged himself to the passenger side of my car. I looked away to hide my smile as he climbed in and fastened his seat belt

"I told your parents I'd try to find you a job, but I haven't told them that I talked to Mike. I thought you'd like to check it out first," I said casually.

He looked over at me and said nothing.

I swung the car back out onto the street and said, "You like to fix things, and you could probably use the cash, right?"

"Yeah, maybe."

"He could use the help—the shop is a mess. I told him you'd be willing to help him get it cleaned up." I said this with a grimace, knowing that cleaning up the shop wasn't going to be his favorite part of the job. I shrugged and went on before he could object. "I had to tell him you'd be good at stuff like that. The place is a mess!"

He sat as if frozen, with his eyes fixed on the road ahead.

"Here's what I'm thinking," I said. "You have to go before the judge in less than eight weeks. We have to be able to show the judge proof that you're better off being allowed to stay where you are. Otherwise, he's going to recommend that you go to some correctional program or something."

He shrugged again, as if to say, *So what?*

I ignored him. "You and I have to keep track of your attendance at school and the hours you've worked. As long as you improve your attendance and stay out of trouble, we should be able to persuade the judge that the counseling you're doing now is working. If we do that, he won't order anything that would interfere with it."

Still no answer. I decided to grab his attention. "Now, there is a catch, Tom."

He took his eyes off the road and looked over at me. I quickly glanced at him to let his gaze have its desired effect.

"Mike understands that you have too many absences. He's willing to give you so many hours for the days that you spend in school. If you go to school Monday through Wednesday, you can work for six hours on Saturday, no matter what. If you go Thursday and Friday as well, you can work an additional three to four hours after school on Wednesday."

"Man?" he whined.

"What?"

He shook his head. I smiled. He continued to shake his head. I laughed.

"Jerk!" he said, spitting the word out.

"Who? Me?" You are calling me a jerk after I went to all of this trouble?" I teased. I acted like I was real proud of myself in a playful thing I did with my head and shoulders. He slid down in the seat. The bike shop was just up ahead on the right.

"Do you need time to think it over? I can take you on home if you'd rather." I slowed the car down to give him time to decide. "So, want to give it a try for a couple of weeks?"

"Yeah, I guess," he muttered.

"Cool! Wise choice. You're gonna be rich and have more time out of the house."

He didn't comment.

We pulled into the parking lot of the shop and found Mike tinkering on one of the old bikes. After a few minutes they started talking about how Tom was going to get back and forth from home. When Mike heard of the problem he was having with his bike, he offered to give him a ride home that night. He said he could look at Tom's bike and drop it off at the shop on his way home. They could fix it together if he wanted to come by the next afternoon.

This was turning out to be a good day for Tom. He was getting a job *and* his bike fixed. Mike talked to him about cleaning up the place, too. Mike impressed me when he did, because he didn't say Tom could do this or that. When he talked about separating and organizing everything and about sweeping and scrubbing, he said "we." He let Tom know that they would be doing the job together.

"I used to have this place in pretty good shape," Mike said with a sigh. "I had everything in separate piles and boxes or shelved over there in those cupboards. I guess I've kind of let it go. Once we get this cleaned up, we'll be able to find parts I forgot I had. It's easier when I know where things are at, especially when someone comes in here off the street and needs their bike fixed in five minutes or less. You get that around here a lot because this road is a major path for long-distance bicyclists."

He paused and looked expectantly at Tom, giving him a chance to respond. Tom, as usual, clammed up.

"Maybe if we get it straightened up, more people will stop," Mike went on. "I see a lot of them look in here and then pass me up and go to the garage up the road. You and I can make some good money if they start coming in here the way they used to."

Mike was male bonding at this point. He was telling Tom that he was going to be as much of a gift to him as getting a few dollars in his pocket would be for Tom. This was a very wise man. He knew how to build trust and get the best out of Tom at the same time.

Tom finally opened up, exclaiming, "This was great!" more than once. I was happy to see his exuberance. It made all the time I had spent on him that day worthwhile. I knew it would be a good end to the day for his parents as well. When they saw him coming home with Mike tonight, they would see that I hadn't wasted any time in following through with my plan. Mike agreed to take him home right away since his mother would be expecting him. It would give them a chance to talk about things.

Over the next few months, Tom's attendance and overall school performance did improve. He was given community service hours and was ordered to attend school. His case would be brought again before the judge if the school notified the court of any absences or if any other charges were brought against him for fighting at home, at school, or in the community.

The next task I had to accomplish with Tom—which I did early on in the intervention—was to convince him that there was no way, rhyme, or reason to wait for his parents to change. I let him know that I would be working with both of them in family therapy with him and that they had agreed to go to counseling on their own but that he needed to focus on what he could do to change his own destiny.

I told him that he could either expect to turn out very much like his parents, or he could see that he was passing through them. And then I added, "I see you as coming from something much greater, much more vast and wonderful, with far more infinite possibilities than you ever imagined before. Where you end up is entirely up to you, and who you want to be."

I encouraged him to begin to ask questions about the direction he would take in improving the potential and quality of his life in the present and in the future. "What do you want out of life for yourself?" I asked. "Where are you going now? Who are you? What do you want to do once you're out of school? What kind of car do you want to own? How much does it cost? How much would you have to make in order to keep up with the payments? What kind of job pays that much? What do you like to do?"

I presented more questions for him to consider. "Do you like working with your hands, kids, computer, tools, trucks, cars, food, people, merchandise, sales? Whatever it is, you can do it and be as good at it as you need to be, to get the kind of money you want for yourself. That's what it's all about."

I took him to a local community college and let him take the aptitude and personal interests tests. He was surprised to see so many jobs actually matched his interests.

I kept Tom's attention because I focused on him and what he wanted out of life. I didn't give him complicated and compromising ultimatums and platitudes. I talked shop. Just talking to him about a job some day out there in the real world wouldn't have kept him hooked. He'd been hearing about that elusive real world since kindergarten. He was already in the real world. The real world to him was bleak and full of struggle and pain.

I let him know that I was there to show him that the real world was whatever he wanted it to be. Before we met, he didn't have two cents of his own to rub together. Because of the decision he made to work at Mike's, he gained a job and a bike. He could hold his head up a little higher. He had a good relationship with Mike that only got better as they worked on bringing in more and more cyclists as the weeks went by. He started to feel that he was no longer a loser who would never amount to anything. Even his dad started talking to him man to man.

My supervisor called me into his office to get an update on Tom's progress. After I filled him in on what had been happening, he shook his head and asked, "What is it with you? How do you do it? How do you get some kid no one has ever been able to help and turn himself around like this? It's amazing! I'd have written him off as a lost cause. I never would have accepted a case like this."

"I tend to see people as they were prior to their life experience, and I start there," I said with as much humility as I could muster. "I reflect back those intrinsic qualities. Once they begin to realize their value and potential, they turn themselves around. I don't have to do anything."

"You know," he said, "I forgot about that. You are so right—good for you! You taught me something today, or at least reminded me of something I guess I had forgotten.

You're doing a great job. I'm really glad you are on our team."

"Thank you. That means a lot to me," I said sheepishly.

I continued working with Tom and his parents for several months. I had to restrict our sessions to three times a week, so I would see him individually twice a week and do a family session with the three of them once a week. Their communication improved within the first two weeks. Part of that was because Tom had something to talk about that they both wanted to hear. The more interest they showed in what he had to say, the more he was encouraged to talk to them.

Rick volunteered to receive substance abuse treatment in addition to couples counseling with Trish. Trish enlisted her aunt in an exercise regimen where they agreed to walk every day until they could get up to three miles a day without being sore, and they agreed to play cribbage every Tuesday from noon to three, taking turns at each other's houses. Knowing that they would have company each Tuesday, they were more motivated to keep their homes clean and tidy, which also helped to improve the way they felt about themselves and their home environment.

By the fourth week, Tommy was able to show his parents a progress report from school that had shown improvement in turning in assignments. His quiz and test grades improved slightly too. Still, when he showed it to me I could see that he was disappointed. Even after doing his homework for the first time in years, his grades were below average. I told him to remember that he had all F's before we started. Getting D's and C's was outstanding. If he could bring them up that much in four weeks, just think what he could do by the end of the quarter!

I also told him that we would look into what it would take to get him into a regular school so he could earn a high school diploma. That diploma would mean more to him than a certificate of completion from the special education school he was attending. I suggested that he make an appointment with his guidance counselor and assured him that we could talk with the counselor together. This was even more incentive for him to continue with the progress he was making.

School personnel saw the progress and changes in Tommy and implored me to take on several other students. I had to tell them that they could make referrals to our agency, but there weren't enough counselors to go around.

It took more than a job and improved communication with his parents to bring about the changes in Tom's school performance. I had to keep prodding him to think about what kind of lifestyle he wanted for himself once he was out on his own. When I first brought the subject up, it was clear that he'd never really thought about it. By the time he had fallen into using drugs and drinking and going through juvenile detention three times, he figured his life was shot. He had given up on the idea of having a productive and fulfilling adult life. He had lost hope.

The only way he had been able to deal with that level of disillusionment was to pretend he didn't care. After a short time of copping that attitude, he really didn't care: by then it wasn't an attitude anymore but rather resignation to the despair and frustration he had felt from the beginning.

I couldn't allow him to resign. He was too young to retire. I had to set a little fire under him. Before I could hope to change his attitude, I had to give him something to care about. Talking and lecturing him wouldn't have helped; he had been talked to and lectured at for years, so it would have been like talking to a wall. He heard but didn't listen because he had lower appreciation for himself than anyone else did. He had lowered his standards of living to suit his immediate self-concept and self-esteem.

I had to help him see his potential. Once I was able to do that, I was able to encourage him to shift his attention from his immediate needs and impulses and to focus instead on his future desires. I couldn't take away his means of escape without taking away his need to escape from his life.

Sitting at a picnic table across from him, outside of his school, I held both of my hands out to him, palms up, as though I were handing him a great and precious gift. I said, "If I held a bright and beautiful future out to you, would you take it?"

"You're weird!"

"Humor me. Imagine that I'm holding a future out to you that promises everything you will ever need and much of what you want out of life. Would you take it?" I extended my reach a little closer toward his heart center. Despite his resistance to imagining such a thing, my persistence held his attention. In that moment I created a picture that he would remember for a very long time.

He shifted his weight and let out a nervous laugh, expecting me to join in the laughter and thus admit that I was being absurd, but I wouldn't relent, and I didn't laugh. Instead, I caught his eye and asked, "Do you know where we can get a paper around here?"

"A newspaper?" He seemed relieved that I had introduced something tangible to ask about.

"Yeah. Is there a newspaper stand anywhere around here?" I had already gotten his parents' and the school's permission to take him off school grounds the last hour of the day.

"There's a 7-11 up there," he answered skeptically.

"Let's go and see if we can get a paper."

"Now?"

"Yeah. I let your parents know we might be late, but that I would take you home today if we found something to do. Right now, I want to go and get a paper. Do you want to come with me, or do you want to go back to class?"

"You'll have to sign me out."

"It's up to you."

"Yeah."

"Okay, where do I sign you out? Lead the way."

He wasted no time in taking me to the office.

"Now, where's that 7-11?" I asked a few minutes later as we walked toward my car.

"Just up the street. I'll show you."

"Okay, get in. We have a lot to do and it's getting late."

He opened the car door, but before getting in, he had to know why we needed a paper. I leaned over the top of my car and said, "So we can check out the cost of living."

"The what?"

I had developed a practice of referring to the want ads when I felt it necessary to motivate a teenager to finish or even to improve his performance in school. We'd build a scenario of a lifestyle that included a car, a home, and, finally the type of job or career that would support the lifestyle the teen had chosen. We would look at the numerous jobs advertised and then at the wages and salary potentials. We would discuss how much you could earn just starting out and what kind of training or education you would need to qualify for various jobs.

I would take them out to job sites and talk to foremen or to offices and stores—all kinds of places where men and women had jobs and careers. I was always able to find somebody who would stop and talk to them about what it took to get there. We also looked at apartments and houses, talking to the landlords or property managers about how much it would cost to live there. We went to the electric and gas companies, and asked for an estimate of monthly costs for the areas we had chosen. We'd take an afternoon and test drive all kinds of cars from the new and used car lots.

I encouraged teenagers to dream. We went from extremes to realistic possibilities. And then, I'd take them to areas in town where a majority of people made less than minimum wage, were unemployed, on SSI or AFDC, or otherwise compromised financially. I would say, "This too can be your future. It's entirely up to you. The choice is yours. What you do now, the habits you form, the attitude you wake up with and go to bed with at night, will inevitably determine where you live one day when you're out on your own."

Tom was extremely receptive to the intervention, but I could tell he was still smoking pot and hanging out with peers who smoke and drank and partied with other drugs. My work with him wouldn't be done until I had shown him how difficult it would be to maintain the future lifestyle he had chosen while wasting himself in those ways.

I did for him what I did with all of the teens on my caseload. I took my beer drinking, drug toting, wheeling and dealing hotshots to drug rehab facilities, where I sat with them in the day rooms, silent and alert. I wanted them to know what losses the patients had suffered and how unfit so many of them had become—physically, emotionally, and mentally

Now and then, I'd strike up a conversation with some of the more weathered alcoholics or addicts. At what age did they start using? What were their withdrawal symptoms like? How harmless is the use of marijuana? Did it in fact lead to harder drugs? Each one would tell how the high from one hit of pot soon took half an ounce to achieve. Before long it took a quarter of a pound. Pills were cheaper, easier to tote, and lingered in the system longer, creating an altered state of consciousness

I took them to facilities funded by the state as well as those funded out of pocket by the more affluent alcoholics and addicts. We explored the populace of professionals, from surgeons and anesthesiologists to attorneys, judges, and bankers, whose careers were hanging by a thread due to their abuse of illegal substances and the toll it had taken on their lives. My clients would see some who looked to be in their late forties or fifties but actually were only in their late twenties or mid-thirties. They had lost their homes, cars, wives, husbands, children, everything—and some were in the rehab for the fifth or sixth time.

I would always make a point of turning to the teen and remarking, "Cool, huh?"

I'll never forget the day I was sitting with a teen in one of these rehabs. We were talking to a surgeon who had just been accepted into the professional rehab program. She was from a big city and was complaining about having to give up her cell phone. She said her dealer had called her three times while she was in the waiting room, waiting to be screened for the program. He didn't want her there. She questioned why she was there and repeatedly said that the program probably had nothing to offer her.

"The only reason I'm here is that I had a dirty urine. The drugs weren't a problem. They didn't affect my role as a surgeon at all," she said.

Her drug of choice had been crack cocaine. She stood about five inches from the schedule of groups tacked to the wall. I overheard her whining, "God, are they expecting me to go through all of this? I need to get out of here. This isn't for me."

I sized her up. She could have been a beautiful woman, aged early thirties, but she looked as if she were pushing mid-forties. She had on street-wear—skin-tight black stretch pants and a halter top that revealed her midriff. She wore thick-soled high heels that gave her a height of five feet one inch. She weighed all of about ninety pounds and looked as emaciated as hell.

I couldn't resist. I walked up behind her, bent down to her ear, and said in a whisper that was loud enough for my client to hear, "Why don't you do this: the first time you wake up in the morning, look in the mirror, and if you like what you see, you can leave."

She had the intelligence left to appreciate what I said. When I saw her again weeks later, she thanked me.

Substance abuse is not a disease of the underprivileged alone. It's rampant on every level of the economic stratosphere. The difference is that we hear about the street users, but many of the professionals are protected from public view. I believe we would eliminate a lot of problems if these users were also exposed. I think they should have to come down to the level of those who are doing time or facing the possibility of getting caught and reveal themselves and all that they have lost.

A man on the street is arrested and put in prison. His children live without his financial support and with the humiliation of his incarceration. The professional pays for a luxury treatment center and is hugged by like professionals, ending each day in a circle of holding hands. Those who have thrown their professions in the toilet after repeated trips to the rehab centers should be sanctioned by the courts to serve 'X' number of community service hours in the schools and detention centers, giving lectures on just how uncool addiction is.

Sitting with a teen in an office, lecturing him on the penalties of drug use and abuse, couldn't compare to the effectiveness of these field trips. Teens on my caseload who were raised in substance dependent homes saw, for perhaps the first time, that they were not alone. Others no longer felt so comfortable with using poverty and the fact that they were one of the have-nots as an excuse for resorting to alcohol and drugs.

I would say to Tom, "The idea that pot and other drugs are okay is an outright lie. Those who are against it aren't trying to keep you from the good effects; they're protecting you from the side effects and cost of the drugs." I showed Tom the financial risks. We discussed the relations and occupations, education, lack of structure and organization, and incredible sacrifices that are made to support habits that never should have been formed in the first place. I reminded him that there's more to this than simply being against the law. They need to be made aware of the potential detriments to them personally.

I often tell a teen, "I don't have to ask you if you use drugs, or if you have a drug problem." I will ask those carrying a banner for the legalization of pot, "Are you functioning at the best of your potential?" If not, then I will suspect they have a drug problem. If they are failing in school, unable to keep a job, at odds with everyone they know who has any authority, surrounded by peers who are in trouble with the dean, their parents, and the law, I'll say they have a drug problem.

I also teach them that if they use because they feel good, they are less likely to develop an addiction than if they use to feel better when they're miserable and depressed or angry and in conflict with their elders.

When we focus on the legal issues, the teen focuses on not getting caught. We haven't given them a good enough reason, from their naïve and inexperienced point of view, to not use. We have simply given them a good reason to be more discreet and deceptive. We inadvertently teach them to lie and hide.

When we do that, they no longer feel free to talk to us. They aren't able to discuss the side effects with us, or any other of the numerous complications involved with obtaining and using drugs. This isn't a good population to force such a breakdown of communication. They could become depressed, self-defeating, and even suicidal, or frustrated, enraged, assaultive, and homicidal. Many feel more and more entitled to lie and steal.

I let them see for themselves that the whole lifestyle we have explored and that could be theirs can be blown up in smoke. I don't condemn them for having used drugs and alcohol because I'm against using shame and blame as corrective tools. I believe shame and blame weigh down the spirit, clouds their perception of themselves and of their potential, and lowers their energy level. I'm there to lift their spirits, to improve their self-perception, and to raise their energy to a higher level.

To make my point, I simply encourage them to look on those who are still into using drugs and alcohol with a statement that reflects their present, more enlightened attitude. I get them to practice saying the words with more and more conviction, spunk and sparkle: "No thanks. Been there! Done that! Moving on now!"

Chapter Fourteen

Ana — Under the Rug

Ana, a nine-year-old fourth grader, was referred to our community mental health agency by her teacher for under achieving. She had earned E's for Excellence in first through third grade, but now all of her E's had dropped to U's for Unsatisfactory.

Despite numerous attempts to reach her mother, the teacher had been unable to get her to come in for a single conference or to return any of her calls. Mark, a case manager, had been going to the home once a week for a month before a counselor could be assigned to them.

Mark told me that the mother was going through a divorce and that she sat around all day letting the kids and the house go. He felt the children would be better off with their dad or in a foster home and that the mother should lose her parental rights. He had done all he could to provide outlets for each of the kids so they would have a network of community support, but he determined that the mother's attitude and failure to provide care and supervision for her children or to tend to the upkeep of her home was sufficient grounds for removing the children from her.

He took Ana and her siblings to the park once a week and arranged transportation for all of the children to get to church on Sunday and to youth group on Wednesday. Despite these interventions, Ana's grades continued to drop. He was preparing a report to substantiate his concerns to the Department of Children and Families; I was to go into the home to confirm his findings.

No one was home when I arrived at the house for my first visit. I waited around for twenty minutes or so and then drove off to take care of some errands. By the time I returned, there was a car in the driveway, so I parked, went up to the door, and knocked.

Ana's mother, Rachel, came to the door, opened it a few inches, and listened as I introduced myself and reminded her of our appointment. She apologized for forgetting and asked if we could reschedule, as she was running behind and the children were in the middle of dinner.

I interrupted her, saying dinnertime was one of my favorite times to visit. It gave me an opportunity to see how the children behaved with each other when they were restless and hungry. That can be one of the most difficult times of day for a lot of families. After some pleasant but unrelenting persuasion, I was invited into the house and introduced to each of the children.

Just inside the door to my right was a mahogany table that was placed between the kitchen and the living room. The ten-year-old, Stephanie, was opening a can of soup. Ana was making a peanut butter sandwich on the table, without a plate, in a little space she had cleared to make room for one piece of bread. The other piece of bread was balanced on top of a pile of clothes that had been left, perhaps on their way to the laundry room that was just off the kitchen. The youngest child, Beth, age three-and-a-half, was waiting on the floor for her dinner, which turned out to be a piece of bread "whiff jelwie" on it.

Rachel said she wasn't hungry. After introducing me to each of her daughters, she invited me into the living room to sit and talk about our program. I scanned the living area as I entered the room. The shades were drawn, there were no lights on. An odor swirled around me like a small tornado as I looked around for a safe place to sit. I asked the mother if she would mind turning on a light. She tried two lights before she found one that didn't have a bulb burnt out. With the light on, I could see what I had smelled: the carpet was ingrained with huge, black spots of grease and dirt from spilled food and drinks. Plates encrusted with food and catsup and silverware were scattered about on the coffee table and the arms of the chairs. One plate, which sat on the top of the TV, had a very zealous roach on it. I chose to sit as far from that plate as I could.

Once I did sit down, I didn't lean back because I could see there were little baby roaches crawling around on the back of the overstuffed chair I was sitting on. (In my profession, one rarely sits *in* a chair.) In that moment, I contemplated other professions that might have been more suited to me. Why hadn't I chosen to pursue that law degree? What made me take a turn halfway through my masters program and decide to earn a degree in clinical psychology? Why—so I could sit in an arena of roaches and filth and…? But these ruminations slipped into the background of my mind as I mustered up the courage to get down to the task at hand.

I studied the mother. She was so thin you could see bones protruding through her paper-thin skin. Her hair, bleached blonde and uncombed, was pulled together in a ponytail at the base of her neck. Her tennis shoes were dirty and tied with laces that were unraveled at the tips. She wore no socks. I looked into her tired blue eyes.

"You have beautiful daughters," I said.

She rolled her eyes and nodded.

"Do they usually get along this well?"

She laughed and said, "Oh no! Wait until they're done eating."

We both chuckled, and I looked at her more intensely. "Do you have anyone close to you that helps you with them? Is their father actively involved in their lives?"

"No, not anymore."

I asked her to tell me what she meant by "not anymore."

She then explained that the girls' father had stayed with them while she went up to Ohio to bury her mother. While she was away he had "shacked up with some bimbo that was, no doubt, half his age," and then he asked her for a divorce. She said her trip was bad enough. Her siblings had divided up all of her mother's possessions before they told her of her mother's passing. And then, after going through all of that, up there, she came home to find out her husband had left her.

All of these events occurred just over three months ago. I could see that she had been struggling with the grief of her mother's passing and the loss of her marriage. Her siblings and her husband had betrayed her at the same time. I forgot about the roaches and moved across the room to sit beside her on the edge of the couch.

"I don't think I would be telling such a story as calmly as you have. I would expect you to feel mortified and enraged."

"Oh, I am!"

"I'm sure! Who wouldn't be? Are you getting any sleep? Are you eating?"

"I sleep all day, usually. I get up and get the girls ready for school. I go back into my room and lie there until I have to go pick them up. If two of them have activities, the case manager arranges transportation for one, and I take the other one and wait around with the baby until it's over and then I drive home. I just sit here when they're home. If they get too rowdy or start arguing, I go and shut myself up in my room, until I can't take their bickering anymore. Some nights they fall asleep out here, on the floor, in front of the TV. If they get to arguing about who is going to watch what, which they do most nights, I send them all to bed and turn the TV off."

"Rachel, you are grieving over the loss of your marriage and your mother. Have you thought of getting some counseling for yourself to help you get through all of this?"

"No, not really."

"Would you be willing to try? You're grieving the loss of your marriage, your mother, and the relationship you had with your sisters. It's important for you to get back on your feet and to begin addressing how you're going to share in the care and custody of the children with your husband. You could use the extra help with them, couldn't you?"

"I guess. I thought I would feel better by now, but I wake up each day feeling worse than the day before, and I can't talk to their father. I don't want to hear his voice or see his face ever again."

"I understand how you must feel, Rachel. You've done the best you could under the circumstances, but I think you could use some counseling. The girls are exhibiting signs of being stressed out by everything going on with you, and I'm sure they're missing their father." I paused to give her a moment to consider what I was saying.

Children feel powerless, hurt, and confused when their parents suddenly separate. When the one they're living with is hurt and angry, they feel hurt and angry too, and frustrated from not being able to fix it. It's natural for children to want both of their parents to be happy and to be where they are supposed to be and to do what they are supposed to be doing with regard to the home and parenting. When their parents fail, the children become so overwhelmed that they often stop doing what they are supposed to be doing. They see and feel their very lives are so far beyond their control that they begin to lose control of things they used to be able to manage effortlessly.

Children need to know that while their parents have agreed to divorce each other, neither parent is divorcing them. They want both of their parents, and they need to know that both of their parents want them. It was important for each of Rachel's children to know that the pain and anger their mother was feeling wasn't their fault and that it wasn't their responsibility to fix it. They don't want to have to take sides with one parent against the other; yet, children begin to feel that if they show any affection or allegiance to one, they will be betraying the other parent.

Rachel was so affected by her own grief that she couldn't see what an impact she was having on them. All she could see was how they were adding to her own stress and misery with their arguing with each other and their defiance of her rules and expectations.

This mom needed to get a better grip on her emotions in order to help her children get through the separation and divorce with the least amount of distress. I continued speaking to her with empathy but also in a more directive way, in the face of her resistance to seeking help.

"Ana's grades are dropping and, as you say, all of them are arguing with each other and staying up late on school nights in front of the TV. You aren't taking care of yourself very well, either. You would benefit from having some help with them from their father, but you can't bear to even hear his voice, let alone communicate about shared custody and co-parenting.

"I'll give you a phone number to call. Just tell the receptionist that you'd like an appointment with a therapist to address issues related to grief and loss, divorce, and co-parenting. Our program addresses the needs and behaviors of the children, but I believe your needs are equally important. We can't get any movement in here until we get you back in touch with the strengths and attributes that have helped you keep things together in the past. And we need to find a way to get their father back into their lives. I can't help the girls while their father is off in nowhere land and your world crumbles at your feet."

While it is understandable that a parent would feel angry toward the parent who has left, it's not okay to shut that parent out of the children's lives. Barring any proof of the absent parent being unfit, parental alienation isn't accepted by any court of law, because it could compromise the psychological and emotional well-being of the children.

I was telling Rachel that while it's normal to grieve, she had the strength and attributes to improve her mental status and home life. I let her know that, by seeking counseling, she would be able to find what she needed inside herself to help her cope with the healing that would need to take place before she could make things better for herself and her children. I explained that there are times when we feel hit from so many different directions that we forget what our own strengths are. We lose faith in our ability to make decisions or to function. Our pain and anguish begin to cloud our own judgment. It's imperative that we reach out to get the support we need to make it through such trying times

With these directions, I placed the focus on her situation, rather than on her. It wouldn't have served any purpose to blame or condemn her for the state of her house, for her inability to exercise effective parenting skills, or for her alienation of the father. She already felt condemned enough. Deep down, she was probably blaming herself as much as she blamed her husband for the loss of her marriage. She already felt hopeless and helpless.

The cries of the children, their failing grades, and their challenging behaviors were just more of the same to her. When things piled up to the point they had in this house, it was as if she had given up and said, "What's the use? If nobody dies it's been a good day." By the time I left, I was able to convince her to make the appointment with a counselor for herself. I said a little prayer for her as I drove home.

My first visit had been on a Monday. Late in the afternoon on Tuesday, I called her to see if she had made the appointment. She hadn't gotten around to it yet. I suggested that she try to make it for Wednesday, when the girls were busy with youth group. I gave her my phone number so she could call me if she had any trouble getting an appointment for that day. She agreed to try and said she would text me and let me know how it went.

In less than fifteen minutes I received a text saying she had made the call.

"Hurray!" I exclaimed to myself as I dialed her number. As soon as she answered, I said, "You got one already?"

"They can get me in for an intake assessment and my first appointment a week from Wednesday at 6:30 p.m."

"Great! The youth group is from 6:00 to 8:00, so that should work out perfectly." I reminded her that I would be there early on Thursday so we would have a chance to talk before she picked up the girls from school. She agreed that would be best, and we hung up.

On Thursday she let me in and led me back into the living room where we had sat on our first visit. I was just as susceptible to the atmosphere of gloom in that house as I had been on the first day. I couldn't see how anyone could not be depressed in there. If something didn't change in the condition of the house, she would never recover.

I asked her if she had thought of taking out the carpet. She said it had been the way it was since she moved in. She said she got the house for free rent because of its condition. The landlord was her husband's uncle. He had let her move in there with her husband when they moved into town from Ohio, while her husband did his residency. He had merely asked that it be occupied to ensure it wasn't vandalized. She then added that there had been two break-ins during the last month.

Well, one couldn't argue with the rent deal, but still—how could any of them have any pride living in such filth? How could they feel safe at night?

I said, "I would ask him if you could take the carpet out."

She said she had on the first day and he had said no, because it protected the hardwood floors underneath.

"There are hardwood floors underneath?" I visualized how beautiful the room would be without the carpet. "Why don't you ask him if you couldn't put a protective stain on the floors? Maybe he would go for that and you could have nice floors in here. Hardwood floors are easy to sweep. You could throw a braided rug in here to cover the main surface. All of you would feel better about living here if we could get it looking nicer."

"Yeah, and then he'd start charging me rent."

"You don't have any means to pay rent?"

"My pay was prorated to cover the summer months and then, after applying for FMLA, I drew from my accrued paid leave, which was substantial since I had never taken a sick day. I guess I could pay rent, but I'm afraid the money will run out before I'm ready to go back to work."

"Where did you work? What do you do?"

"I'm a middle school science teacher. I've been teaching eighth grade science for twelve years. I've earned the teacher of the year award twice in the past five years, and my classes have earned the regional Science Fair award three times in the past four years."

"Wow! That is impressive. I understand middle school kids can be very challenging on your best day. We need to get you back on your feet so you can get back to doing what you've dedicated your life to doing all those years."

"That's the thing. Those kids need a teacher who's grounded and capable. It takes a lot of patience and effort to arouse an interest in a subject many of them think they will never use in real life. Not everybody wants to be a doctor or a scientist when they grow up."

"Well, I'm proud of you for all those awards. We need to get you back in there for another round, girl! You can't throw all of that away. Those kids need you, and your kids need to see their mommy back on her feet, too. We'll get this place back in order, and I'll help your girls get back on track while you work on getting yourself back together with your counselor. I give you six weeks. In six weeks you should be up and running and ready to get back in the game."

"Six weeks?" she moaned. "I'm thinking more like six months! I don't see me ever getting back to where I was."

"Well, I do! I believe it will take less than six weeks once we get things rolling in here. I just said six weeks to give you a little time to breathe once you are back on top of things, before you get back in there. Now that is that! I would go ahead and let the school know that you will want your job back in six weeks. Tell them you will be back on October first."

"October first?" she exclaimed. "No way!"

"Absolutely. I mean, you won't want to end your counseling in six weeks. You will be able to continue counseling once you get back to doing what you do, and your counselor will help you to meet the challenges of returning to your job for as long as you want. But, yes! Six weeks is more than enough time. I have a lot of faith in you. Anybody that can teach middle school kids and earn all those awards is more than capable of thumbing their nose at a few minor real life bumps in the road." I patted her arm. "Now, stop arguing with me and let's get started. Why don't you give your landlord a call to see how much rent he would charge if you fixed the place up?"

"I guess I could. He was supposed to come in and fix the latches on the doors and a couple of the windows. There's a window in the girls' room that we had to board up because the rain got in and soaked their beds."

"How long ago was that?"

"A few months ago, right after my husband moved out."

"Uh-huh. Nice of him. What about the latches? Are you telling me you've had two break-ins and you can't lock the doors?"

"Yeah. Stephanie used to sleep in that front bedroom, but she won't because the front door is unlocked. She gets in bed with her sister."

"Were you home when these break-ins occurred?"

"No! Not yet, at least I don't think so, but I'm waiting for that to happen."

"That's not good, Rachel. He needs to get over here and fix the doors and windows, or you need to get somebody in here to do it. That is dangerous for you and the girls."

"Oh, we know who's doing it. We saw one of them running from the house the last time he was here. We just can't prove it. We called the police, and they said unless we can catch him with stuff in his hands, we couldn't press charges. It's just a teenager from up the street. He wouldn't hurt any of us."

"Have you thought of getting a dog? If you left a dog in here when you were out, he might be less inclined to trespass."

She laughed. "That's true, but I couldn't afford to keep a dog, and the girls wouldn't take care of it. They can't keep up with their chores now."

"Rachel, for your peace of mind, I'd feed and water the dog myself, if I were you. Why don't you think about it? Stephanie must think they could break in while she is sleeping in her room. She might feel more secure if there was a dog who would bark if someone approached the house."

"That's true. Ana actually said she saw two teen boys in here one night, but nothing was missing. I thought she had probably imagined she heard them or she dreamed that they were here because we had been talking about it that afternoon."

I had more than one reason for pushing her to get a dog. It was important for them to feel secure in the home at night, and a dog would alert them if someone approached the house while they slept. But, even more important, they each felt the absence of their father in that home. They had gone from a family of five to a family of four, and that absence was felt. It was very unsettling for each of them. Simply by adding a dog, they would have a family of five again. Moreover, a dog can be a healing companion that can help a family deal with their loss and depressed feelings.

"I'd get a dog, Rachel—I'd get a very big dog. There are free dogs in the paper all the time. Can you have pets in here?"

"On his hardwood floors?"

"You've got a point. But we were asking if we could put a protective surface on the floors, remember? And a lot of the dogs in the paper are already trained. I'd still look into it. I wouldn't spend another night in here without a dog if I had three precious little girls. What would you do if something happened to one of them? It's scary! When you call him about the floors, tell him you have had break-ins and that you're getting a dog for protection. See what he says."

"Okay."

"Where's the girls' room?"

"At the end of the hall."

"May I see it?'

"It's a mess. They throw everything all over the place. I can't get them to clean it up. They take their folded clothes and toss 'em in there on the floor. I gave up trying to get them to keep it up."

I got her to let me go down the hall to see it for myself. When I got there, I stood at the door and just looked. I saw a double and a single bed separated by about three feet of floor space. At least, I imagined there was floor space, beneath about a two-foot-high pile of clothes, toys, dishes, and garbage that ran the full length of the room. Neither of the beds had sheets or pillows. The little bed had a huge wet spot on the blanket that was covering part of the mattress. The smell was atrocious.

"I see what you mean," I said. "This is awful! They sleep in this? It would give me nightmares."

"They seem to like it that way. I've grounded them from the TV and from going outside. I've tried everything. They just get in here and shove the stuff aside."

"I think it has gotten too far along for them to tackle. Do you have any boxes or trash bags?"

"There are some boxes on the porch and a few garbage bags in the kitchen."

"Good! Bring me a couple of boxes and let me see if I can't put things in order in here."

Rachel tried to argue against my cleaning the place up, saying that it wasn't my job, but there wasn't a better way to effect a change in the atmosphere of that house than to try and put some order back in there. Once I got it to where it was livable, I would be able to help her draw up a list of chores for them that would help them keep it nice. She finally agreed and went to get the boxes, bags, and a broom. I needed the broom to shovel the stuff out from under the beds once I'd made room for it between the beds.

I handed her the sheets and pillowcases that I had found under and on the beds, and both blankets, and asked her to put them in the washer while I put a pile of dirty clothes together.

I sifted through clothes, dried food, broken toys and dolls, more dirty sheets and underwear, spoons, forks, and a butcher knife. I wondered if that was in there for protection. Three very active roaches, the size of Rhode Island, nearly had me running out the door and half way home without my car, but I managed to give them a squirt of some 409 that I found in the kitchen. Two squirts of that was all it took to exterminate them. I found little bracelets and necklaces, marbles and pennies, dimes and a quarter. I found jewelry boxes and shoe boxes, and used those to separate tiny things I knew the girls would want to keep.

By the time I was a third of the way done, I saw that there was an end table with three little drawers between the two beds. Fortunately, for my purposes, the drawers were practically empty. I filled one of them with paper, pencils, pens, color crayons, and magic markers. I filled the other two with the youngest child's T-shirts, underwear, and socks.

At the opposite end of the space between the beds was a five-drawer dresser. It stood empty, next to a wall closet. The closet had nothing hanging in it. It had four feet of stuff piled on the floor, though. I sorted and sifted out clothes that were torn, stained, or too small for any of them, and Rachel took the dirty clothes to the laundry room. I brushed off stuffed animals and put ribbons in the dolls' hair that I had dressed up to put on the top of the dresser. I found a radio to put on top of the end table and even an outlet to plug the thing in.

I was feeling good as things began to shape up.

Rachel helped me haul out six giant garbage bags of clothes that could be sorted, saved for the youngest one, or sent to Goodwill, and two four-foot-long boxes of trash and broken toys. Clothes were hung up or folded and put away. Fortunately, the beds had plastic coverings on the mattresses that were easily washed off. We made up the beds with fresh sheets and fluffed pillows. Pictures they had made were tacked to the walls. The room was a masterpiece by the time they got home from school.

As I had explained to the mother, it was part of my role as a therapist to model behavior. If that meant rolling up my sleeves and doing a little work, so be it. That was what I was there to do. I said it in a "no nonsense, don't even bother to argue with me" posture and attitude that I half believed myself. I wasn't going to be able to bill for the extra time I spent that day, but I knew it had to be done.

The girls couldn't believe their eyes when they saw their room, and eagerly agreed to keep it nice for my weekly inspections. Whatever discipline they had to exercise to hold to that promise would be generalized to other aspects of their daily lives. By cleaning their room, I had said to them that they were worth whatever it took to make their lives better. A message that could have taken numerous therapy sessions to impart was conveyed in that one afternoon.

Much to my surprise, when I returned to their house the following Tuesday, the mother was on her hands and knees, ripping up carpet where it had been tacked to the peripheral areas of the living room. She had boxed up books and knick-knacks and had moved furniture out of the way, and was nearly done by the time I arrived for our appointment. I was so proud of her. Nothing could be more therapeutic for depression than an activity that would improve her whole living situation.

She looked up and told me to let myself in. As I entered, I could see that she a big, bright smile on her face. I applauded her and asked if I could help. She told me that she had sprayed pesticides inside and all around the outside of the house too, to tackle the roach problem, and that she had arranged for her husband to come over to get the rug out of there.

She said he was so surprised that she had finally contacted him after telling him to "drop dead" and to "rot in hell," that he agreed to come over right that minute. She wasn't ready to see him without someone there, so she asked him to wait until she knew I would be there. He was to arrive in a minute or two. It was wonderful to hear, not only that he was near enough and willing to help, but also that he would be coming over while I was there. That was an opportunity I would not pass up.

"Has he been asking to see the girls?

"Not really," she said dryly. "I didn't want him bringing them around that woman he shacked up with, and I didn't know how to tell the girls about her, so when I told him to get out and stay out, he did. Since then we haven't really discussed his seeing them."

"Has he filed for the divorce?"

"Not that I know of. He said we're getting a divorce when I got back from Ohio, but he hasn't said when. Knowing him, he won't want to spend the money it's going to take to get a divorce and wouldn't know how to go about it on his own. He probably is enjoying his freedom and doesn't want to have to deal with them. This way, he can run around like a bachelor, without the responsibility of raising his kids. Why would he want to mess that up?"

"They must miss him. Do they ask for him? Have they asked you where he is?"

"They were right here when we had the big blow out. They heard me tell him to get out and stay out. They cried and asked for him during the first few weeks, but I was in no mood to discuss it. I guess by hushing them up then, they haven't wanted to stir the pot since."

"Oh, I see." Not knowing him or his side of the story, I didn't want to give her the impression that I agreed he was the scoundrel she was making him out to be. Yes, he apparently had betrayed his vows, and yes, he had picked a self-serving, lousy time to do it, but what was his relationship with each of his daughters? Did he miss them? Was he staying away out of a selfish interest in leading a bachelor life, as she thought, or was he staying away to protect them from the fighting?

He could have thought it was better for him to stand back and let the dust settle before approaching her for equal time with his daughters. This was something I would have to scope out. I had planned on her addressing the custody arrangements with her counselor but with him on his way over to their house, I was being given an opportunity I didn't want to pass up.

"Rachel, have you given any thought to what you will agree to in terms of sharing the care and custody of the girls with him?"

"He chose that bimbo over his wife and family—he doesn't need to worry about the care and custody of anybody," she snapped.

"Let's take a break for a minute and talk about this. Come sit down." I patted the seat next to me on the couch. She slowly stood up and took the seat beside me. I could see her bright smile disappear and the energy drain out of her as she reluctantly complied.

"What's to talk about? He made his bed and now he should lie in it. No one told him to go gallivanting around like a tramp, picking up girls and walking out on his family. He doesn't deserve them, and they don't need a man in their life that behaves like that. I don't want them thinking it's okay to do what he did to me."

"I understand he did betray you. And, yes, if what you say is true, he did choose that woman over you. That is very painful for you, I can certainly agree with that. I can also agree with your wanting him to handle the divorce since he's the one who left. Is he helping out with the expenses?"

"His brother brings a check over once a week."

"That's good. But has he made any effort to contact or to see his girls?"

"He blew my phone up the first couple months, but I wouldn't let him talk to them, and I didn't want him coming back around. I told the girls he didn't deserve to talk to them or to see them, and I guess they've learned to accept it. They've stopped asking about him, and that's fine with me."

Hearing this was unsettling to me. While it was understandable that she didn't want him around after what he had done to her, it wasn't okay to shut him out and deny him his rights to share in the care and custody of his daughters. It wasn't okay to deny them their rights to grow up with their father in their lives, either, unless he had been an unfit parent—and so far, I hadn't heard that he had been anything but a good husband and father until she left for Ohio. No, her shutting him out of their lives appeared to be based on what he had done to her, and that wasn't fair to him or to them. She was expressing her anger toward him in vindictive and vengeful ways, without even realizing it. In her tit-for-tat response to him, she was depriving her daughters of a father.

It was as if she were saying, "If I can't have you, then you can't have your daughters."

Again, it's not okay to turn children against a parent.

Children don't need to hear what one did to the other. They don't need to hear that one parent is bad unless he or she has caused them harm, and even then, things need to be explained in objective terms so they can develop an objective understanding of the situation and not feel responsible for any harm done to them or to their mother.

Children internalize critical comments made about one parent by the other parent. They come from both parents and see each parent inside themselves. When one parent is criticized by the other parent, or by extended family members and friends of the family, they take that criticism personally, as if it were being said about them. They might even begin to fear that if they do something bad or make even the slightest mistake, they too will be rejected by the custodial parent and kicked out of the house.

I had to find a way to turn things around so that he was back in their lives, and I had to do it now. After explaining all of this to her, she agreed to let me help them come up with a co-parenting plan that would be in the best interests of her children, despite the pain and anger she felt toward him. I had convinced her that, to serve the best interests of her children, she would have to put their differences aside and at least appear to be on the same team when it came to parenting the girls.

Just then, I heard a rapid knock on the door behind me and turned to see a man in scrubs, standing there, peering in through the screen. He was a male version of his daughter Ana. He had the same dark hair and big brown eyes and pronounced cheekbones and chin.

"Come on in, Sam," Rachel called out.

When he came in, she introduced me. I reached out to shake his hand and then asked if he had a few minutes to sit down with us to talk about his daughters. He glanced over at Rachel to see if it was all right with her, and then, once she nodded, he took a seat opposite her on the couch.

"Rachel and I were just talking about how important you are to each of the girls," I said to him matter-of-factly.

"They are important to me, too," he said excitedly. And then, turning to Rachel, he said, "Listen—I know I've been irresponsible, and I regret hurting you. You have every right to be angry with me. I'm angry with myself for hurting you and them. I'm miserable without them. I miss them so much!"

He turned away from both of us and dropped his head in his hands. It took a moment for him to compose himself so he could speak again. I looked at Rachel and could see that she was surprised to see him show so much emotion. She truly had thought he didn't care about any of them.

Rachel glared at him and, forgetting she had just moments ago agreed to set her pain and anger aside, began to speak in a voice that began as a whisper and escalated to a roar. "If you cared so much about them, how could you leave like that? How could you walk out on us like that? Their grandmother died, and you didn't even stick around to see them grieve over that before you threw another wrench in the mix by leaving them! You didn't care about anybody but yourself! Yes, I was and I am still angry with you." She turned away from him and shook her head in disgust.

I couldn't allow her to turn this into a bashing session where he was under attack and on the defensive. He had apologized and shared that he regretted hurting her. She had to be content with that for now. I had to shift the focus from how they felt toward each other back to the girls.

Addressing them both, I intercepted her questions and said, "It'll take time to adjust to what has happened between you both. I don't know enough about your marriage to begin to know what, if anything, was missing in the relationship that might have contributed to the dissolution of your marriage. Hopefully, notwithstanding the very hurtful way it turned out, Rachel will be able to sort things out in the counseling you are doing, and perhaps Sam would be willing to engage in some couple's sessions to help with that." I looked over at Sam for some assurance that he would agree to participate in any counseling.

"I think that's a good idea. I don't want to hurt them any more than I have already."

"Good," I said, "because it's important for both of you to make the transition from being a nuclear family to being two separate households in a way that will cause the least amount of stress for the children. The best possible outcome for all of you would be one of mutual understanding and accountability, acceptance of the way things are now, and forgiveness for what has gone down in the past. A counselor can help you get past the pain and anger you're both feeling toward each other. The girls have been increasingly more difficult to manage, and they've been struggling with rules and limitations at home and at school. Ana's grades have fallen from E's to U's. We have to address their needs right now.

You both have to put your pain and anger aside and put your heads together to decide what's best for your little girls."

Neither of them protested, so I continued, "Sam, what's your work schedule like? Do you have time to see them during the week, on weekends, or what?"

Before he could answer, Rachel interjected, "See them where? I don't want him bringing them around that woman. I don't even know who she is or what kind of person she is, and I'm not about to allow them to be exposed to some sleazy, low-life bimbo."

"She's not a sleazy, low-life bimbo!" he said defensively. "She's a pediatric nurse practitioner and a very sweet person that I think you would like very much, under different circumstances. Believe it or not, she has her own home but hasn't once invited me over. She won't step foot in my townhouse either. She has insisted that all of our time together be spent out in public. She has refused, from day one, out of respect to you, to take things any further until our divorce is settled.

"In the beginning, before we even started seeing each other, I explained to her that I was unhappy with our marriage and that I felt too much resentment to make it work. She tried to get me to try marriage counseling, but I had already made up my mind. I was too despondent and angry to even consider it, and then, well, things just happened."

"You never said anything about being so miserable. Why didn't you tell me that? Why did you go and tell some total stranger and not tell me? I had no idea you were that unhappy with me. I thought you were just overworked and stressed out about your residency and having to work the night shift in the emergency room, and the traffic to work and back. That's all you ever complained about. I would have done anything to make it work. We have the girls to think of."

"I am sorry, Rachel. You were a wonderful wife and a beautiful mother to our children. We were very happy in the beginning, but over the past four years, you know as well as I do we weren't getting along. I was angry with you, and you would turn around and get angry with the girls for no reason at all. I knew I was causing it, and I couldn't do it anymore. I couldn't fake it, either. I was done."

"I wish you had communicated that to me," Rachel cried. "We could have gotten counseling and learned how to communicate with each other. I had no idea you were so disappointed in me. Instead you go and look for someone to take my place? You just throw in the towel and go find someone else to marry?"

"No, Rachel, you don't understand! It wasn't planned—it just happened. Annabelle and I clicked right from the beginning, yes, but it was a surprise to both of us. Neither of us was thinking about starting anything up with anyone, when we met. She was widowed just over a year ago, when her husband was killed in Afghanistan. She wasn't at all eager to attach to anyone, any time soon. I was angry all the time and unhappy with the way my feelings were affecting you and the girls.

"When you left for Ohio, the anger just went away, and the girls and I talked and played like the old days. I realized then that it wasn't working between us, and I had to move out. I didn't want to create any more tension in the house. I realize, by handling it the way I did, that I made things worse for you all, and I'm deeply sorry for that.

"You have to understand," he went on, "I didn't know what to do. I wanted a divorce, but I didn't want to hurt any of you. I was between a rock and a hard place. I couldn't stay, and I didn't know how to leave in a nice way. I have to admit that I've been dragging my feet with filing for the divorce since then, but I felt it was for a good reason. I knew you needed time, and I wasn't about to push you into anything. I just felt we needed to chill out before we took the next step in the divorce process."

"I guess I should thank you for that," Rachel said, while sniffing and blinking back her tears. It seemed he had changed her perspective from seeing him as the scoundrel that ran off with some bimbo half his age, without an iota of regard for her or his daughters, to one who was remorseful, thoughtful, and sensitive to the pain he had caused her. It was hurtful enough for him to leave, but she had been compounding the impact of his decision, hurting herself even more, by making false assumptions about why he left, what he was thinking and feeling when he chose to leave, and the character of the woman he was seeing.

Those false assumptions contributed to the level of depression and subsequent dysfunction that had plagued her family and her home life for the past several months. Again, communication would have dissuaded her from jumping to those conclusions, but, in retrospect, they seem to have agreed that they hadn't been able to communicate effectively for years.

While I wanted to focus on the co-parenting plan rather than on their relationship issues, I allowed time for them to open up to each other. They were both hurting. She benefitted from being able to vent to him what she had been feeling for the past several months and from having her assumptions challenged in a non-offensive way. He had to convey that he was hurting too, and he needed to clarify his reasons for leaving in a way that gave a historical context of why he left by speaking to the truth of what their relationship had been like over the past several years. He also needed to address the character of the person he would be introducing their daughters to, once the divorce was final.

I felt by allowing them to clear the air, they would both be less reactive and, therefore, more amenable to developing a co-parenting plan that would best serve the needs of the three girls. Before he could respond to her remark, I spoke to both of them.

"I'm encouraged to hear both of you communicating without excessive negativity. You're both sounding very credible. I hope we can move forward and build a co-parenting plan that satisfies both of you and meets the needs of all three of the girls."

"What is a co-parenting plan?" she asked, as if glad we were shifting from the subject of the dissolution of her marriage.

I explained it in a way that would help them to make decisions that would let the girls know they were being parented by both Mom and Dad, regardless of who had them on any given day.

"I hope that you two agree to share in the decisions to be made on behalf of each of the girls and all the particulars that would meet their needs. A good parenting plan is one where both parents agree to keep the other parent informed about what is going on with the children. By that I mean, if something is going on with one or all of the children that would concern you, it would most likely be a concern to the other parent as well, and therefore should be shared. Can we all agree to that?"

They both nodded.

"And then there's the matter of who has them when. Sam, do you have room for them where you're living now? Could they spend the night at your place and have separate sleeping quarters, privacy, and sufficient space for their things?"

"Yes! I rented a three-bedroom townhouse. The two oldest ones could share a room, and the little one could have the smaller room for herself. I made up the rooms to accommodate their interests and needs. I have wanted them to come over and to feel at home in my place. I just didn't want to rush things." He said the last sentence to Rachel, to emphasize that he had taken her feelings into account.

"That sounds like you've put a lot of thought into this. Now about the schedule—are you both willing to share in the care and custody of the children fifty-fifty?"

"What do you mean by fifty-fifty?" Rachel grimaced.

"Rachel, I know it sounds awful not to see them every day, but it's just as awful for their father. A fifty-fifty arrangement is the most equitable arrangement. There are alternative ways to handle it, but none are as good for the children as a fifty-fifty agreement. They need both of their parents. If the two of you can accommodate that need, you'll be making a worthy sacrifice that will cause the least amount of distress to your daughters."

As I spoke, I could see tears welling up in Rachel's eyes. She knew I was right but was reeling with her objections to the whole situation. She hadn't wanted any of this to be happening, but she could see there was no way to stop it. I gave her a moment to compose herself, watching her with a sympathetic expression on my face. Once she was composed and looking back up at me, I continued speaking.

"I suggest you both agree to move forward in peace." I reached into my briefcase for three copies of a handout that would give them the tools they needed to help them and their children make the necessary adjustments in their lives. "Let's read through this together, and then you can tell me if there's anything suggested in here that you don't agree with."

They each took turns reading the handout, *Acronyms for Parenting and Co-Parenting,* with me. The text of the handout is shown in the next few pages.

Acronyms for Parenting and Co-Parenting

Foster Peace Be Fair Have Mercy

P.E.A.C.E

Peace is an acronym I use to describe the way parents can both work together that will honor their rights as parents and meet the needs of their children. The five letters stand for the following: P) Polite Negotiations, E) Empathy, A) Accept present circumstances, C) Cooperative Parenting styles, and E) Encouragement.

Polite negotiations

Negotiate scheduling, as well as parenting practices, with each other in a polite, non-incriminating manner.

Empathize

Empathize with each other when deciding how to handle the children when the unexpected happens, such as an illness, or some work related changes. Recognize that children and other stress factors in life can be challenging, and agree to help each other get through trying times.

Accept Present Circumstances

By putting objections and negative emotions aside, you will be able to stabilize your relationships with the children. The more accepting you are of the present circumstances, the easier it will be for your children to make the adjustments they will need to make.

Cooperative Parenting Styles

Avoid falling into or imposing Good Cop/Bad Cop roles. Cooperate with each other when deciding on rules, limits, and expectations for the children.

One parent cannot undermine the other more responsible parent by allowing the children to have whatever they want, stay up as late as they want, or misbehave without consequences, while the other more responsible parent holds them to a structured routine with consistent and reasonable rules and limits. Parents need to cooperate with each other and agree to set down and endorse the same rules.

Encourage

If one parent has been overwhelmed with their child's behavior, rather than criticize that parent for not being able to effectively manage the child, encourage the parent with a "You can do this" kind of response, or offer to speak to the acting out child on that parent's behalf. Parents need to have each other's backs.

Avoid triangulating. To avoid consequences for their misbehavior, kids have a way of pitting one parent against the other. By complaining to one parent about the other parent, they change the subject from their misbehavior to that parent's behavior. The two adults start going at each other while the kid slips away, under the radar. Once kids learn they can get away with that, they become experts at creating such diversions. The best approach is to address the child's behavior and then, later, once the child is out of hearing range, talk to each other about how the situation might be avoided next time or handled better.

F.A.I.R.

In order to sustain that peace, parents have to agree to be FAIR. The letters in that acronym stand for F) Flexible, A) Agreeable, I) Invested, and R) Responsible.

Be Flexible

While it is important for the children to have structure and for there to be a routine for them to settle into, it is also important to have some flexibility. You can't be so rigid with each other, the children, or the schedule that you can't accommodate the unexpected.

Be Agreeable:

The antecedent of being agreeable is to be argumentative and unyielding, no matter what the circumstances. By committing to being agreeable, you are each agreeing to actively listen and consider the whole situation before pressing for things to go a certain way.

Be Invested

You will both want to be 100 percent invested in the mental, emotional, and physical well-being of each one of your children. Personal interests, desires, and objectives will take a back seat to whatever is necessary to promote the healthy development of your children.

Be Responsible

I tell my clients they can choose to be responsible parents. Some parents, in trying to be good, give in to their children and try to keep them happy by letting them break the rules and have whatever they want. Contrarily, the responsible parent weighs their requests and considers them in the light of what is best for the children. Parenting is difficult when children set their minds to getting something or to having something go their way. Some parents buckle under the pressure of their demands, thinking the child won't like them if they don't give in to them. Sometimes the parent will give in, in order to overcompensate the children for mistakes that parent has made, in the past, which may ultimately cause the child to develop an impossible sense of entitlement. Responsible parenting is fair and consistent and doesn't foster the same degree of entitlement.

M.E.R.C.Y

The letters in the acronym MERCY stand for: (M) Model, Guide, and Teach; (E) Expect, Explain, and Endorse; (R) Be Reliable, Reasonable, Reachable; (C) Be Caring, Creative, and Consistent; and (Y) Say "Yes," "Yay," and be Youthful.

Model

When I say "model," I mean demonstrate what you expect from them. If you want them to be polite, be polite. If you want them to be diligent, be diligent. If you want them to be honest, be honest with them even when the honesty puts you in less than the best light. Let them know it is human to err and that errors can be corrected and forgiven.

Guide

Nudge and guide them in the direction that you want them to go. Don't order them to go this way or that, or yell to them from across the room. Go to them, pull them close to you, get behind them or beside them, and nudge them with kind words and gentle hands to move them in the direction you want them to go.

Teach

Teach them right from wrong. Don't assume they already know and that they are just trying to contradict you or be difficult. For the most part, children want to please you. Teach them what pleases you. Don't assume they already know.

Expect

Children need to know what you expect. Be kind and clear in conveying what your expectations are. Do not incessantly admonish or lecture your children without letting them know what you expect from them. See to it that your expectations of them are challenging, yes, but also that they are age appropriate.

Explain

Explain things using words and examples of what you mean that are appropriate for their age.

Endorse

Endorse rather than enforce right relations and good behavior. Give them approval and support in making the right choices. Catch them doing something right. Children crave praise and acknowledgement. They will want to keep doing the things that cause you to show your approval, and they need your support.

Be Reliable

Reliability fosters security in each of your children. They have to know that you will be there for them when they are down or struggling with something. They will learn to be reliable when you are. If you say you will do something, do it. If you say you will take them somewhere, follow through with it. If you aren't sure of your ability to follow through with a promise, then don't promise it. Use qualifying terms instead, such as, "if the weather is nice" or "if I don't have to work that day."

Be Reasonable

Don't ask them to do one thing and then send them off to do one or two other things before they've accomplished it. Don't ask them to take on tasks that are above their competency level. Don't keep them out late at night and then admonish them for being tired and cranky the next day. Acknowledge that they are tired and cranky because they were out late the night before. The former makes them feel they are a disappointment to you. The latter conveys that you understand and are sympathetic to how they feel. The former fosters a sense of being bad and unlovable. The latter fosters a spirit of understanding, respect, and cooperation.

Be Reachable

Even when you are unhappy with one or all of your children, avoid distancing yourself from them or scaring them away from you with loud and harsh reprimands. Get down to their eye level instead. Gently reach out and pull them to you, and make eye contact, with warm and approving eyes. It is their behavior that you disapprove of, not them. Let them know you love them when you correct their behavior. Explain why you are unhappy. Tell them what they can do to regain your approval versus listing all the things they have done to earn your disapproval.

Be available to them physically as well as emotionally. Children thrive on one on one time with each of their parents. Take turns keeping one up a little longer than the others for some quiet "you and me time." Designate a family game night during the week and a family dinner production day on the weekend. Some traditions are worth keeping, no matter what your lifestyle entails. All of this can be accomplished whether you live in a nuclear family or a single-parent home.

Be Caring

Even in the most upsetting circumstances, show them that you care. Children need to know that no matter what they have said or done, you care about them deeply. Use nurturing tones that convey acceptance and appreciation for their faculties and abilities, for it is from those attributes that they will draw to achieve what you want them to achieve, to be how you want them to be, and to learn what you want them to learn. If your tone convinces them that they are stupid, weak, or unlovable, how then will they believe they can do better?

Be Creative

Introduce subjects and activities that are challenging and fulfilling. When children are occupied with creative endeavors, they aren't hanging around idle and restless. When you see a child doing something you don't want him to do, make a creative suggestion of something he could do instead.

Be Consistent

Barring an unexpected event, children should know what the daily routines are. Getting up, going to bed, meals, chores, outings, etc., need to be scheduled so the children know what is expected of them. If you say you'll do something, follow through with it. If you plan something, see that the plan is carried out. If you consequence one child for a certain misbehavior, be sure to consequence the other children if caught doing the same behavior. Be careful not to correct one child more than all the others. Don't target one child or pit the children against each other by showing favoritism. Be fair and consistent in your approach to correcting them.

Say "Yes!"

Be mindful of how many times you say no in any given day. Count your yeses. Frame your no in a way that suggests an alternative of what they can have or can do, as much or more than you are saying what they cannot have or do.

Say "Yay!"

Applaud your children no matter how young or old they are. Don't hesitate to say "Hurray!" "Great job!" "Good for you!" Parents tend to make such a big deal over irritations or the mistakes children make, but then let their minor to major successes and attributes go unnoticed. Whether it's a new idea, a performance, or simply a gesture of kindness, let them know that you noticed it, right then!

Be Youthful

It's okay to play! Play to your heart's content. You'll be happier, healthier, and live longer the more you let yourself play. Don't take yourself, your position at your job, or your life so seriously that you forget to play.

Laugh, dance, run, skip, and hoola hoop if you can. Bat a ball, dive for a water toy, ride a bike as fast as you can, feeling the wind in your hair.

Play with your children. Step into their world, even if that means getting all the way down to the floor. Make the roar of a Mack truck. Be the siren for the police cruiser. Waaaaa and coo for the baby doll. Without driving recklessly, make sounds as if you were. Screech as you put on the brakes. Say "Wheeeeeee!" when you turn a corner or go over a tummy-turning bump. Play like there's no tomorrow. Your kids will love you for it, and you'll enjoy them more.

The more you work to Foster PEACE, to Be FAIR and to Have MERCY when parenting your children, the easier it will be to parent them

Once Sam and Rachel finished reading the handout out loud, I said, "If you can both agree to bring these tools to the table, we should be able to come up with the best possible plan. You'll get better at it as time goes on, of course, but for now, it will help to at least work toward creating an atmosphere of peace, to be fair to each other in your approach to establishing the co-parenting plan, and to show mercy when disciplining your daughters. This is important not only for your own healing, but also for the stability and security of each of your children."

"I'll do whatever you think is best, Rachel," Sam said.

"I don't even know what your schedule is," Rachel replied. "When are you going to be available? If you're working nights, you can't have them sleeping at your place alone."

"I'm working days now, and there's a day care for Beth, right on site, where the girls could go until it's time for them to go to school. There's a shuttle that picks up the kids and takes them to their schools, and I would be able to pick them up after school since I get off at three o'clock."

"How nice!" Rachel snapped. "If you could have worked days before, we wouldn't have had to feel like we were single parents, left holding the bag every day. We would have had time together, and we could have been more like a real family."

"That's true," Sam said regretfully.

"Let's stay focused on moving forward, you two," I said. And then in a gentler tone, I continued. "Parents can choose to switch off every other week, or divide each week up in a way that gives them equal time. I actually think the every other week arrangement is the least confusing for the kids. When it's one parent's turn to have them for the week, the other parent gets them on a Wednesday after school and then returns them in the evening in time for them to do what they have to do to get ready for school the next day. Since they're in the youth group on Wednesday, you two might want to pick Tuesday or Thursday evening instead."

After suggesting the weekly exchange, I paused to let them work it out with each other. Once they had an agreement to exchange weeks, I asked, "So, when do you want to start?"

Sam took in a deep breath and looked over at Rachel with an air of anticipation. "Let me start this weekend," he implored. "I've been out of the picture way too long already, and you could use some time for yourself."

Rachel sat there, staring down at the packet in her lap and shaking her head for several seconds before she spoke. "I guess this weekend is as good a time as any, if it's going to happen at all. I just never thought this would happen. I never thought a day would come when I wouldn't have my family home with me. So what happens? Am I just to forget I have children for days at a time? Am I going to be allowed to talk to them? Will I be able to say good morning and good night at least? Are you going to be able to get them to their after-school activities? Can I still come to their games on the weeks that you have them, or what? I don't know! This is all happening so fast."

"This will be hard for all of us," Sam said. "I'll see to their afterschool activities, and I would welcome you at their games and so would they, and you can call them anytime you want. They'll want to hear from you, too, I'm sure."

"Well, that's settled then, I guess," she said with a sigh. "So he'll be picking them up this Friday after school, and I'll be seeing them when?"

Both of them looked at me for the answer.

"Most parents begin their week in the late afternoon on Sunday, so they can get them back in a routine for the start of the school week on Monday. Since you haven't had them this week, Sam, you could start Friday night and either return them Sunday or keep them until the next Sunday late afternoon. That's something you two will have to decide."

"Why couldn't we keep it on Friday nights?" Rachel asked. "He can pick them up Friday, and keep them until the next Friday. That way, the parent that has them for the weekend will have their book bags and know what homework and any projects they'll have to do over the weekend, and the girls won't have their stuff scattered between two houses when they get up to go to school on Monday."

"Good idea," Sam replied enthusiastically. "I hadn't thought of that. I think that would work out much better.

Should we pick a day for us to see them during the week when the other one has them?"

"Well, if you're going to have them from Friday night through the whole weekend, I'd like to see them Tuesday night. I'd really like to see them more than that, but I guess that wouldn't work out so well, huh?"

"Tuesday sounds good, and you'll see them at their activities. And we could pile them all in one of our cars and take them out for pizza on a game night together too, if you would like to. I think it would be good for them to sit with us for a meal together once a week, and I would have no problem with that if you don't—as long as we're getting along and not arguing or getting into any serious discussions about anything. We might have to trade off so we aren't missing the same child's activities every week."

"I would like that. Tuesday then, and yes! I think it would be great if we could get along well enough to share a meal together as a family, at least once a week. That sounds great! It would certainly make the week go by a little easier than if I didn't get to see them at all."

"I'll feel the same way when it's your turn," he said.

"Okay! We've made some progress," I said, smiling. "You guys have come full circle, and I'm proud of you. There will be other things to work out as time goes on, such as holidays and little trips that might occur on three-day weekends where there will need to be some flexibility on both sides, but I think we've done enough for now. The girls should be coming home soon. Would you like me to stay and help you get things in order in here and then let them in on what's going to happen? Since Sam will be picking them up this coming Friday, after school, they'll have four days to adjust to the idea and to look forward to the new arrangement."

Both parents agreed I should help them tell the girls, and then we all got up and started dusting, sweeping, and putting the living room furniture back in place, in time for them to come home. I felt lucky to have a couple that could work things out so amicably.

Beth and Ana were delighted to see their father. Stephanie was reluctant to approach him at first. But after seeing him interact with the others—with Mom's approval—and after hearing about the new arrangements, she warmed up to him too—especially after hearing that Dad would help them pick out a dog to take his place when they were at Mom's house and to keep Mom company when they were at his house.

The landlord had said the floor already had a protective covering on it and that he had no problem with them getting a dog. In fact, he encouraged her to get one and promised to come over and fix the latches when he was in town the next weekend.

It took three more sessions to get the rest of the house in order. During the first week the girls were back from their dad's, the five of us worked together after school. We cleaned the kitchen, the sunroom (which had been a storage area or, more fittingly, a dumpsite), and the bathrooms. In less than six weeks, Rachel was back in her classroom, the girls had developed better study habits (which showed in the improvement of their grades at school), and everyone had joined together in improving and maintaining the atmosphere and cleanliness of their home. The Friday night pickups were carried out without a hitch, and everyone seemed to have adjusted to the changes. The family and I agreed that my work was done.

Since the father was now involved with his children again and their mother was back in the swing of things, Mark (the case manager) discontinued his services. He had been kept abreast of our activities and progress and had reported that everything that needed to be done to get things moving in a positive direction had been done.

On my last day, Sam and Rachel participated in one last family session with all of the girls. As I stood up to leave, they all agreed to let me know if they needed to see me for anything at all in the coming months. Mighty Paws, their black-and-white, tail-wagging collie-spaniel mix, sniffed, nudged, and teased my foot for the last time as we hugged each other and said our good byes.

Chapter Fifteen

Susie

I drove over three bridges, crossing two rivers and a beautiful lake, on my way to where Susie lived with her family. As my car rose up over the rushing or still water, I felt renewed and refreshed with a welcome wash of energy and peace. The view was breathtaking. I considered that experience, both ways, to be one of the greatest perks of my job. I was so calmed and meditative, so refreshed and energized all at once for the tasks that lay ahead, that I made it a point to visit her house last whenever possible. That way I could take some of that energy home to my own family at the end of the day.

When given the referral, I received a report that said Susie was being held at a runaway shelter until the judge could decide whether to allow her to return to her family home or be placed in a home for ungovernable girls. Her mother, Maria, had asked the court to remove Susie from her home permanently because this was the fifth time in four months that Susie had run away from home.

In that report, Maria complained that whenever Susie was grounded, she would remove the screen from her bedroom window and escape as soon as her mother and stepfather were asleep. Her parents had tried boarding up the windows and even put a lock on the outside of Susie's bedroom door, which only kept her from escaping in the middle of the night. Once they had barred her escape in the night, she began to plot her escapes in broad daylight. She'd wait until her mother went to the bathroom or out in the yard, and then poof! She'd be gone.

When I received her referral, she was not only on runaway status with the Department of Children and Families, but quite possibly sexually active. Susie was only thirteen years old.

Before meeting Susie at the shelter, I arranged to meet the mother at home first to get all the necessary intake information and papers signed. At the same time I made that appointment, I was able to get the mother to agree to get her whole family to participate in a family session at the shelter the following day.

I took my first mind-altering, spirit-lifting drive over the three bridges and out to the country road, where I was to wind around sharp and gradual curves for miles and miles, until I came to her triple-wide trailer. It sat off the dirt road some fifty yards or so, behind tall pecan trees and a beautiful garden, in the middle of which hung an inviting cedar swing.

I wouldn't mind living here, I thought as I approached the front door. The silence was sweet, compared to the hustle and bustle of city traffic and sirens. I stood on the porch, waiting for the mother, allowing myself a moment to imagine having the time to sit on the swing and simply enjoy the peace and beauty of the country. It had also puzzled me to think that a girl of thirteen would run away from such a tranquil place. Where could she go? It was miles from town.

Maria was a petite woman of thirty with long, curly, black hair. She wore shorts and a blouse and was barefoot when she came to the door. She let me in and led me past a bench, to the right of the foyer, that was decorated with smiling blue- and brown-eyed Victorian and Spanish dolls, all dressed up in flowery dresses and lace. We then walked through a very tidy living room of overstuffed furniture placed in front of a TV and entertainment center. I was led finally to the dining room, where we sat, sipped tea, and went over the intake papers that would allow me to speak with Susie, her school, DCF, and the staff at the shelter.

As we went through the stack of papers, I encouraged Maria to vent her thoughts and feelings about Susie's behavior. It took little to no persuasion. She sputtered and fumed as she relayed to me the problems she was having with her daughter. Her body language, facial expressions, tone, and content expressed the disgust, anger, and hatred that she felt toward her oldest daughter. She was clearly fed up. She said Susie was a bad influence on her son, age five, and her two younger daughters, ages seven and eight. She added that none of her other children behaved like Susie.

"She curses at me," Maria complained. "She slams doors and refuses to follow directions. She's failing at school, in her special education classes. She's had multiple unexcused absences for refusing to go to school and numerous referrals and suspensions for fighting with peers. She disappears until all hours of the night to God only knows where, doesn't introduce us to her friends, and then complains because she isn't allowed to hang out with anyone."

At the end of her rampant spiel, in an air of disgust and defeat, Maria mumbled that Susie had been ungovernable since she was three years old. She let me know that she and her husband had given up and were waiting for the courts to relieve them of the burden of parenting her. She didn't want Susie to be returned to the home. She said she hoped that, in the course of my intervention, I would be able to document proof that such a return would be a mistake for all concerned.

Throughout her entire speech, Maria put so much bitter emphasis on her daughter's name that she made "Susie" sound like a curse word.

The incident that had inspired her most recent escape had begun with a little temper tantrum Susie had while hanging up laundry on the clothesline in the backyard. All the clothes ended up on the ground, wet and caked with sand. The argument had started with the mother's first request that her daughter hang up the clothes. By the third or fourth request, they were shouting at each other.

Somewhere in the course of Susie's eventual defeat and compliance, something her mother said triggered her again, causing her to change her mind. In a last-ditch fit of defiance, Susie tore down all the clothes she had hung up and threw all of the clothes left in the basket out on the ground. When she did that, she was ordered to go her room, but Susie refused to even go inside the house. When her mother attempted to pull her into the house, the two of them got into a scuffle.

Maria showed me the bruises on her wrists where Susie had grabbed her to get her to stop pulling on her hair. Maria appeared to be flustered and frustrated, showing absolutely no remorse for the physical escalation of their altercation as she spoke of the incident. When I pursued that aspect, she demanded that I give her some alternative—while implying, in thick overtones, that there was no such alternative. She felt she had been pushed to the edge of her wits and had shown considerable restraint in not beating the child to a pulp.

Anyone witnessing the hatred in that mother's eyes could easily have labeled her with that infamous "B" word and would have felt nothing but pity for the poor child who was forced to live with her. There was no evidence of love in the mother's description of their relationship. At the same time, her accounts of the relationships she had with her other children were filled with love and pride. It appeared as though Susie wasn't at all safe in that environment.

I listened attentively without allowing my facial expressions, body language, or verbal responses to carry any hint of negative judgment. I had to allow the mother to feel safe in disclosing her thoughts and feelings so I would know how she might have been perceived by her daughter. And then, without making any judgments that would have compromised our therapeutic relationship, I was able to change the focus of our discussion to the mother's own childhood and early adult years.

Maria's mother had been an alcoholic and had been a single parent when she raised Maria. As a child, Maria had lived in her mother's house until she met Susie's father, Rodrigo.

Maria described Rodrigo as a "wheelin' and dealin' businessman by day and an abusive, raging lunatic by night." She then explained that he swept her off her feet and got her pregnant when she was only seventeen. She admitted she had seen him as her ticket out of her mother's house.

It wasn't until after Susie was born that Maria learned how abusive and controlling he could be. He didn't allow Maria to go out or to receive phone calls. He called several times a day to make sure she wasn't answering the phone. He humiliated her in front of her family and his friends (she wasn't allowed to have any friends) and physically abused her whenever she argued with him.

She confided that she had left him "hundreds of times." But he would go to her mother's house, where she would take Susie to get away from him, and beg for her to forgive and return to him. She felt trapped. Maria said her mother was just as controlling as Rodrigo. Moreover, she asserted that her mother was overbearing and a disgrace, qualities to which she did not want to subject her baby. She then said she and her daughter were very close whenever neither of them was around.

She looked out through the window toward the back yard as she told me of the hours she had spent playing outside with Susie and all of her little friends. But then Rodrigo would come home, grab the baby from her arms, and demand that Maria wait on him hand and foot. He never let her participate in their time together. He would tell her to leave them alone, and if she dared protest, he'd tell her to shut up.

She then said that her mother and Rodrigo spoiled Susie. They wouldn't allow Maria to have any say in the way she was to be raised. "They let her get away with murder!" she exclaimed. "He bought her presents and treated her like she was his little princess. When he was home, he spent all of his time with her. When we escaped to my mother's house, he would come over at first just to see Susie, but then he would threaten to take custody of her if I didn't return home with him. My mother thought he was the cat's meow and took his side against me, never believing he abused me without good cause."

The last time Maria left Rodrigo, Susie was three years old. Her mother said Susie would do nothing but sit in the window and wait for him to come for her. She refused to eat or go to bed. When Maria tried to get Susie to come to the table or get ready for bed, she would have to physically drag her from the window, kicking and screaming.

During the last few times Rodrigo had come after them, Maria had refused to let him in to see Susie. She would run and lock the door, leaving him banging on the door and threatening to tear it down. He also threatened to take Susie someplace where she would never see either of them again. Meanwhile the grandmother would yell at Maria to let him in. Despite his threats and her own mother's interference, Maria had held her ground until he finally stopped coming around.

Several weeks had passed before Susie totally abandoned her roost by the window. The wear and tear her daughter's obstinacy presented, together with the absence of support from her own mother, took its toll on Maria and on their relationship. It appeared to me that it was a toll to be reckoned with as Susie entered puberty.

They each had harbored deep-seated anger and resentment toward each other that had, until now, never been identified and resolved. Susie began to develop in ways that would be attractive to men, in the way that her mother had been at her age. She also entered the stage of life where young girls begin to oppose their mothers in every way possible. The combination seemed to have stirred the pangs of jealousy and the sense of acute powerlessness Maria had felt when Susie had been Rodrigo's "little princess that could do no wrong," along with the betrayal they both felt had been inflicted by the other when he was prevented from coming around.

Susie may have held it against her mother that he wasn't allowed to be a part of their lives. Maria had clearly resented her daughter's allegiance to the man who had physically abused her. The close bond they had enjoyed in the first years of Susie's life was fragmented by the emotional aftermath of that separation—and all of the elements that led up to it.

Although Susie had received counseling throughout her childhood, apparently no one had connected the dots that would reveal the whole picture of what went wrong with their relationship. Already in her young life, Susie had been labeled with several different diagnoses and put on three or four different kinds of medications for behavior disorders, including hyperactivity, none of which had helped. Her mother had lost faith in counselors and doctors and had determined that nothing could be done to repair the situation. It was only getting worse.

The courts terminated the father's rights after he had been repeatedly put in jail for domestic violence against Maria. Although it may have been the best thing for the child, the separation from her father was a blow her fragile emotional state couldn't withstand. She continued to present with a serious emotional disturbance that severely compromised her ability to accept authority at home and at school and severely limited her capacity to concentrate well enough to learn.

Had her home life been more stable, she might have had the strength and wherewithal to learn and assimilate the skills to grow through the separation. But it wasn't stable—not by a long shot! The result was that she didn't grow emotionally from age three. She was stuck. Redirecting her or denying her anything, even at the age of thirteen, caused her to act out as a three-year-old would if you were to snatch away a favorite toy or a piece of candy.

As I connected the dots, I shared my interpretations with the mother. In sharing interpretations, I never say, "This is so." Instead, I try to generate some thinking in a new light by asking, "Is this possible?" "What do you think?" "Could this dot be in any way connected to that dot over there?"

From Maria's own report, Susie had been acting out against her mother's authority since age three. That fact caused me to want to know what had happened at age three that spawned the seeds of hostility that existed between them now. Maria was aghast when she first understood that Susie's acting out had been rooted in circumstances she had long tried to forget. She kept dropping her mouth and widening her eyes, looking at me in astonishment, as if each revelation was a godsend or something.

She confided that, until now, she had avoided speaking of the father with her daughter—or anyone else for that matter. She admitted that Susie asked about him, but she wouldn't respond with anything but an attitude of resentment. She felt that Susie only brought him up to undermine her authority.

The whole subject of Maria's marriage to Rodrigo triggered so much resentment and anguish that Maria wouldn't speak of it herself. Her current husband, Antonio, as devoted and supportive as he was, knew little of all that had transpired in that marriage. She had never received counseling for domestic violence or the spousal abuse that had occurred—which had in fact occurred at the end of an era where spousal abuse wasn't talked about. Or, when it was talked about, the abused spouse was erroneously thought to have deserved it.

Maria understood, after talking with me, that the counseling her daughter had in the past could have been more effective, if Maria had been more truthful and forthcoming in her own disclosure. She had always expected the counselors to make the child change her behavior and that such a result would solve the problem. She admitted to blaming the child for being too obstinate to change her behavior. She had always thought Susie was out-smarting the counselors and that they were a waste of time and money.

The results weren't all Maria's fault, since none of the counselors included the mother in their play therapy with Susie. None of them had connected the dots between the present and those earlier years when Susie was caught in the middle of a controlling father, a meddling maternal grandmother, and a too-young-to-know-better mother who was only seventeen to twenty years old.

After pausing to reflect on the information she had disclosed, I explained how I would like to proceed. I wanted to make every effort to build on the bond they had with each other prior to the separation and divorce from Susie's father. It would be necessary for the mother to begin relating to Susie at her actual emotional age in the same way she would if Susie were still only three years old. The communication between them had been lost for ten years. It wouldn't be repaired overnight.

I let the mother know that if she was interested in participating in treatment and allowing her daughter to return home, I would be working with them on those aspects of their relationship in the first few weeks of our intervention. I explained that I would use role-play to examine their current interactions and also so they could practice more productive communication. Fortunately for Susie, her mother had the intelligence to follow my lead in trying this approach to the problem.

I saw the love and concern behind the mother's rage. She laughed when I told her that. She even denied that she had felt any love for Susie for a long time. I was able to point out to her that her daughter felt and was acting on the same void in their relationship. In response to that understanding, her hardened glares and fiery rage dissolved into tears that streamed down her face. She said she would do anything to improve their relationship.

Now I was ready to meet Susie and to observe the family session at the shelter.

The following day, I went to the shelter to meet with Susie, half an hour earlier than the scheduled family session. I waited in the conference room while one of the counselors went looking for her. My plan was to soften her in time for the family session and to let her know that my intervention might be just a little different from what she was used to.

Susie had the same agenda. She entered the room with skepticism written all over her face and threw herself into the chair with all the grace of a truck driver. She of course chose the chair that was the farthest away from me. She wore an oversized coat, camouflage pants, and heavy black boots. Her lips were covered in black lipstick. Her eye makeup was so thick on her eyelids that she could hardly lift them. Her hair was tied up in a ponytail in the back with more than wisps hanging down around her face. The top of her hands had doodles and phone numbers inked on them; her nails, layered in black nail polish, were chewed nearly down to the cuticles. She couldn't have made herself any less attractive or any less feminine if she had tried.

I wondered if she wasn't trying to offset some of her mother's jealousy by dressing and clomping around in that way. I made a note to look into that a little more as we got further along in treatment.

I began by telling her that I thought it only fair that she have a chance to talk to me before the session, since I had already talked to her mother. She demanded to know what her mother had said about her. Before I could answer, she shot the question, "Is she going to get me out of here or what?"

"She wants to, but she thinks you'll run again."

"Yeah, well—she's just a bitch!" With that she stood up as if there were no point in talking and she had better things to do than sit around "B-S-ing" with me. I could have feigned astonishment at her using such language, but would that have been productive? In admonishing her, I could have let her know, in no uncertain terms, that I wouldn't tolerate such language. I could have stated the obvious, but why change the words without first changing the sentiments expressed in them? To what end? Why repeat rules of proper conduct when the child had half a mind to throw herself and her whole life in the toilet? There will be plenty of time to examine and extinguish the words and other forms of communication they each used to trigger the most anger in the other. Now was not the time.

Without moving a facial nerve or muscle, I said, "Yeah, I know!" And then, in a dramatic tongue-in-cheek manner, I added, "The woman gave me the creeps when I first met her!"

This was true. When I first sat down with Maria, her hatred and the disgust in her tone and facial expressions as she spoke of her daughter did give me the creeps. I couldn't help but imagine what it felt like to be the daughter, having to look up at that face and hear her mother's venomous speech.

Susie held her post at the door, turned her head so she could almost see me, and asked, "What'd she say?" Her tone said, *Hurry up, like, I haven't got all day,* with as much sarcasm as she could convey in three words.

"Well, I thought I'd get here a little early so I could tell you what we said, but you seem to be leaving. If you want to wait until everybody is in here, that's fine. I can wait." I laced my tone with a little sarcasm too, just to let her know two could play that game, but with enough tongue-in-cheek to bring out an involuntary smile on her face.

She turned so I could see her eyes for the first time since she entered the room. I looked away as if to say I had all the time in the world and had no investment in whether she stayed in the room or not. I then rolled my eyes a little and started tapping my fingers on the table while swinging the one leg I had crossed over the other in exaggerated circles.

All of a sudden this wasn't about her and her mother.

"What are you here for, anyway?"

"I'm supposed to see if you can go home from here or if you need a residential placement for ungovernable girls."

"She won't let me go home."

"She thinks you'll just run away again."

"Yeah. She's stupid."

"Why do you want to go back there?" I put an emphasis on the word "there." I continued to test her. "You two can't even talk to each other?"

"Nobody can talk to her—she's a bitch! I got nothin' to say to her. She can stay out of my face, and I'll stay out of hers."

"Okay, now that we've got that worked out…" I stood up and pretended to be about to leave the room as I said that. She laughed, but it was more like a sputter that said I was crazy.

I took a seat a little closer to where she was postured by the door and pushed a chair out for her with my foot, indicating she could sit back down if she had a mind to. She did.

With all the weight she could put into it, she dropped herself into the chair sidesaddle and slung her arm over the back of it, with one foot still aimed at the door.

I sometimes equate these first little encounters with all the originality and excitement to be enjoyed in the first round of a good bullfight. I had this bull rearing for the dance. I could feel her glaring at me as if I were the little red flag, as I watched her front foot pawing at the ground.

"I'm going to be working on that, if I decide to take this case."

"On what?"

"The way you two talk to each other. Sheesh! Aren't you paying attention?"

That got a huge smile out of her.

"What?"

"Nothin'."

"Yeah. We need to work on the way you communicate with each other. You two are mean, down, and dirty."

The idea must have spooked her, as she dropped the smile down to a sour scowl and said, "I got nothin' to communicate." She spread out the word "communicate" so I heard each and every syllable, as though it were a word by itself.

She was apparently of the opinion that no communication was necessary. If she had drawn up the treatment plan at that point, her objective would have been to eliminate that aspect of their relationship altogether. In her mind, it couldn't be fixed. She knew one thing and one thing only: her mother hated her. Why did it matter how she conveyed that to her? It was still hate. She understood this in her gut. Any argument from me about that would have been a waste of time.

But then, I had a lot of time to waste.

"She cried at the end of our session," I mumbled.

"She what? She cried? About what?"

"About the way she's been treating you for the past ten years."

"Yeah, right!"

"I'm serious! Alligator tears. All of that anger and disgust just disappeared and dissolved into alligator tears."

"What do you know about the way she's been treating me?"

"I could see it in the way she talked about you. This isn't all about you, ya know. She has some changes to make too."

The idea of her mother having cried seemed to melt her somewhat. Her face softened and her posture improved slightly as she continued to interrogate me about the conversation I'd had with her mother. I shrugged as if to say it didn't really matter.

"That's quite an outfit you've got on there," I observed. "Does she let you wear that black lipstick, or do you need a few minutes to wash your face and tidy up before she gets here?"

"I ain't tidying up nothin'. She don't like it, but she got nothin' to say about it, while I'm here."

"Ooh! Tough girl." I smiled.

"What's she comin' here for if she isn't going to take me out of here?"

"I told you, we have to decide if you can go home or not. To do that, we have to see if the two of you want to learn how to communicate better. She's coming in to see if you'll agree to participate in family counseling with her."

"What for?"

"Susie…"

"Oh yeah!" And then, in her best rendition of Disney's Goofy, she answered her own question: "So we can learn how to communicate."

"Right! See, I knew you were smart," I teased.

Although it might have appeared to an outsider that we were just shooting the breeze, something much more profound had taken place in the half-hour we shared prior to joining the family for therapy. She had dropped her facade and allowed her very thirteen-year-old self to emerge. She understood that her mother had changes to make too, and that both of them would have to improve the way they talked to each other. By the time we met in the family room, she had washed her face and put on a blouse. Granted she still wore the boots, but hey, they were quite fashionable for the times.

The most remarkable thing about the family session was in the way the younger ones vied for the mother's attention. By the time the session was over, I could see the dynamics of the two camps in that house. Susie occupied one camp. The mother and her other two daughters occupied the other camp. Susie's stepfather of eight years danced a two-step in between the two camps, with the little brother running up behind to catch the crumbs.

Susie's stepfather admitted the mother was often too harsh, but that he only made things worse by trying to stand up for either one against the other. The sisters admitted too that they spent a good part of their day trying to catch their sister at something they could then run and tattle to Mom.

Mom admitted that she never allowed Susie to help her in the kitchen or with any of the chores at home. They each had their own chores and ne'er the twain shall meet—except by some unfortunate accident. The whole family system seemed to function on the premise that Susie was the core of all of their problems and that with her gone these past few days, things had been wonderful on the home front.

I couldn't let the session end without each one being assigned something they would personally have to work to improve. To do that, I had to make everyone stop and think. What was really the case? Did the others truly do no wrong? After some probing questions, I managed to scavenge a list a foot long of what the others did to contribute to the dysfunction in that family system.

The siblings played rivalry games with the brother. The brother wailed for no apparent reason at bedtime and every morning. The youngest sister always left her clothes on the floor, and the oldest cheated in card games. None of them did their homework without ear-shattering reminders and reprimands from their mother. Both of the younger sisters picked on and teased their brother until he got in trouble for slamming his door, or calling them names.

The mother never invited Susie to help her with anything. She had never thought of inviting her into the kitchen to learn how to cook, or to iron, or to help her with the meal planning or the shopping. That was the most disturbing thing—how would she ever learn to run a home once she turned eighteen and was out on her own if her mother didn't expose her to these things? Here was a wonderful opportunity to strengthen the bond between them during her teen years, and at first her mother wouldn't hear of it.

"That is my kitchen! Nobody comes into my kitchen."

"But you let her in there to do up the dishes."

"Well, yes. But I'm not in there, then."

"Exactly!"

After what seemed like a millennium, she finally agreed to let Susie help one night a week. I knew I could get more nights down the road, after she saw how much fun it could be.

We spent the first few weeks working on improving the way they expressed their disagreements and disapproval, using role-plays. They were more and more enlightened by this activity as time went by.

Here is how it went: I would ask them to tell me if an argument or negative verbal exchange had occurred between sessions. Of course, there had been such exchanges. I would then ask them to play it out for me, only by reversing the roles this time. One example is when Maria and Susie recalled a struggle a few nights before our session. Maria had asked her daughter to get up and do the dishes.

In the reversed role-play of that event, Susie, playing her mother, ordered Maria, who was playing Susie, to get up and do the dishes. Maria then acted out the way Susie did when she refused and then ran her mouth until she was sent to her room.

Susie played the perfect mother. She snapped at her mother to get up and get in the kitchen because there were dishes that had to get done. Maria immediately argued that she hadn't sounded that harsh, but the other children nodded and said that indeed she had. Then the mother, acting as Susie, whined that she would do it in a minute and that she wanted to finish watching her show. When Susie persisted in the tone that her mother had used with her, the mother played back Susie's nasty attitude and retorts, and got herself sent to Susie's room.

They both laughed at themselves as the other portrayed the way they each were in real life. I had to hold my stomach as I laughed, watching the mother acting out the way Susie did, throwing herself down the hall to Susie's room, muttering the B-word, among other equally explosive adjectives, every step of the way. Then we all cringed as she slammed the door shut so hard it rattled the whole trailer.

They learned a lot from those role-plays. They learned how it felt to be on the receiving end of whatever the other was putting out. That alone gave them insight that helped in softening their tones with each other. They also learned not to take those things so personally or so seriously anymore. I think that was the most valuable part of the lesson.

We did the role-plays during the first couple of sessions, and then I let them take a break—not because I didn't think they were important, but because it would be a good way to see if any progress had been made. If they knew we would role-play every argument, they would have been on their best behavior for the time that I was involved with them, but no longer. I needed to let some time pass and then call for a role-play when it was least expected.

In order to address the problem of tattling on Susie, I bought three boxes of stars and gave a box to each of her siblings. I then taped a piece of construction paper on her bedroom door, with a list of ways she would earn them. Smiling was number one on the list. Getting up in the morning and coming home after school, sitting with them in the living room, saying hello or goodbye to someone, getting up and answering the phone, and just being nice at the table were all behaviors that I included on her list.

They found that giving her stars was far more fun than tattling to Mom. It was so much fun that they started giving stars to everyone. I decided that would be okay, as long as it was only for when they were caught smiling or being kind to someone. Even the mom and dad were given some.

In order to satisfy Susie's need to be coddled as her mother had wanted to when she was three, I set it up so that she could sit up with her parents a half hour later than the other kids. Her parents agreed to sit with her during that time, doing something she wanted to do. Sometimes they read.

Sometimes they sat and watched a TV show. Other times they simply sat and talked about people in her class or things that were happening at school.

Their relationships improved. The family home atmosphere was better than even I had imagined it could be. But, I was still concerned about Susie's choice of friends. Her peer group consisted of those who were in special ed or who had dropped out. She had expressed to me, on many occasions, how they made her feel. She wanted to be accepted by people her age who were successful in school.

We talked about how she might be able to connect with peers who were successful in some other areas, as well. There had to be something about her that was special, other than that she couldn't make it in regular classes.

I thought and thought about this, and then finally I came up with it. I introduced her to the idea of taking dance lessons. Feeling comfortable in her own body, at an age where awkwardness and self-consciousness is at its peak, would do wonders for her attitude. Dance lessons could give her a sense of pride in herself and a more graceful way of moving. While taking dance lessons, she would have an opportunity to make friends with girls from other schools, too. I told her she would make friends with girls from regular and special ed classes, where she would be recognized for her ability to learn the steps and to dance as well as any of them—if she put her whole self into it.

She liked the idea and said she would ask her mother.

It turned out better than I thought. Much to my surprise, Susie and her mother began to take jazz lessons together. They began weekly jazz classes and made it a mother-daughter night, stopping for something to eat and talking and spending quality time together on their way home.

They started their lessons that same week and began practicing in their living room together on weekends. Every now and then, they would show me some steps they had learned together and tried to teach them to me. After weeks of practice and preparation, the whole atmosphere in their home was crescendoing to remarkable heights as the event of their very first dance recital drew near.

I had been implored to attend, so I arranged to meet with them for one last time, after school, on the day of the recital. That way we could get through our termination session, and then, I could help them dress and fix their hair for the big event. I thought it best to get our goodbyes out of the way early, so that when the recital was over, they could return home, riding the waves of jubilation from a successful performance, together with their family and without any interference from me.

It was a wonderful recital. During two intermissions they met me in the lobby, beaming and brimming with excitement. Both of them had their arms around each other as they praised and celebrated each other's performance.

And then, at the end, as I joined the audience in a standing ovation, they both blew me a kiss from the stage. With tears of joy and pride streaming down my cheeks I heartily applauded them, as the final curtain was drawn.

Afterword

I have placed the sometimes heart inspiring, sometimes heart wrenching details; some of the best and the worst of my experiences with Troubled Kids and the adults in their lives, in your hands. What you do with them is up to you. For centuries we have encountered such children whether from the fictional accounts of them in Charles Dicken's portrayal of the workhouses, orphanages and streets leading up to the 1600's and beyond, to the non-fictional report of the countless children beaten and buried in the 20th century boot camp grounds of a town in Florida. The images startle, shock, outrage and humble us momentarily but then we manage somehow to quickly turn to other more pressing and personal matters of seeming greater significance such as getting dinner on the table, shopping for that new sports coat or evening dress and matching accessories, catching that playoff game in the comfort of our living room, or tossing that football with one of our own little angels.

Why? Why are we so quick to turn away? Are we so cold and calloused that we can't care or is it that we are so fragile, sensitive and vulnerable that we can't bear to dwell on the images long enough to consider how we might rise up against such maltreatment? My hope is that you will take the book to heart, talk about it, and pass it on.

I began recording facts and impressions of the plight of troubled kids, back in the mid-nineties. I would start and stop writing sometimes for a year or more at a time. And then, on September 11, 2001, I had placed the entire manuscript in a large manila envelope addressed to a publishing company, and was about to walk out the door on my way to the post office, when I saw and heard the news of the terrorist attack on the Twin Towers in New York. I was devastated. I looked down at the envelope in my hand and thought to myself, "How trivial the plight of these few children will seem to anyone now." And then, I placed it in a cupboard where it sat for another seven years.

During that seven years, I continued to record my work with troubled kids and I wrote two more books. One I called How to Raise a Rebel: A Satire on Raising Rebellious Kids, was a tongue in cheek parenting guide designed to help parents avoid making mistakes in the rearing of their children, from who they select to be the 'other parent,' to how they treat them throughout each of their developmental stages. All the experiences, and wit, recorded in that book, were lost when my computer broke down. Had I known at the time that experts could have found a way to retrieve it, I most certainly would have jumped at the chance, but alas, I didn't know it could be done.

The other book was called, "Boys Behind Bars." It was a heart wrenching account of the lessons I learned and taught while working as a therapist in a High Risk-level eight juvenile correctional facility for boys aged 13 to 21. That one seemed to write itself. I was done in record time and so scared it too would be lost that I took extra care in preventing the same outcome. I took my old computer processor that flickered and threatened to shut down, to Best Buy and asked them to put the whole book on a CD. I planned to upload it on a brand new computer, make some final edits, and send it off to a publisher. I even had my inquiry letters written and ready to go. I had them put on the CD too.

And then, with great speed I hurled that old computer into the scrap bin at the city dump! Aha! I said as I heard it thump against the metal bottom of the bin! I felt victorious to have been able to hurl it before it consumed my laborious but worthwhile work of art. And then, I took my brand new lap top and my CD home and set it all out on my dining room table, with a Cheshire cat grin on my face and a surge of excitement running through me from head to toe. But it was late and I had to get up and back to the correctional facility, early the next morning, so I patted it and said good night to it and let it sit there, alone in the dining room, all that night and into the next day, thinking I would get back to it, the minute I got home from work.

It wasn't there! I got home to find that my apartment had been broken into. My brand new computer, and my CD were gone! I called the police and canvassed the apartment complex for days. I put out signs offering a $1000 reward for the return of the CD alone, but I got no response, from anyone. It was gone! All I have left are my handwritten notes; no more than a skeleton of all that I had written. I thought then and still say now, "I hope the thief or thieves had at least taken the time to read what was on that CD." Both books still flicker off and on in the back of my mind. Perhaps I will revive some semblance of them, in time. But will I ever be able to recapture the heart and soul of the work? I tell myself to think, "I can!"

About the Author

Clarissa Star Crystal-Belle is the Co-Founder and Clinical Director of two Counseling Centers in Florida; the Star Point Counseling Center and the Affordable Counseling Center of Florida, located in Tampa, and Brandon. She is a qualified supervisor overseeing all services provided by Interns and she provides counseling services to Individuals, couples and families. She earned a Bachelor of Science Degree in Psychology with Honors of Distinction at the Johnson State College of Vermont, and a Master of Arts Degree in Clinical Psychology at the Vermont College of Norwich University. She holds an active license to practice Mental Health Counseling in the state of Florida and she is a member of the American Mental Health Counselors Association.

When I am not providing counseling services, I enjoy catching up with my three daughters and sons in law, and my four granddaughters and two grandsons. I also enjoy writing, reading non-fiction as well as poetry and arm chair mysteries, walking along the beach, swimming in the pool, cooking, playing chess, and even pool on occasion although I get three turns to my opponents every one if I am to have any chance of winning.

I strive to achieve and maintain a balanced lifestyle that includes spiritual mindfulness, personal growth and care, fostering strong family ties and keeping myself in good company, promoting the health and happiness of others in my practice, and keeping myself active in ways that are healthy, interesting, fulfilling and fun.

CPSIA information can be obtained
at www.ICGtesting.com
Printed in the USA
LVOW11s0929250717
542517LV00001B/141/P

9 781621 833284